The Holy Land

An Archaeological Guide from Earliest Times to 1700

The Holy Land

An Archaeological Guide from Earliest Times to 1700

JEROME MURPHY-O'CONNOR, OP

École Biblique et Archéologique Française, Jerusalem

Drawings by Alice Sancey

Oxford New York Toronto Melbourne

OXFORD UNIVERSITY PRESS

1980

Oxford University Press, Walton Street, Oxford OX2 6DP

London Glasgow New York Toronto
Delhi Bombay Calcutta Madras Karachi
Kuala Lumpur Singapore Hong Kong Tokyo
Nairobi Dar es Salaam Cape Town
Melbourne Wellington

and associate companies in
Beirut Berlin Ibadan Mexico City

British Library Cataloguing in Publication Data

Murphy-O'Connor, Jerome
The Holy Land.
1. Palestine – Antiquities
2. Palestine – Descriptions and travel – Guide-books
915.694'04'5   DS111   80–40113
ISBN 0–19–217689–7
ISBN 0–19–285088–1 Pbk

Set, printed and bound in Great Britain by
Cox & Wyman Limited, Reading

CONTENTS

Part 2: The Land

INTRODUCTION

Scope of this Guide

The most useful guide-book caters to a specific interest. This guide focuses on the historical sites of the Holy Land and is designed to help the visitor find and appreciate the visible remains.

The history of the Holy Land is so long and so much archaeological work has been done that to attempt complete coverage would be self-defeating. A guide-book is not intended to be an encyclopedia; it is a practical aid. A selection has to be made and three criteria have determined which sites (of many thousands) should be included: antiquity, accessibility, and intelligibility.

'Antiquity' covers everything from the beginning of human history in the Holy Land to AD 1700. The only justification for this limit is a legal definition: nothing created after 1700 is classified as an antiquity.

'Accessibility' normally means that one can drive to the entrance. Places at some distance from a tarmac road have been included if the site has a unique feature and if the walk to it is in itself interesting. To acquire the 'feel' of the Holy Land one should walk as much as possible. Some sites that would otherwise merit inclusion have been omitted because physical or political obstacles make access unusually difficult if not impossible.

'Intelligibility' is perhaps the most difficult criterion. In the context of this guide it means the presence of a coherent complex of remains; there must be something significant to *see*, and 'significant' is interpreted with the average seriously interested visitor in mind. Certain sites which have made very important contributions to our understanding of the history of the area have been omitted, either because they had been eroded to nothing or because they are such complicated mixtures of apparently unrelated elements that only a professional archaeologist could draw profit from visiting them.

How to use the Guide

The guide is divided into two parts, the City of Jerusalem and the Land, each being organized on different principles.

The City of Jerusalem

In this part the sites are grouped in areas (see the Table of Contents) because Jerusalem and its vicinity will most naturally be explored in this way. Each section is accompanied by a detailed sketch-map showing the precise location of each site described. Where appropriate, the visit to particular sites is preceded by a general historical survey of the area in which they are found.

Two maps published by the Survey of Israel will be found useful. 'Jerusalem' (1:14,000) covers the entire urban area, and the larger scale 'Jerusalem: The Old City' (1:2,500) shows every street in the walled city. They are available at virtually all bookshops and bookstands in addition to the offices of the Survey of Israel (1 Heshin St., Jerusalem; 1 Lincoln St., Tel Aviv; 28 Yafo Road, Haifa; Merkaz HaNegev Building 22, Beer Sheva). The map on p. 10 shows in outline that part of Jerusalem covered by the guide, marking only the main areas (as listed in the Contents) and a few other focal points to help the visitor get his bearings.

To facilitate travel in Greater Jerusalem the Egged Bus Company publishes a map (available at its offices and in bookshops) with all the bus routes superimposed on the street-plan.

The Land

In this part sites scattered throughout the Holy Land are listed alphabetically, to obviate the need for frequent reference to an index.

A letter and a number appear in brackets after the name of each site. These refer to the grid on p. 114 and on the 'Israel Touring Map' (1:250,000). Published by the Survey of Israel and updated every two years, this map is extremely accurate and clear; with it one can find the way to any site. Those who intend to be a little more adventurous in their exploration are advised to buy the English overprint edition of the Israel 1:100,000 map; it comes in 23 sheets sold separately or as a neatly boxed set. Before buying these maps check the revision date in the bottom right-hand corner.

The spelling of place-names follows that of the Israel Touring Map; this will sometimes differ from the version found on signposts or in other publications; e.g. *c* instead of *k*, *z* instead of *s*, *v* instead of *b*, or vice versa. As a general rule, if the names *sound* the same when read aloud, presume identity. The reason for such difference is that the English version is always a transliteration from Hebrew, Arabic, or Greek, and not all the various official bodies follow the same principles.

Types of Entries

There are four categories of entries in the second part:

(1) *Entries on General Areas.* A general presentation of certain areas (e.g. Jericho, Golan, Sea of Galilee) has the double advantage of directing attention to interesting sites which might be ignored and of showing them as representative of different stages in the historical development of the area.

(2) *Entries on Individual Sites.* In each case a summary of the history of the site is followed by information for a detailed visit.

(3) *Entries on Specific Subjects.* Such entries (e.g. Crusades, Monasteries) provide the general information on a particular social phenomenon and direct the visitor to sites where it has left traces.

(4) *Entries on Social Groups.* These provide a survey of the history of particular groups (e.g. Essenes, Samaritans, Nabataeans) which appear frequently in the presentation of a number of sites.

Cross-References

Names in small capitals in the text indicate that more information is given under that entry or that it refers to a comparable feature.

Bibliography

Works on the history and the archaeology of the Holy Land are legion. The following selection is limited to primary sources which have an immediacy and impact that commentaries lack.

Archaeological Sites

Over a hundred years' work on 180 sites has been conveniently summarized in the *Encyclopedia of Archaeological Excavations in the Holy Land* (4 vols., London: Oxford University Press; New Jersey: Prentice Hall, 1975) edited by M. Avi-Yonah and E. Stern. Most of the articles are written by the archaeologists who dug the respective sites, and good photographs, plans, and bibliographies are included. This authoritative work is the source for the dates given in this guide.

Old Testament Period

The basic text is, of course, the Old Testament whose religious message is set in a well-defined historical and geographical context. Frequent references to the OT have been provided because, when read on the site, they often provide the human dimension which brings the ruins to life.

Extra-biblical texts are equally illuminating. Rulers of the great states adjoining Palestine, whose armies marched through the country century after century, left detailed records of their battles and conquests. Petty kings of city states wrote to their overlords. Merchants noted their dealings. Schoolboys copied exercises. These documents have been published in *The Ancient Near East; An Anthology of Texts and Pictures* edited by J. B. Pritchard (Princeton University Press, 1958; reissued in two volumes paperback 1975). Excellent indices make it easy to find the texts and pictures relevant to a particular site.

Josephus

Detailed information on places and people of the New Testament period is provided by the Jewish historian Flavius Josephus (AD 37–100). Born Joseph ben Matthias, he was made governor of Galilee at the beginning of the First Revolt (AD 66) but as soon as possible turned traitor and sided with the Romans. As an Imperial pensioner he wrote four books: his autobiography, an attack on anti-Semitism, and two historical works, *The Antiquities of the Jews* and *The Jewish War*. *Antiquities* is dull and long-drawn-out because it covers the whole period from Creation to the outbreak of hostilities against Rome in AD 66. *The Jewish War*, though sometimes inaccurate and written with a clear pro-Roman bias, is always interesting because it concentrates on a much more limited period, 170 BC to AD 75. I have given references to it wherever possible. Available in a Penguin Classics translation, it is an excellent guide to any Herodian monument and the best to certain sites (e.g. Masada); a detailed index ensures that it can be used for this purpose.

References to Josephus are given to book and paragraph. Thus *War* 5: 24 means paragraph 24 in Book 5 of *The Jewish War*. In the Penguin edition this system of reference appears in the inner top corner of each page.

Byzantine Pilgrims

The conversion of the Empire to Christianity in the early C4 AD brought about the first tourist boom in the history of the Holy Land. Pilgrims came in increasing numbers until the Arab Conquest in the C7 created obstacles which deterred all but the most persistent. Many of these visitors wrote accounts of their tour of the country and described the buildings they visited. These narratives have been presented by J. Wilkinson in two books which do not overlap, *Egeria's Travels* (London: SPCK, 1971) and *Jerusalem Pilgrims before the Crusades* (Jerusalem: Ariel, 1977); the translations of

Byzantine authors in this guide are taken from these two volumes. The translator has made the narratives intelligible by providing numerous maps and plans, and the Gazetteer appended to *Jerusalem Pilgrims* condenses (and critically evaluates) all the Byzantine information regarding each site under its name.

Islamic Period

From the publication of Ibn Khurdadbih's *Book of Roads and Kingdoms* in AD 864, Arab authors wrote voluminously on the geography and history of the Holy Land. The texts of 31 authors ranging from the C9 to the C18 have been collected and translated by A.-S. Marmardji, OP, *Textes Géographiques Arabes sur la Palestine* (Paris: Gabalda, 1951). Arranged according to sites, many of these texts vividly portray events which the authors witnessed.

Medieval Period

Being admirable chroniclers and administrators, the Crusaders produced reams of documentation on every aspect of their lives in the Holy Land, and virtually all of it has survived. Many of these documents are presented in Latin with an Italian translation by S. de Sandoli, *Itinera Hierosolymitana Crucesignatorum (Saec. XII–XIII)*, Jerusalem: Franciscan Press. The first volume (of four) appeared in 1979. Visitors will also derive profit from accounts written by two of their predecessors, one a Spanish Jew, the other a German Dominican friar. Both ostensibly came on pilgrimage but they were men with a sharp eye for the unusual and possessed the ingenuity to satisfy their curiosity.

Benjamin of Tudela passed through the Holy Land in the course of a long journey throughout the Middle East between 1166 and 1171. His account has been translated by M. N. Adler, *The Itinerary of Benjamin of Tudela* (London: Oxford University Press, 1907). Friar Felix Fabri made two pilgrimages to the Holy Land, the first in 1480, the second three years later when he also managed to get to Mount Sinai. He wrote more than 1,500 pages about his experiences because he was in truth nine parts observant tourist to one part pious pilgrim. This mass of material has been condensed with grace and wit by H. F. M. Prescott in two books, *Jerusalem Journey* (London: Eyre and Spottiswoode, 1954) and *Once to Sinai* (London: Eyre and Spottiswoode, 1957; New York: Macmillan, 1958).

Modern Period

From the beginning of the C18 a new spirit begins to permeate writings about the Holy Land; the natural curiosity of the traveller gives way to critical inquiry. This is first evident in H. Maundrell's *A Journey from Aleppo to Jerusalem in 1697* (Oxford, 1703; reprinted Beirut: Khayats, 1963). For over 200 years it served as the guide-book to Syria and Palestine. The rhythm of scientific investigation steadily increased during the C19 and C20, culminating in the publication of the two-volume *Géographie de la Palestine* by Fr. F.-M. Abel, OP, in 1933 and 1938 (Paris: Gabalda). In addition to his own personal contribution the author synthesizes the contributions of all his predecessors both for the physical description of the country and for the identification of ancient sites.

Practical Advice

Travel and Lodging

Most countries have Israel Government Tourist Offices, normally located in the capital city or financial centre, and all major towns in Israel have Tourist Information Offices. These will supply up-to-date information regarding all modes of travel to and within the country as well as the location and prices of hotels, youth hostels, and camping sites. In the UK the address is 59 St. James's St., London SW1A 1LL, tel. 01-493-2431; in the USA, Empire State Building (19th floor), 350 Fifth Ave., New York, NY 10001, tel. 212-560-0650, with additional offices in Chicago, Atlanta, and Los Angeles.

National Parks

Some of the most important archaeological sites have been transformed into National Parks. Those who intend to visit a number of these sites within a two-week period will save considerably by buying a general admission ticket, available at the ticket office at some National Parks and at the offices of the National Parks Authority in Tel Aviv (3 Het St., Hakiriya).

Opening Hours

Opening hours have been given for each site wherever possible, but these should be used with caution because local conditions may impose unforeseeable modifications. Religious feasts may mean that the site closes early or is not open at all. Sites under Jewish control close one hour earlier on Fridays and two hours earlier on the eve of major feasts and do not open at all on Yom Kippur. Admission to Christian sites is normally restricted on Sunday mornings and to Muslim sites on Fridays. Where no times are given the site may be visited at any hour.

Dress

Once pavement is left behind the ground is rough and stony; rubber soles (the thicker the better) are strongly recommended. Climatic conditions can vary considerably within a relatively small area; one can freeze in Jerusalem and swelter in Jericho only thirty minutes later. It is advisable to dress in layers that can be shed and replaced at will. Winter in the hill country is usually cold and wet; a warm windcheater is essential.

Desert Areas

When visiting sites in desert areas basic safety precautions should be observed. Always take at least one canteen of water. Always tell someone where you are going and at what time you expect to return. Never go alone; always take an experienced companion. All the important trails in the Judaean Desert and in the hills north-west of Elat are marked with colours corresponding to those on special maps issued by the Society for the Protection of Nature in Israel (4 Hashfela St., Tel Aviv) but they can still be difficult to follow and you should not set out without a guide who knows the area. These maps are only in Hebrew but since the scale is 1 : 100,000 it is easy to relate them to the English overlay edition of the same scale. The Society for the Protection of Nature also organizes desert hiking and driving trips; a brochure is available on request.

Export of Antiquities

No object fashioned by man before 1700 can be taken out of Israel unless a written export permit has been obtained from the Department of Antiquities and Museums which is located in the Rockefeller Museum, Jerusalem: telephone (02) 285-151 for an appointment. The fee for the permit is 10 per cent of the purchase price. Fakes greatly outnumber genuine articles in the shops and it is risky to buy without expert independent advice.

Acknowledgements

All that I know of the Holy Land rests on what I learned from two of my professors who later became colleagues and friends: Fr. Pierre Benoit, OP, introduced me to the City and the late François Lemoine, OP, to the Land. It is a pleasure to be able to acknowledge publicly all that I learned from them. I must also thank Fr. Benoit for his ready response to innumerable questions during the writing of this guide.

One's knowledge of history and archaeology tends to remain vague and ill-defined without the opportunity to communicate it. Hence, I am also conscious of a debt to three groups whose eager questions over a period of ten years have stimulated research and discovery: the United Nations Truce Supervisory Organization, the students of the École Biblique et Archéologique Française, and the members of the Sunday Group. All deserve my gratitude but none more than the Sunday Group to whose members I dedicate this guide. They are friends of many different nationalities whose duties have now taken them to other parts of the world, but when they lived in the Holy Land their energy and enthusiasm for out-of-the-way places brought me to sites that I probably would never have explored otherwise.

Other friends have also made essential contributions and to them I express my deep gratitude: to John Wilkinson for suggesting my name when Oxford University Press recognized the need for a guide such as this; to Peter Janson-Smith my editor at OUP; to Alice Sancey who expended such care and patience on the drawings; to Etienne Nodet for his translations from modern Hebrew; to Rachel Lepeer for many photocopies; to Dominic Baldwin for classifying all my drafts; to Jim Poston, Michael Stark, and Michael Burgoyne for their advice and assistance; and finally to my brethren at the École Biblique who freed me from other duties so that the guide might be finished in a reasonable time.

Jerusalem, March 1980.   Jerome Murphy-O'Connor, OP.

A BRIEF HISTORICAL OUTLINE

Human history in Palestine extends over half a million years, and is more complicated than that of other regions because Palestine is a narrow land bridge between the vast land masses of Africa and Asia; peoples from north and south have moved back and forth across it continuously. The purpose of this outline is to highlight the salient features of the major historical periods.

The Stone Age 600,000–4000 BC

The oldest part of a human skeleton found in Palestine is dated to about 600,000 BC. People would then have lived by the shores of rivers and lakes which were numerous because the area received much more rain than it does today. Here pluvial and dry periods corresponded to the glacial and inter-glacial periods in Europe. Large animals abounded in the savannah-type landscape, and as the technique of making flint tools improved the hunters could move further from sources of this basic raw material in search of game. By the end of the Stone Age a good artisan could get 6 m of cutting edge from the kilo of flint that at the beginning produced only 10 cm of cutting edge. Evidence of fire first appears about 200,000 BC, but the major revolution occurred about 14,000 BC when the economy shifted from food-gathering to food-producing. The domestication of animals and the production of grain permitted nomads to settle, and this forced them to develop new skills and a new type of social organization; villages replaced camps, and pottery took the place of stone vessels.

The Copper and Bronze Ages 4000–1200 BC

The first settlements were near springs because the recession of the Ice Cap resulted in a much drier climate in Palestine. Trade in a new raw material, copper, lessened the isolation of the villages and fostered the spread of culture and ideas. Villages blessed with a strategic location on a trade route grew to fortified towns. Urban life facilitated the development of specialized skills; the potter's wheel was introduced and copper was combined with tin to produce a much harder metal, bronze.

Evolution progressed much more quickly in the great river valleys of the Nile and Tigris-Euphrates. Empires grew up in Egypt and Mesopotamia while Palestine remained a mosaic of city-states. Energetic Pharaohs assumed control of the coastal plain and had held it for several hundred years by the time (*c.*1800 BC) a group of nomads arrived from Mesopotamia led by Abraham. His tribe ranged freely in the mountains until famine forced them to migrate to the great granary of Egypt. The Israelites remained there until Moses led the exodus *c.*1250 BC. While Joshua was carving out territory in the hill country, the People of the Sea, repulsed by Egypt, installed themselves in the coastal plain, Philistia.

The Iron Age 1200–586 BC

The Philistines and the Canaanites had developed the use of iron and their chariotry controlled the plain and the wide valleys that penetrated into the mountains. The pressure they exercised eventually forced the Israelites to abandon their loose tribal system in favour of a centralized monarchy. The success of the first king, Saul, was limited, but David (1004–965 BC) made the new system work; he conquered a new capital, Jerusalem, and made it an effective centre by installing there the Ark of the Covenant, the religious symbol to which all gave allegiance.

Solomon (965–928 BC) consolidated the victories of his father but the price demanded – tight bureaucratic control and heavy taxes – proved too much for his people. On his death the northern portion of his realm seceded and became the kingdom of Israel in which bloody uprisings became the normal means of succession to the throne. In both Israel and the southern kingdom of Judah prophets cried out for purity of faith and condemned blatant social injustices.

In the C8 BC a reborn Assyria swept out across the Fertile Crescent subduing the Aramaean kingdoms of Syria which had frequently threatened the two Israelite states. Their turn was soon to come. After dismembering Israel in 721 BC, the Assyrians laid Judah under tribute and made themselves masters of Lower Egypt. As Assyria gradually weakened Babylon grew strong and by 600 BC controlled all Mesopotamia. Jerusalem fell in 586 BC and the people of Judah suffered the traumatic experience of the Exile.

The Persian Period 538–332 BC

The Jews were permitted to return to their homeland (538 BC) by Cyrus, king of Persia, whose army had taken Babylon the year before. Syria and Palestine became but one remote province of an empire that covered the whole of the Middle East. The Jews had to suffer the hostility of the Samaritans until a Jewish governor, Nehemiah, was appointed in the middle of the C5 BC. His political manoeuvres achieved a quasi-independence, and the morale of the people was strengthened by the religious reform of Esdras.

The Hellenistic Period 332–63 BC

Alexander the Great brought the Persian Empire to an end in 331 BC, having campaigned in Palestine the previous year. After his death in 323 BC his generals carved up his short-lived empire: Ptolemy acquired Egypt and Palestine while Syria and Babylon fell to the lot of Seleucus. Palestine became the battleground of these two dynasties, but the Ptolemies held it until 200 BC when it passed into the hands of the Seleucids.

Since the Exile the High Priest had been obliged to assume many of the functions previously discharged by the king. In order to guarantee their dominance the Seleucids had to control this office. Their nominees displaced the traditional Sadokite dynasty, but the extent of foreign influence, particularly in so far as it touched religion, eventually sparked off a revolt led by the three Maccabaean brothers in 167 BC. What began as a struggle for religious freedom soon became a successful fight for political independence. The bloodline of the Maccabees evolved into the Hasmonaean dynasty which extended Jewish dominance to the whole of Palestine, the Golan, and the east bank of the Jordan, almost the extent of the empire of David and Solomon.

The Roman Period 63 BC–AD 324

A strong Jewish state served the interests of Rome as a buffer against the Parthians, but when internecine struggles paralysed the Hasmonaeans the Romans had to step in and take control in 63 BC. They preferred, however, to have a client state and when a strong Romanophile ruler emerged in the person of Herod the Great they gave him autonomy and, where possible, added new territories to his domain. Herod's sons lacked the qualities of their father, forcing the Romans to resume direct control in AD 6. Political authority was vested in a Procurator who resided in Caesarea.

The ministry of Jesus of Nazareth (AD 27–30), destined to have such tremendous consequences for the world, was at the time but one factor in an intense religious and political ferment which, under Roman mismanagement, exploded into the First Revolt in AD 66. In reprisal Titus and Vespasian laid waste the land. The destruction of the Temple in AD 70 precipitated a major shift within Judaism; sacrificial worship was no longer possible and the old priestly aristocracy ceded their primacy to legalists convinced that a scattered community could only be held together by obedience to a common law.

Jerusalem, however, remained central, and when it showed signs of becoming the focus of renewed nationalist aspirations the emperor Hadrian resolved to raze it completely. This provoked the Second Revolt (AD132-5) led by Bar Kokhba whom some considered to be the Messiah. A Roman victory permitted Hadrian to carry out his plan; Aelia Capitolina was built on the levelled ruins of Jerusalem. Refused entrance to Jerusalem and harassed in Judaea, Jews began to move north, founding villages and building synagogues in Galilee and the Golan. Palestine became a backwater which the Romans did not disturb as long as taxes were paid.

The Byzantine Period AD 324-640

The shift from the Roman Period to the Byzantine Period is explained by the transfer of the capital of the empire from Rome to the Greek city of Byzantium which was renamed Constantinople (AD 330). The political significance of this move was less important to Palestine than Constantine's decision to legalize Christianity (AD 313) and to foster its development. His consecration of the sites associated with Christ's birth, death-resurrection, and ascension by great churches awakened interest in the Holy Places. Pilgrims flocked to the Holy Land, stimulating development in all spheres; churches sprang up everywhere and monasteries made the desert a city. Jerusalem grew again to the size it had been under Herod the Great.

Palestine, though rife with theological controversy, was troubled by serious violence only twice during these centuries, the Samaritan revolt in AD 529 and the Persian invasion in AD 614. Both were short-lived but proved extremely destructive.

The Early Arab Period AD 640-1099

Divided by internal intrigues and exhausted by the struggle against Persia, the Byzantine Empire could offer no resistance to the highly motivated cavalry who swept out of the Arabian desert inflamed by the new faith preached by Muhammad (AD 570-632). For Palestine the end came at the battle of the Yarmuk on 20 August 636. Two years later the second caliph (successor of the Prophet) Omar accepted the surrender of Jerusalem.

Recognized as a holy city because sacred to the two religions of the book (Judaism and Christianity) regarded as the predecessors of

Islam, Jerusalem became a centre of pilgrimage. It was protected and embellished by successive dynasties (Umayyad, Abbasid, Fatimid) until 1009 when the mad caliph Hakim unleashed a savage persecution of Christians and many churches were destroyed.

Organized groups of pilgrims came regularly from Europe until the capture of Jerusalem by the Seljuk Turks in 1071. These refused to co-operate and the frustrated religious fervour of Europe expressed itself in overwhelming assent when Pope Urban II, in 1095, called for a crusade to liberate the Holy Places.

The Crusader Period AD 1099–1291

Once set in motion the great enterprise could not be halted, even though the Fatimids had retaken Jerusalem at the beginning of 1099. The Crusaders occupied the Holy City on 15 June 1099. Their first act was to massacre all the Muslim inhabitants, and from such unthinking fanaticism was born the inflexibility of Islam. The memory of the massacre forever stood in the way of a permanent *modus vivendi*.

The first king, Baldwin I (1100–18), gave the new realm a solid territorial base. The feudal system which the Crusaders brought with them furnished a highly effective administration. Palestine was never so efficiently governed on the local level and full use was made of the alms which flowed from Europe. Castles, abbeys, and manor houses were surrounded by fertile fields.

Decisively defeated by Saladin at the Horns of Hattin in 1187, the Crusaders recovered parts of their former territories through treaties in the first part of the C13. In 1250 the Bahri Mamelukes toppled the Ayyubid dynasty of Saladin and began a series of campaigns which culminated in the capture of the last Crusader stronghold, Acre (Akko), in 1291.

The Mameluke Period AD 1250–1517

A continuous internal struggle for power in Egypt and the need to defend Syria against the Mongol hordes gave the Mamelukes little leisure to occupy themselves with Palestine. Once again it became a backwater; the great currents of power ran elsewhere. Jerusalem, the Holy City, attracted pilgrims and scholars, and became a political limbo to which out-of-favour emirs were banished.

The Ottoman Period AD 1517–1918

The Ottoman Turks took Constantinople in 1453, and Egypt fell to them in 1517. The first two sultans were vigorously effective administrators: Suliman the Magnificent rebuilt the walls of Jerusalem. Then followed a series of incompetents whose minimal energy had to be concentrated on trying to keep in order the independent Egyptian pashas. Palestine was left to fend for itself under the capricious authority of pashas whose only concern was to meet their tax quota and to have a little over for themselves. Lack of effective control permitted petty chieftains to carve out independent domains, and bedouin from the desert raided unchecked into the town. A sense of total insecurity led to a decline in population; villages and fields were abandoned, parts of Jerusalem fell into ruins.

The Jews were the one community to grow during this period. Refugees from persecution in Europe and Russia found fragile security in Palestine where outbursts of anti-Semitism occurred infrequently.

The Modern Period AD 1918–

The Turks sided with Germany in the First World War, and the victors dismembered their empire, Britain being given a mandate to govern Palestine in the name of the League of Nations. Able administration gave the country a modern infrastructure which facilitated rapid development. Increased Jewish immigration led to racial strife which grew in intensity to the point where the British could no longer control the situation. They turned the problem over to the United Nations which, in 1947, recommended that Palestine be partitioned between Arab and Jew. Jewish acceptance was nullified by a flat rejection on the part of the Arabs. War broke out when the British withdrew on 14 May 1948. An armistice was accepted on 18 July 1948 leaving Jordan in possession of the West Bank and the Old City of Jerusalem and the new state of Israel in control of the western part of Jerusalem and the rest of the country. Israel was victorious in the war which erupted in June 1967 and since then has occupied the Old City of Jerusalem and the West Bank.

Significant remains from the above periods are visible at the following sites:

Stone Age. Amud Caves, Arbel Caves, Carmel Caves, En Avdat, Tel es-Sultan, Wadi Khareitun.

Copper Age. En Gedi.

Bronze Age. Aphek, Arad, Gezer, Hazor, Jerusalem (City of David), Megiddo, Tel Balata, Tel el-Farah.

Iron Age. Beer Sheva, Gezer, Hazor, Izbet Sartah, Jerusalem (City of David; Jewish Quarter; Kidron Valley), Jib, Lakhish, Megiddo, Shiloh, Tel Dan, Tel el-Farah.

Hellenistic Period. Bet Guvrin, Jerusalem (Citadel; City of David; St. Anne's), Lakhish, Samaria, Tel er-Ras.

Roman Period. Ashqelon, Bet Shean, Bet Shearim, Caesarea, Gamla, Hebron, Herodion, Jerusalem (Citadel; Damascus Gate; Ecce Homo Arch; St. Anne's; Temple Mount; tombs in New City), Khirbet Mird, Kypros, Maale Aqrabim, Mamre, Mamshit, Masada, Qasrin, Qumran, Samaria, Shivta, Solomon's Pools, Susita, Tel es-Samrat, Tulul Abu al-Alaiq.

Byzantine Period. Ashqelon, Avdat, Bet Alpha, Bethlehem, Bet Shean, Bet Yerah, Capernaum, Chorozain, Eshtemoa, Hammat Gader, Hammat Tiberias, Heptapegon, Jerusalem (Bethany; Dominus Flevit; Holy Sepulchre; Nea; St. Anne's; St. John the Baptist; excavations around the Haram esh-Sharif), Kefar Baram, Khan el-Ahmar, Khirbet Mird, Khirbet Shema, Khirbet Suseya, Kursi, Latrun, Mar Saba, Mamshit, Meron, Mount Gerizim, Mount Tabor, Shepherds' Fields, Shivta, Susita.

Early Arab Period. Khirbet al-Mafjar, Jerusalem (Dome of the Rock; excavations around the Haram esh-Sharif).

Crusader Period. Abu Ghosh, Akko (Acre), Ashqelon, Belvoir, Caesarea, Hebron, Jerusalem (Bethany; Cathedral of St. James; Holy Sepulchre; St. Anne's; Virgin's Tomb), Latrun, Nabi Samwil, Nimrud, Qubeiba.

Mameluke Period. Jerusalem (Citadel; Haram esh-Sharif; Muslim Quarter), Nabi Musa.

Ottoman Period. Akko (Acre), Jerusalem (Walls and Gates), Tiberias.

Note. Centuries are indicated by a capital C followed by the number: thus, the C15 = the 15th century.

PART 1
The City of Jerusalem

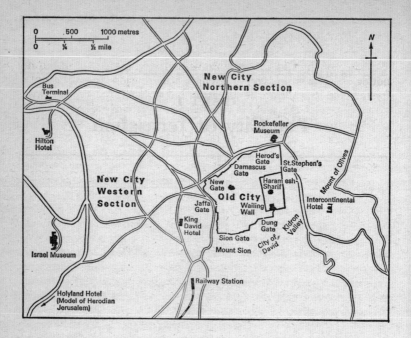

N

New City
Northern Section

Bus
Terminal

Hilton
Hotel

Rockefeller
Museum

Herod's
Gate
Damascus   St.Stephen's
Gate   Gate

New City
Western
Section

New
Gate

Haram esh-
Sharif

Mount of Olives

Old City

Jaffa
Gate

Wailing
Wall

Intercontinental
Hotel

King
David
Hotel

Dung
Gate

Kidron
Valley

Israel Museum

Sion Gate

City of
David

Mount Sion

Railway Station

Holyland Hotel
(Model of Herodian
Jerusalem)

WALLS AND GATES

The walls of the Old City enclose without dominating, limit but do not define. The impression of strength is an illusion; the city is not a fortress and its walls are not a barrier but a veil. The visitor is drawn forward, challenged, and finally embraced. The city inspires passion, and the expansion and contraction of its walls (fig. 1) show how it has struggled to accommodate the expectations it has aroused.

The city of David [1] was a small settlement on the eastern hill, close to the only spring and defended on two sides by deep valleys. By bringing the Ark of the Covenant within its walls, David made it the symbol of a religious ideal which transcended the petty jealousies of the twelve tribes of Israel. To underline this dimension his son Solomon (965–928 BC) built the first temple to enshrine the Ark. He had to extend the city, and the valleys gave him no choice but to move northwards along the ridge [2].

In subsequent centuries suffering caused the city first to expand and then to contract. The Assyrian invasion of the north in the latter part of the C8 BC sent refugees flooding towards Jerusalem. Failing to find space, many built outside the wall to the west. As they had to be protected when Sennacherib menaced the city in 701 BC, a new wall was built to enclose part of the western hill [3], almost tripling the size of the city. The exact line of this wall is problematic because only 40 m have so far been exposed. This was the city devastated by the Babylonians in 586 BC. After its inhabitants returned from exile some fifty years later they were refused authority to rebuild the walls; it was accorded to Nehemiah (445–443 BC) but a greatly reduced population forced him to revert to a line which encompassed less than the city of Solomon [4].

Only after the Maccabaean revolt in the first part of the C2 BC had restored Jewish independence did the city grow again. Under powerful Hasmonaean kings, such as John Hyrcanus (134–104 BC) and Alexander Jannaeus (103–76 BC), it spread first to the west [5] and then to the north [6]. It was destined to grow further to the north and to the south, but the lines of the eastern and western walls have remained constant ever since.

Herod (37–4 BC), surprisingly, does not appear to have touched the walls, concentrating his attention on buildings within the city. One of these, the Temple, naturally affected the eastern wall which was replaced by one side of his great platform. According to Josephus

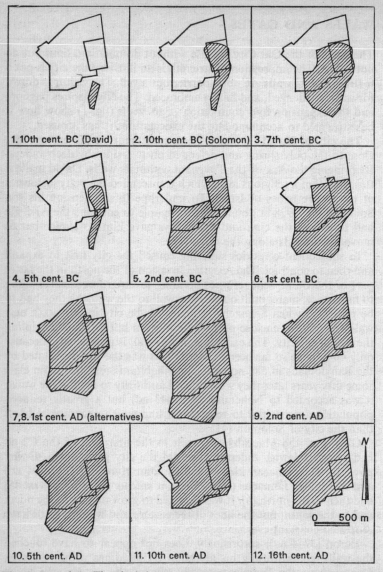

1. 10th cent. BC (David)
2. 10th cent. BC (Solomon)
3. 7th cent. BC
4. 5th cent. BC
5. 2nd cent. BC
6. 1st cent. BC
7,8. 1st cent. AD (alternatives)
9. 2nd cent. AD
10. 5th cent. AD
11. 10th cent. AD
12. 16th cent. AD

N

0   500 m

Fig. 1. Jerusalem. The shaded areas represent the size of the walled city at different periods.

(*War* 5: 147–55), Herod Agrippa I (AD 37–44) laid the foundations of a new north wall which was completed only during the First Revolt (AD 66–70), but his indications are so vague, and the archaeological evidence so ambiguous, that the exact trace of this famous 'Third Wall' is still disputed. Some claim that it follows the line of the present north wall [7] but others insist that it enclosed a much greater area [8].

After his victory in AD 70 Caesar ordered the walls of Jerusalem to be razed, 'leaving only the loftiest of the towers, Phasael, Hippicus, and Mariamne, and the portion of the wall enclosing the city on the west: the latter as an encampment for the garrison that was to remain and the towers to indicate to posterity the nature of the city and the strong defences which had yet yielded to Roman prowess' (Josephus, *War* 7: 1–2). The destruction begun by Vespasian was completed by Hadrian in AD 135. It is not clear if his new city, Aelia Capitolina [9], was walled, but its dimensions were very close to those of the present city whose street plan (such as it is) is conditioned by the lay-out of Aelia; the main arteries are still the same.

The small city, deadened by the absence of Jews who were forbidden to enter it, acquired a new lease of life when Christianity received the public support of the emperor Constantine the Great in AD 313. The places made holy by contact with Jesus drew pilgrims from all over the known world and the city was forced to expand. In the C5 the empress Eudokia confirmed this development by walling in Mount Sion and the old city of David [10]. The caliph Omar's desert riders flowed over these walls without damaging them in the C7, but Jerusalem was not as central to Islam as it was to Christianity. Pilgrimage continued but the stable population of Jerusalem decreased steadily, so that when the caliph el-Aziz felt that John Zimisces threatened the city (AD 975) he abandoned the area added by Eudokia, retaining only the northern portion [11].

The city thus acquired the dimensions it has today [12], but a whole series of walls were built and torn down before the Ottoman sultan Suliman the Magnificent erected the present rampart. He began in the north in 1537 and continued down the east and west sides. The south wall was completed only in 1540, apparently because there was a dispute whether or not Mt. Sion should be included. The authorities objected to the expense involved in extending the wall for the sake of one building, the Cenacle, and tried to get the Franciscans to bear the cost. They had no money and so were left outside. Suliman's anger (he had the architects executed) shows that he intended

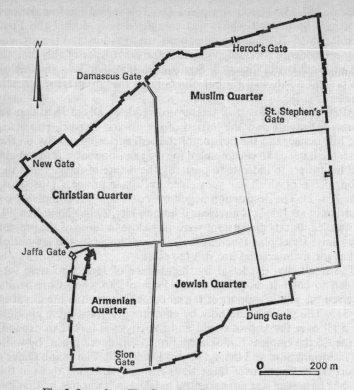

Fig. 2. Jerusalem. The Gates and Quarters of the Old City.

his wall to honour and protect the places of popular veneration. The depredations of modern urban development reveal more clearly every day that no one ever gave Jerusalem a finer gift.

Visit (fig. 2). It is possible to walk round most of the Old City on top of the walls. Not only is this the best way to appreciate their negligible defensive strength, but it offers a unique perspective on the life of the Old City. One can go all the way from Jaffa Gate to St. Stephen's Gate without descending, and for a certain distance on either side of Sion Gate. There are convenient stairways at all the gates save one; inside St. Stephen's Gate a path running to the north brings one to a point where it is easy to step up to the walkway. The rampart walk is open from 10 a.m. to 4 p.m.; women are advised not to go alone. It is best to begin at Jaffa Gate.

The Gates

Suliman the Magnificent set six gates in his wall, and it is obvious that all were designed by the same hand (fig. 3). Only three retain their original shape – Damascus Gate, Jaffa Gate, and Sion Gate. A straight or slightly curved joggled lintel bearing an Arabic inscription is set slightly inside a higher broken arch, and the entry is always indirect; the L-shape of the gate gave the guards an advantage by forcing those entering to make a right-angled turn which broke their momentum. Such entrances worked well as long as all goods were carried on pack animals but once wheeled traffic developed, modifications became inevitable. Herod's Gate and St. Stephen's Gate lost their turn and became direct entrances. The Dung Gate was originally only a postern but was widened after World War II.

0   4 m

Fig. 3. Jerusalem. Two C16 Ottoman gates. Left: St. Stephen's Gate. Right: Damascus Gate.

Suliman gave all six gates official names, but in fact the names vary according to language and religious community (fig. 2).

The official name of *Herod's Gate* is Bab ez-Zahra, 'the Flowered Gate'. It got its present name because pilgrims of the C16–C17 believed a Mameluke house inside to be the palace of Herod Antipas (now within the Franciscan Monastery of the Flagellation). It was at this point that the Crusaders established themselves on the wall at noon on 15 July 1099. The original entrance was in the east face of the tower.

Damascus Gate is the most elaborate of the six, and is the finest example of Ottoman architecture in the region. Its Arabic name is Bab el-Amud, 'the Gate of the Column'. Hadrian is reputed to have erected a column in the area and one is in fact represented in the C6 Madaba Map just inside the gate. It is the only gate to have been excavated. Running above an angled Crusader entrance, the present bridge permits one to look down at the beautifully moulded base of the wall built by Herod Agrippa I in AD 40–1. The small side entrance was part of this wall but its arch and capping stone may date to Hadrian's reconstruction in AD 135.

New Gate was opened in 1887 by Sultan Abdul Hamid in order to facilitate access to the Old City from the new suburbs developing outside the north wall.

Arabs still call *Jaffa Gate* by its official name Bab el-Khalil, 'the Gate of the Friend', the reference being to Hebron which takes its Arabic name from Abraham, 'the Friend of God'. The wall between it and the citadel was torn down and the moat filled in by Sultan Abdul Hamid in 1898 in order to permit Kaiser Wilhelm II and his suite to ride into the city. According to legend the two graves behind the wrought-iron fence just inside the gate are those of the architects executed by Suliman for leaving Mt. Sion outside the walls.

Sion Gate is the only one whose name is the same in all languages. Its pockmarked outer face bears mute testimony to the fierce fighting for the Jewish Quarter in 1948.

The official name of *Dung Gate* is Bab el-Magharbeh, 'the Gate of the Moors', because immigrants from North Africa lived inside in the C16. The small Ottoman arch above the ugly modern lintel shows that the original gate was much smaller. The Jordanians widened it to take motor traffic during the 20 years (1948–67) when the Jaffa Gate was sealed.

Suliman called *St. Stephen's Gate* Bab el-Ghor, 'the Jordan Gate', but this name never took root. It became known as St. Stephen's

Gate only after the fall of the Latin Kingdom (1187). Earlier this name designated the present Damascus Gate, but the Arabs only permitted Christian pilgrims to leave the city by the gate facing the Mount of Olives. In consequence holy places which the Byzantines and Crusaders located north of the city moved to the east side, and the name of the gate moved with them! Its current Hebrew name, 'Lions' Gate', is derived from the heraldic emblems of the Mameluke Sultan Baybars which Suliman re-used. According to legend they represent the lions prepared to eat Suliman's father if he carried through his project to level the city. The original back wall of the gate, creating an L-shaped entrance, was removed under the British Mandate to enable cars to enter.

For the series of sealed gates, the Golden Gate, the Triple Gate, and the Double Gate, see the section on the Haram esh-Sharif (Temple Mount).

The South Wall

Extensive excavations on both sides of the wall between Sion Gate and Dung Gate (fig. 4) have brought to light interesting remains of all periods in the city's history. Those outside the wall are beautifully presented; all important elements have explanatory signs and are easily accessible, for the path runs beside the wall. Those inside the wall are not ready for visitors and are best seen from the top of the wall; there is an entrance inside Sion Gate, and further east, where the wall runs beside the road, it is easy to step up to the walkway.

Inside the wall. The great square with two masonry piers [1] belong to an Ayyubid gate tower built in 1212 and destroyed in 1219; part of it just projects outside the present wall. It cuts through a Crusader wall [2] running east-west. This wall is built on a Byzantine wall running parallel to a paved street whose slabs are still clearly visible. The large building [3] just beside the interior road has in the centre a great hall with four columns; built during the Crusader period, it was re-used by the Mamelukes.

Further to the east a very deep trench [4] reveals the massive foundations of the Nea, the 'New Church' built by Justinian in AD 543 and depicted in the Madaba Map (1 in fig. 23). The identification is confirmed by an inscription on one of the walls, and by the description of Procopius of Caesarea (before 558): 'There was not enough space on the hill for the building the Emperor wanted,

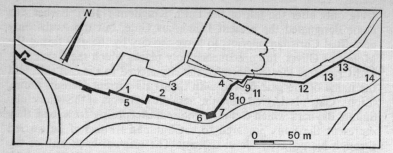

Fig. 4. Jerusalem. Excavations on both sides of the South Wall with outline of the Nea. Sion Gate is shown near the west end of the wall.

and a quarter of the site was missing on the south, and also on the east .... Those in charge of the work therefore contrived this plan: they laid their foundations right out to the edge of the high ground, and then added to the hill an artificial platform of the same height as the rock.' The south-east corner and part of an apse of the Nea project outside the present wall [9]; it was destroyed by an earthquake in the C8 AD.

Outside the wall. Just beside the path [5] one can see about 15 cm of the Ayyubid gate-tower. Part of the C1 AD lower aqueduct bringing water is visible [6] near the tower Burj el-Kibrit. The signs of frequent repair are obvious. The ceramic pipe dates from the Turkish period when the aqueduct was still in use. The aqueduct can also be traced through the medieval Sulphur Tower [7], and picked up again in the deep narrow channel [11] running under the wall to the Temple area. This section also contains part of a house [10] destroyed by the Romans in AD 70, but the most significant remains are on a higher level right under the wall. The two parallel walls [8] belong to a hospice attached to the Nea church. The massive blocks in the five courses of the corner of the Nea [9] are very suggestive of the magnificence of the edifice; according to Procopius of Caesarea, 'They made special wagons the size of the stones, put a stone in each and had it drawn up by 40 oxen.' The curve of a lateral apse is evident on the east side.

The rock surface running towards Dung Gate has been cut to create a great number of baths and cisterns which formed part of the basements of dwelling houses. East of the medieval tower [12] are two ritual baths [13]. Note that each *mikve* (bath) has two pools connected by a pipe; pure water stored in one was permitted to drip into the stepped pool where one bathed. Beside Dung Gate is another medieval tower [14] which guarded the Tanners' Gate (so called because the cattle market just inside furnished hides to pungent tanneries nearby). It rests on a paved Byzantine street going down to Siloam; this street linked up with the other paved street of the same period inside the present wall [2].

The Citadel and the West Wall

The west side of the Old City is dominated by the minaret and towers of the Citadel which has been its bastion since the time of Herod the Great (37–4 BC).

Israelite settlement in this area is attested as early as the C7 BC, but it was first brought within the city walls 500 years later (compare 3 and 5 in fig. 1). The Hasmonaean wall is mentioned by Josephus in his description of the three towers which Herod named in memory of his friend Hippicus, his brother Phasael, and his wife Mariamne. 'While such were the proportions of these three towers, they seemed far larger owing to their site. For the old wall in which they stood was itself built on a lofty hill, and above the hill rose as it were a crest 30 cubits higher still (*War* 5: 173). He continues, 'Adjoining and on the inner side of these towers, which lay to the north of it, was the king's palace, baffling all description' (*War* 5: 176). Remains excavated in the Armenian garden show that the palace extended almost to the present south wall.

When the Romans assumed direct control in Palestine in AD 6 the Procurator, who lived in CAESAREA, used the palace as his Jerusalem residence; it was the praetorium in which Pilate judged Jesus (John 18: 28–19: 16). In September AD 66 Jewish revolutionaries attacked and burnt the palace (*War* 2: 430–40). Titus, after his victory four years later, preserved the towers as a monument to the valour of his troops whom he garrisoned in the area of the old palace (*War* 7: 1–2).

Considering the western hill to be MT. SION, the Byzantines inevitably identified the site with the palace of David; today Phasael is still known as David's tower. They incorporated the remains of the west wall of the palace into their city wall, but whether they rebuilt the fortress is unclear. A fortress certainly existed in the C10 AD and in 1128 it became the residence of the Crusader kings of Jerusalem who extended it to the west. From the battlements on an October

day in 1187 Saladin watched two lines of Christians leave the
defeated city, one going to slavery, the other (the ransomed) to
freedom. In the following century, as the Crusaders struggled to
maintain a toe-hold in Palestine, the Citadel was rebuilt and dismantled more than once. Only when the Crusaders had clearly
relinquished all hope of return did the Mameluke Sultan Malik
an-Nasir give the fortress its present form in 1310. He retained the
line of the Crusader walls but levelled the old city wall which had
divided the interior into an inner and outer ward. Suliman the
Magnificent contributed the outer gateway, the stone bridge, and the
western terrace between 1531 and 1538. The minaret was added in
1655.

Visit (fig. 5). Open: 8.30 a.m. – 4 p.m.; closed Saturdays. The building is now a civic museum; all the exhibits are well marked.

From the platform of the ornamental outer gate [1] General
Allenby proclaimed the liberation of Jerusalem in 1917. The bridge
to the barbican [2] spans the moat, which now goes only as far as
the north-west tower [15] but originally went right round the citadel

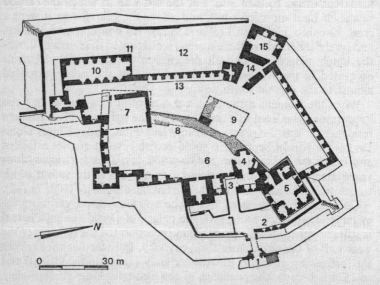

Fig. 5. Jerusalem. The Citadel (after Johns).

on the west. The glacis is medieval. The C16 stone bridge leads to the angled Mameluke main gate [3]. The entrance to the courtyard is from the C14 hexagonal room [4], but it is better first to climb the outside stairs to the roof of the Phasael tower [5] in order to get a bird's-eye view of the excavations.

The network walls in the deep trench [6] were designed to hold the rubble brought in by Herod to create the platform on which he built his palace. On the west it was held by the C2 BC Hasmonaean wall [8] which had two towers [7 and 9]. The orientation of [7] was altered in the Middle Ages, but the masonry visible in [9] is original. The difference between the great rough Herodian blocks at the base of Phasael [5] and the smaller stones above is striking; the Ottomans built for display while Herod built for eternity. The Romans had little choice but to leave this tower standing since the base is solid all the way through.

There was a Crusader gate [11] at the corner of the Mameluke mosque [10] and from it a wall ran to the middle of the north-west tower [15] whose exclusively medieval foundations make any identification with the Herodian towers, Hippicus or Mariamne, impossible. The Mamelukes moved the west wall [13] inwards, but the bailey outside [12] is due to Suliman the Magnificent who is also responsible for the gate [14].

From this gate it is worthwhile to go out on to the street and follow the city wall to the south-west corner. In this section it has been cleared to bedrock and it is easy to appreciate the various building periods. The C16 Ottoman wall is built on the remains of the C2 BC Hasmonaean wall which is visible in places. Outside this line Herod built his wall. How high it went is unknown; it may have been intended only to protect the foundations of the earlier wall.

THE MUSLIM QUARTER

The Muslim Quarter covers 76 acres in the north-eastern sector of the Old City (fig. 2). The delapidated buildings huddle wearily together and only the domes bubbling up everywhere suggest the intensity of life within. The population is estimated at 14,000. Although within the city walls since AD 40 the quarter has little to show for its long history, but what it does have can be shown with pride. There are striking Roman and Crusader remains along the street inside St. Stephen's Gate (fig. 6), and marvellous Mameluke façades in the warren of little streets beside the Haram esh-Sharif.

St. Anne's

Crusader Jerusalem is seen at its best in the simple strength of St. Anne's (AD 1140), certainly the loveliest church in the city. According to Byzantine tradition, the crypt enshrines the home of the Virgin Mary and her parents Joachim and Anne. Next to it are the ruins of miraculous medicinal baths where clients of the god Serapis (Asclepius) gathered in hope of healing; Jesus there cured one, a man ill for 38 years (John 5: 1–13).

The high priest Simon constructed two great pools about 200 BC to supply water to the Temple (Sir. 50: 3). Towards the middle of the next century a number of natural caves east of the pools were adapted to serve as small baths; their function can only have been religious or medicinal, and at this time the two were inseparable: health was a gift of the gods. The twin pools were taken out of commission when Herod the Great (37–4 BC) dug the Pool of Israel closer to his new temple, but they continued to fill with water during the winter rains and perhaps served to wash the animals brought for sacrifice in the temple.

John begins his account of Jesus' miracle with the words, 'Now at the Sheep-Gate in Jerusalem is a pool with five porches; its name in Hebrew is Bethesda' (5: 2). The name may mean 'House of Mercy', a very appropriate designation for a healing sanctuary. After AD 135

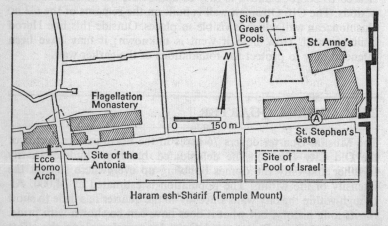

Fig. 6. Jerusalem. The area immediately inside St. Stephen's Gate.

when Jerusalem was paganized into Aelia Capitolina the sanctuary expanded into a temple; votive offerings of the C2 and C3 AD show that it was dedicated to Serapis (Asclepius). In Hadrian's grid-plan (reflected in today's streets, fig. 6) a street ran across the dike dividing the ancient pools to terminate in front of the Temple.

Origen (*c.* AD 231) was the first to relate the five porches mentioned in the gospel to the shape of the double pool, 'four around the edges and another across the middle'. The hypothesis is an obvious one; it is doubtful that he actually saw anything. By the middle of the C5 AD a church had been built; its west end projected out over the dike dividing the pools. It was dedicated to the Blessed Virgin whose home was believed to be in the vicinity.

The Crusaders found only the ruins betraying the destructive passage of the caliph Hakim in AD 1009. They erected a small chapel in the middle of the large Byzantine church; a stairway down to a corner of the northern pool permitted pilgrims to venerate the miracle of John 5. Just beside that they built the beautiful Romanesque church of St. Anne to enshrine the home of the Virgin and to serve as the conventual chapel of a community of nuns. Soon too small for the growing community, which included members of the royal family, the church was enlarged by moving the façade out 7 m.

On 25 July 1192 Saladin transformed the church into a Muslim theological school; his inscription is still above the door. Other rulers were not so careful; they did not destroy but neither did they protect and by the C18 the church was roof-deep in refuse. It recovered its former glory only when the Ottoman Turks presented it to France in 1856 as a gesture of gratitude for aid in the Crimean War.

Visit. Open: 8 a.m.–12 p.m. and 2–5 p.m. (winter), 2.30–6 p.m. (summer). Entrance at A. The museum containing the more important objects found in the excavations is not open to visitors, but those really interested should ask the guardian.

The location of the medieval cloister is preserved by the garden around the bust of Cardinal Levigerie, founder of the White Fathers to whose charge the church is entrusted. Around are various objects brought to light by the excavations. A narrow stairway protected by a railing permits a view of the plastered south-east corner of the southern pool (200 BC); it is 13 m deep.

The church deserves silent contemplation. A joint in the north wall betrays the medieval extension. The crypt is older than the church; the foundations of the pillars interfere with the original shape of the caves which once formed part of the sanctuary of Serapis; only one section is open to the public.

Before visiting the excavations examine carefully the plan affixed to the railings; it is the only way to grasp the relationships of the various elements which come from several different periods. The tri-apsidal church was built directly above the healing sanctuary. Part of the west end lay on the dike dividing the two pools but the sides were supported by a series of huge arches founded on the bottom of the pool; a perspective drawing opposite the shop at the street entrance facilitates visualization.

In the excavation the various remains are clearly labelled and dated, making a detailed guide unnecessary. Note in particular the section in the centre furthest from the apse of the medieval chapel. The curvature of the walls shows that two rooms were vaulted; from one, three steps lead down to a small cave cut in the rock; a rect-angular shallow depression at one end is the bath. After bathing, the client of Serapis slept in a darkened room; drug-induced dreams provided the basis of the priest's diagnosis.

Ecce Homo Arch

From St. Anne's the road runs uphill into the Old City. Just beyond the cross-roads on the crest a two-windowed room is suspended above the street. It rests on an ancient arch whose northern pier with a smaller side-arch is preserved in the Convent of the Sisters of Sion. In this building one can see that the arch is surrounded by a pave-ment made of beautifully trimmed slabs; its support vaulting spans a huge rock-cut pool (broken outline in fig. 6). Part of the pavement is also to be seen in the chapel of the Franciscan monastery of the Flagellation.

For over a generation this complex was identified with the Antonia fortress built by Herod the Great between 37 and 35 BC and named after his Roman friend Mark Antony: the arch was the entrance and the pavement the courtyard. New archaeological evidence showed that the pavement must be dated to the founding of Aelia Capitolina in AD 135 and so it was suggested that the pave-ment belonged to a forum on which stood a Roman triumphal arch celebrating Hadrian's suppression of the Second Jewish Revolt (132–135). Closer investigation, however, revealed that the arch in no way resembled Roman triumphal arches of the C2 AD. On the contrary, it was found to have close parallels in Roman city gates of the C1 AD. Hence it is now thought that the arch was the eastern gate of the city when it was extended to the north by Herod Agrippa I (AD 37–44). On this hypothesis it would have been protected by the long rock-cut ditch running up to the high escarpment of the Antonia fortress. Part of the ditch may have been an ancient cistern; we know that it was still open in June AD 70 because, in order to get their siege equipment up to the Antonia, the Romans had to build a ramp 'across the middle of the pool called Struthion' (*War* 5: 467).

After the Roman victory, on the orders of Vespasian, the wall and gate were torn down, but the debris of the superstructure protected the lower part of the gate. When Hadrian replanned Jerusalem in AD 135 he created a forum here, leaving the ancient gate in the middle of the pavement which now covered the pool, as a monument to his achievement.

Visit. No traces have yet been found of the Antonia fortress, described at length by Josephus (*War* 5: 238–47), but since he says it was 'built upon a rock 50 cubits high' at the north-west angle of the Temple, it can only be located on the escarpment now occupied by the al-Omariya school, reached by a flight of wide steps parallel to the street. Entrance to the courtyard is permitted outside school hours, i.e. early in the afternoon, Fridays, and school holidays. There is nothing to see there, but the grilled windows on the upper level provide an unusual view of the Haram esh-Sharif.

The most extensive remains are preserved in the Convent of the Sisters of Sion whose entrance is just beside the Ecce Homo arch (open: 8 a.m.–12 p.m. and 2.30–6 p.m.; closed Sundays). The sisters provide brief explanatory lectures with models and diagrams, and guided tours.

Via Dolorosa

The first two stations of the Way of the Cross are located in the immediate vicinity of the Ecce Homo arch. These and seven other stations are indicated by numbers 1–9 in fig. 8; the other five are within the Holy Sepulchre.

The Via Dolorosa is defined by faith, not by history. On the night of Holy Thursday Byzantine pilgrims used to go in procession from Gethsemane to Calvary, following approximately the present route, but there were no devotional halts along the way. By the C8 a number of stops had become customary but the route was completely different: from Gethsemane it went round the city on the south to the house of Caiphas on Mount Sion, then to the Praetorium of Pilate at St. Sophia somewhere near the Temple, and finally to the Holy Sepulchre. In the Middle Ages the picture becomes much more complicated as the Latin Christians were divided into two camps. One group located the Praetorium and the palace of the high priest on Mount Sion; the other placed both north of the Temple; in consequence, they followed completely different routes to the Holy Sepulchre. The basis of the conflict was simple: one group possessed churches on the western hill, the other on the eastern.

In the C14 the Franciscans organized a devotional walk to follow the steps of Jesus in Jerusalem; a number of the present stations figured on this itinerary, but the starting-point was the Holy Sepulchre. This remained the standard route for nearly two centuries, and impressed itself firmly on the imagination of European pilgrims. A number of these pilgrims (starting in the early C15) created symbolic representations of the events of the Passion in their home countries in order to foster the devotion of those who could not make the pilgrimage. Inevitably, they followed the order of events in the gospels; independently, religious permanently resident in Jerusalem had begun to do the same but, whereas the Jerusalem tradition had only eight stations (the last being the present Seventh Station), the European tradition had fourteen stations. Since pilgrims expected to find in Jerusalem what they were accustomed to elsewhere, the European tradition gradually prevailed; the Jerusalem Way of the Cross was extended to include stations within the Holy Sepulchre. The actual route was fixed in the C18, but a number of the stations (nos. 1, 4, 5, 8) were given their present location only in the C19.

The present Way of the Cross has little chance of corresponding to historical reality; it is more probable that Pilate condemned Jesus to death on the other side of the city at the Citadel, the highest point in the city, 'Gabbatha' (John 19: 13). This was the palace of Herod where Pilate normally resided when he came up from Caesarea to ensure control during the great Jewish feasts (Philo, *Delegation to Gaius*, 38). According to the gospels, the trial took place on a platform (Matt. 27: 19) in the open (Luke 23: 4; John 18: 28). Such a structure existed at the palace in AD 66, as we know from what Josephus says of one of Pilate's successors: 'Florus lodged at the palace, and on the following day had a platform placed in front of the building and took his seat; the chief priests, the nobles, and the most eminent citizens then presented themselves before the tribunal' (*War* 2: 301); as in the case of Jesus, the affair ended in crucifixions.

If, as seems likely, Jesus was brought through the city on his way to execution, the approximate route would have been east on David Street, north on the Triple Suk (bottom left in fig. 8), and then west to Golgotha.

Mameluke Buildings

For some reason the Crusaders did not build close to the walls of the Temple; the west wall could be seen from a distance. It was only with the advent of the Mamelukes (1250–1517) that the area began to fill with buildings. They erected religious colleges and pilgrim hospices in such numbers that the whole sector west and north of the Haram glowed with clean-cut stone – red, white, and black – whose austere decoration still preserves its dignity. Some streets have changed very little, but they lie off the beaten track and few venture in. Those with the courage to explore will discover a little-known facet of Jerusalem's rich history.

The nature of these buildings is surprising when one remembers that the Mamelukes were for the most part converts to Islam. The Arabic word *mamluk* means 'owned', and the term was applied to boys, bought in the slave-markets of present-day Turkey and southern Russia, who became bond-servants of Muslim rulers. When Saladin was caught behind the Crusader battle line at Mont Giscard in 1177, only the fact that his Mamelukes stayed with him enabled him to fight his way out. The idea behind the practice was to have servants (who eventually became vassals) who had no relationship to any other political faction; they could then have no conflict of loyalties. Promoted to positions of importance as the eyes and ears of the ruler, they grew so powerful that eventually they were able to topple the Ayyubid dynasty of Saladin (1250). Once in power they continued the practice for precisely the same reason.

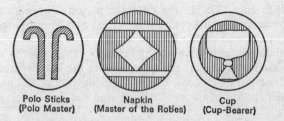

Polo Sticks
(Polo Master)

Napkin
(Master of the Robes)

Cup
(Cup-Bearer)

Fig. 7. Mameluke Blazons.

No matter how high they rose in the service of the state Mamelukes never forgot their origins; the blazons found on their buildings in Jerusalem (fig. 7) reflect the first responsibilities they had at court. Tankiz, the great Viceroy of Syria, always had inscribed on his buildings the emblem of the cup he bore as a young man.

Much is known about these buildings from a British architectural survey still in progress, and from inscriptions still in place which give the name of the founder, the date of construction, and the function of the building. In consequence, they come to life in a unique way.

Most of the buildings are now tenements and are not open to the public; a glance through an open doorway is generally the most one can hope for. Fortunately the most interesting part of a Mameluke building is the ornate façade which normally has but one door highlighted by a much larger recess; the combination offers welcome shade and protection. The conscious use of shadow and silhouette brings out the detail of the embellishment of the door recess, and alternating courses of red, cream, and occasionally black stone give interest to a broad expanse of masonry. The intricate complexity of the ornamentation is a challenge to adequate appreciation. Detailed explanation is no substitute for the discerning eye delighting in discovery.

For convenience the buildings are grouped by streets rather than by date; the initial letter gives the location on the map in fig. 8. All the fountains in the area are due to the munificence of the Ottomans in the C16.

Aqabat et-Takiya

[A] *Serai es-Sitt Tunshuq.* The Lady Tunshuq was a Mongol or Turkish slave forced to live abroad when the Kurdish dynasty of her husband or protector began to crumble under the onslaughts of Tamerlane at the end of the C14. She managed to bring with her enough money to erect this palace (1379–82) in which she lived until her death in July 1398. In the Ottoman period it appears to have been a convent of dervishes and is now used as a Muslim orphanage providing work and shelter for 150 boys.

The building is unusual in having three doors; in order to vary the effect all are framed in different ways. Note the inlaid panel above the left door (now blocked), the intricate joggling of the lintel and circular decoration of the centre door, and the fine dressing of the masonry.

[B] *Turbat es-Sitt Tunshuq.* Six years before her death the Lady

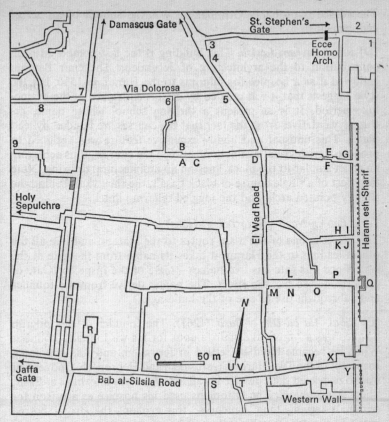

Fig. 8. Muslim Quarter of Jerusalem. Locations of Stations of the Cross (numbers) and Mameluke buildings (letters).

Tunshuq prepared her domed tomb immediately across the street from the palace. In addition to the stone mosaic panel (which differs subtly from its sister across the road), note the voussoirs of black, white, and red stones.

[C] *Imaret of Khasseki Sultan.* Little is known of the history of this building save that it was used as a soup-kitchen for the poor until recently. Anyone who has attentively examined the two previous buildings [A and B] can see that this comes from a later period; no coloured stones are used and the construction of the lintel is different.

The edifice is probably Ottoman; it was the subject of an act of endowment in 1552.

[D] *Ribat Bayram Jawish*. This building is the last notable Muslim contribution to the architecture of Jerusalem. The emir Bayram endowed it as a hospice for pilgrims to the Haram in 1540, but the style suggests that it was created by craftsmen trained in the Mameluke period. It is at present a thriving school whose name, er-Rasasiyya, derives from the fact that the courses are bonded by lead plates. This unusual and highly expensive feature was designed to produce a crisp visual distinction between the courses, thus achieving an effect similar to the black lines on an architectural drawing. Note the effect of a single course of black basalt, the shell vault behind the slightly pointed arch, and the joggled relieving lintel.

Tariq Bab en-Nazir (Tariq Bab el-Habs)

This street is one of the main routes to the Haram, and like all the others leading to the Haram it takes its name from the gate at the end. Since this gate has two names – Gate of the Inspector/Gate of the Prison – so has the street. The names derive from the founder and subsequent use of one of the buildings.

[E] *Ribat Ala ed-Din el-Basir* (1267). The founder of this pilgrim hospice was a Mameluke emir famous for his wisdom and holiness. When he became blind he settled in Jerusalem and was appointed Inspector of the Two Harams (Jerusalem and Hebron); his judgement was so respected that, despite his affliction, he was known as el-Basir, 'the Clear-Sighted'. The Ottomans used his hospice as a prison for criminals serving long sentences; this explains the strong barred gate and the minute cells in the courtyard.

This is the earliest Mameluke building in Jerusalem; no coloured stones are used. Note the chamfering of the left pier, the carved panel over the door, and the bossed stones above the pointed arch.

[F] *Ribat Mansuri* (1282). The construction of this hospice, ordered by the sultan al-Mansur Qalawun, was probably supervised by the emir Ala ed-Din whose own hospice is just across the road. Under the Ottomans it served first as a barracks and then as a prison; the small cells may still be seen in the courtyard.

The projecting entrance narrows the street at this point. The deep vestibule is paved with striated stone slabs reminiscent of those belonging to the forum of Hadrian (AD 135) preserved in the Convent of the Sisters of Sion at the Ecce Homo arch. The basic structure of the entrance is similar to that of [E] but an evolution is perceptible; coloured stones appear in the wide pointed arch and in the relieving lintel above the door, but as yet there is no joggling.

[G] *Muslim Supreme Council*. The columned entrance was erected during the British Mandate. On the first floor one may apply for permission to visit the locked underground areas of the Haram; it is not always given.

Tariq Bab el-Hadid

As seen from the main thoroughfare, Tariq el-Wad, this is a curved uninviting street on the east side which disappears into an ominous looking tunnel leading to the Iron Gate of the Haram. The tunnel is in fact very short and opens into a quiet street lined on both sides with fine Mameluke buildings of the C13–C15.

[H] *Madrasa Jawhariyya* (1440). The founder of this college was an Abyssinian eunuch; most eunuchs were given names of precious stones or substances, and Jawhar means 'jewel'. After being given his freedom, his energy and talent won him the offices of Treasurer and Superintendent of the Royal Harem in Cairo.

The one noteworthy feature of this building is the founder's concern to be in direct contact with the Haram; in order to achieve this he had to extend his structure above the one-storey Ribat Kurd next door. Note the continuity of the courses above the moulding of Ribat Kurd, and the circular ornamentation above the windows.

[I] *Ribat Kurd* (1293). The modesty of this single-storey hospice suggests an impecunious founder. Sayf ed-Din (he was a Kurd by origin) was in fact only a cup-bearer at the time. His promotions began two years later, and he had achieved the rank of governor of Tripoli (Lebanon) before being killed when leading a charge against the Tartars at Homs in 1299. Here entrance is easy but unfortunately recent constructions hardly make it worthwhile.

[J] *Madrasa Arghuniyya* (1358). Arghun el-Kamili was only about thirty when he died an exile in Jerusalem a year before his college was completed. He began his career as Master of the Robes (note the blazon on the inscription above the door, fig. 7) but he had been governor of Damascus and twice governor of Aleppo before being caught on the wrong side in the perpetual Mameluke power-struggle for the throne. After imprisonment in Alexandria he was banished to

Jerusalem, and we are fortunate that his frustrated talent sought expression in architecture.

The original height of the building is indicated by the bold moulding which returns on the right to exclude the entrance to the Madrasa Khatuniyya built four years earlier (1354). Note in particular the entire course of joggling and the elaborate inlay over the openings on either side of the portal.

[K] *Madrasa Muzhiriyya* (1480). When he erected this college Abu Bakr Muhammad ibn Muzhir had been secretary of the Chancery of Egypt for eight years. He was stricken by fever in Nablus in 1488 trying to raise troops for an expedition against the Ottoman sultan of Rum (Constantinople) and died the same year.

In order to bring his college into direct contact with the Haram he extended the upper floor over the Madrasa Arghuniyya. Note the trefoil arch over eight courses of imprecise stalactites, the cream and black joggling above the lintel, and the decoration of the windows.

Suq el-Qattanin

For many years this shopping arcade was full of rubbish; it has now been cleared and restored, making it possible to appreciate a different type of Mameluke architecture. The name means Market of the Cotton-Merchants, and it was built in order to provide revenue from rents to support charitable works.

Though significant work has been done, the history of this complex has not yet been fully worked out. A glance along the shop-fronts reveals two periods of construction: those nearest the entrance from Tariq el-Wad have a simple arch, whereas those at the far end near the Haram have a heavy lintel. The join near the centre is marked by pendentives coming together around a beautiful stalactite oculus. The western part [L] is earlier and originally stood alone; at a later stage the market was extended to the east [P] to join the Haram.

Three inscriptions mention the emir Tankiz. One is on the bands of brass affixed to the great doors of Bab el-Qattanin [Q], the second is on the lintel above these doors, and the third is on the lintel of the entrance to Khan Otuzbir [N]. This latter is not evident from the market so go through a dirty wooden door below a high pointed arch with a metal grille and the farmyard smell will indicate that you are in the right place. The first two inscriptions provide the date 1336.

The blazon on the Khan Otuzbir lintel shows that Tankiz was first employed as a cup-bearer (fig. 7). Having accumulated a vast fortune during his 28 years as governor of Damascus and viceroy of Syria (1312–40), he spent much of it in beautifying Jerusalem. When his loyalty became suspect, he was removed from office and executed in Alexandria in 1340.

It seems likely that Tankiz took over the old western section of the market and incorporated it into a new building project crowned by the magnificent Bab el-Qattanin. In this case he would also be responsible for the two baths, Hammam el-Ayn [M] and Hammam esh-Shifa [O]. Both are still in use today, and may probably be built above much earlier baths.

Tariq Bab es-Silsila

The Street of the Gate of the Chain is the main east–west artery in the Old City and the principal route to the Haram esh-Sharif.

[R] *Khan es-Sultan* (1386). A vaulted entrance leads into a large courtyard. Now a series of workshops, it was once surrounded by shops whose rents were devoted to the upkeep of the Haram. The present name recalls the sultan Barquq, but it seems likely that he did no more than bless a local initiative on the part of the Superintendent of the Two Harams (Jerusalem and Hebron) to increase revenues.

[S] *Madrasa/Turba Tashtimuriyya* (1382). The emir Tashtimur exercised a number of important functions in Egypt and Syria before becoming a victim of the chronic Mameluke power-struggle for control of the empire. In 1382 he retired to Jerusalem where he immediately began to build his tomb; his state of mind is admirably expressed by Shakespeare: 'If a man do not erect in this age his own tomb ere he dies, he shall live no longer in monument than the bell rings and the widow weeps' (*Much Ado About Nothing*, V, ii). He was laid to rest there two years later (1384); his son Ibrahim was buried beside him in 1393. A passage beside the tomb leads to a magnificent cruciform college.

The façade contains three elements, the high door, the two windows of the tomb, and an elegant balcony. Note the intricate joggling surrounding the inscription above the tomb windows and the fleur-de-lis interlock at the end of the inscription; Tashtimur's blazon was the pen-box of a secretary.

[T] *Turba Barakat Khan* (Khalidi Library). A glance at the façade of this building suggests a complicated history. The Romanesque decoration above the window on the right (near the corner of Aqabat Abu Madyan which leads to the Western Wall) originally surmounted the entrance to the mausoleum of Barakat Khan, a curious figure to have a monument in Jerusalem. He was commander of the Khwarizmians, a ferocious Tartar tribe who swept as far south as Gaza in 1244. Two years later, while still very young, he died drunk in battle near Homs. His head was taken in triumph to Aleppo. His two sons, however, became Mamelukes of Sultan Baybars, and one rode against the Crusaders at CAESAREA in 1265. Baybars married Barakat Khan's daughter who, when widowed, retired to Jerusalem and erected a monument to her father and brothers. Given the career of her father, there is a certain poignancy in the Koranic verses she had inscribed on the mausoleum: 'Pure we came from nothing and impure we have become; tranquil we came into this world and anguished we have become.'

Some time after 1280 a series of vaulted structures was added on the east; hence the arches still evident in the façade. In 1390 these were blocked up and the present door and window inserted by one Muhammad ibn Ahmad. He also built a room above; the supports of a balcony project at the top of the wall. In 1900 the original tomb was converted into the reading room of the Khalidi Library housing 12,000 books and manuscripts.

Note in particular the double lintel of the centre window, and the intricate centrepiece (containing the word 'Allah') of the joggled lintel. The blazon at each end of the lintel inscription has no parallel in Mameluke heraldry and may be the personal emblem of Barakat Khan.

[U] *Turba Kilaniyya* (1352). The fine proportions of the monochrome façade show how disciplined austerity can be used to effect. Behind each set of double windows is a tomb-chamber, an unusual feature that has a very human explanation. The emir Kilani left 100,000 dirhems to his nephew to build a tomb in Jerusalem and convey his body there for burial; at his uncle's expense the nephew added a tomb-chamber for himself!

Note the restrained moulding framing both the entire building and the two sets of windows. The course above the lintel of the blocked windows is undercut in a decorative profile to achieve the same effect as a relieving arch. The next course is set back to form a long panel with decorated terminals.

[V] *Turba/Madrasa Taziyya* (1362). Having begun his career as a cup-bearer at the court of Sultan Muhammad (note the blazon, fig. 7), Taz rose to become governor of Aleppo when Arghun el-Kamili (see [J]) was recalled in 1354. He suffered the same fate four years later, and was imprisoned in Kerak and Alexandria before being exiled to Jerusalem; he died in Damascus in 1362. The poverty of his tomb suggests that he had little saved! Only the window of the tomb-chamber remains, the door having disappeared.

[W] *Turba Turkan Khatun* (1352). This unusual tomb was erected for a Mongol princess who died on pilgrimage to Mecca. The inscription gives the name of her grandfather who was a Mameluke of Muhammad Uzbak, the famous khan who ruled the Golden Horde (1312–40).

The façade is striking in its simple elegance; the arabesques in its grey stone are the most subtle in Jerusalem. Note the use of the blunt star first introduced as architectural decoration by the Mamelukes.

[X] *Turba Sadiyya* (1311). This tomb of sheikh Burhan ed-Din, a famous judge, is noteworthy for the fine stalactite corbelling, the earliest of its kind in Jerusalem, and for the mosaic of coloured marble over the door.

[Y] *Madrasa Tankiziyya* (1328). The open square in front of Bab es-Silsila permits full appreciation of the magnificent entrance to the college erected by the emir Tankiz whose career is described apropos of Suq el-Qattanin above. The big inscription is punctuated by three cup blazons (fig. 7). Note in particular the stalactites and the moulding of the semi-dome above.

The street and college rest on Wilson's Arch, a huge bridge (named after its discoverer) built to span the Tyropoeon valley; it can be visited from the Western Wall area (see EXCAVATIONS WEST AND SOUTH OF THE HARAM ESH-SHARIF).

THE CHRISTIAN QUARTER

The Christian Quarter covers an area of 45 acres in the north-west section of the Old City (fig. 2); its population is estimated at 4,500. Just as the Mamelukes clustered their buildings around the Haram esh-Sharif, so Christians erected their institutions as close as possible to the Holy Sepulchre (A in fig. 9). The area is quieter (more clerics, fewer children) and much more affluent than the Muslim Quarter, because Christians had access to a better educational system.

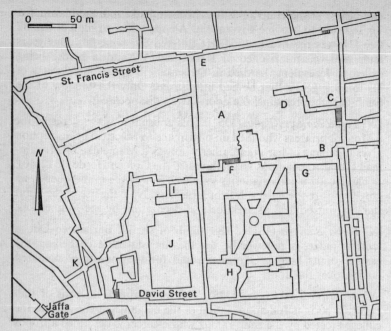

Fig. 9. Christian Quarter of Jerusalem.

Holy Sepulchre [A]

One expects the central shrine of Christendom to stand out in
majestic isolation, but anonymous buildings cling to it like barnacles.
One looks for numinous light; it is in fact dark and cramped. One
hopes for peace, but the cacophony of warring chants is punctuated
by the ring of masons' hammers. One desires holiness only to encounter a jealous possessiveness: the six groups of occupants – Latin
Catholics, Greek Orthodox, Armenians, Syrians, Copts, and
Ethiopians – watch one another suspiciously for any infringement
of rights. The frailty of man is nowhere more apparent than here; it
epitomizes the human condition. The empty who come to be filled
will leave desolate; those who permit the church to question them
may begin to understand why hundreds of thousands thought it
worth while to risk death or slavery in order to pray here.

Is this the place where Christ died and was buried? The answer is a very probable affirmative. At the beginning of the C1 AD the site was a disused quarry outside the city walls ([6] in fig. 1); and tombs similar to those found elsewhere, and dated to this period, had been cut into the vertical surfaces left by the quarrymen. The latter had also cut around a block of inferior, cracked stone standing to a height of some 10 m. These facts are the meagre contribution of archaeology but at least they show that the site is compatible with the gospel evidence. Jesus was crucified at a place reminiscent of a skull outside the city (John 19: 17) and there was a grave nearby (John 19: 41–2).

On the positive side there is the tradition of the Jerusalem community which held liturgical celebrations at the tomb at least until AD 66; it had become the practice of Jews to pray at the tombs of holy men. The memory of the site remained, even after Hadrian (AD 135) had filled in the area to provide a level base for a temple dedicated to Aphrodite. It is unlikely that he chose the spot in order to destroy a Christian site, as Jerome claims; a natural prominence close to the main street would attract the attention of any city planner. The value of the Jerusalem tradition must have been scrutinized very carefully when the emperor Constantine decided to build a church in honour of the Resurrection, because acceptance involved double expense: substantial buildings had to be torn down and a new one put in their place. Had the community been willing to move 100 m one way or the other everything would have been much easier, but they were insistent that it was precisely here and nowhere else. In fact, no alternative location ever won popular support in Jerusalem until General Gordon invented the Garden Tomb in 1883.

Constantine's church, started in 326, was dedicated in 335. It comprised four elements (fig. 10): [1] an atrium at the head of the steps from the main street; [2] a covered apsidal basilica; [3] an open courtyard with the block of stone venerated as Golgotha in the southeast corner; [4] the tomb. The work on the tomb was not quite finished at the time of the dedication because of the immense labour involved in cutting away the cliff in order to isolate the tomb-chamber; it was completed some time before 348.

The reconstruction of Modestus, after the building had been set on fire by the Persians in 614, made no significant changes. When the caliph Omar came to sign the treaty of capitulation in 638 he refused the patriarch's invitation to pray in the church, saying, 'If I had prayed in the church it would have been lost to you, for the Believers would have taken it saying: Omar prayed here.' Such

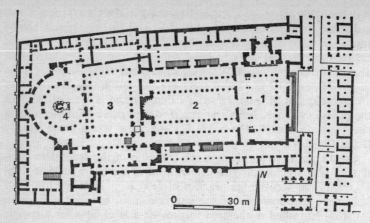

Fig. 10. The Holy Sepulchre. The C4 Constantinian church (after Couäsnon).

generosity had unfortunate consequences; had the church become a mosque it would not have been destroyed by the Fatamide caliph Hakim in 1009. The destruction was systematic; wrecking crews knocked the courses from the walls and attacked the rock tomb with pickaxe and hammer, stopping only when debris covered what remained.

The poor community in Jerusalem could not afford repairs. It was not until Constantine Monomachus came to the throne of Byzantium in 1042 that the Imperial Treasury provided a subsidy for reconstruction. However, it was not enough and a great part of the original edifice had to be abandoned (fig. 11). To compensate for the loss of the basilica an upper gallery was introduced into the rotunda and an apse added to its eastern side. The open courtyard remained much as it had been. This was the church to which the Crusaders went with tears of piety on 15 July 1099.

Exactly 50 years later the Crusaders completed their alterations; the courtyard was absorbed into a Romanesque church joined to the unchanged rotunda. As it stands, therefore, the Holy Sepulchre is a Crusader building. A fire in 1808 and the earthquake of 1927 did extensive damage, but it took until 1959 for the three major communities (Latin, Greek, and Armenian) to agree on a major repair programme now nearing completion. The guiding principle was the replacement of elements no longer capable of fulfilling their structural function; a weakened stone was replaced but its neighbour in

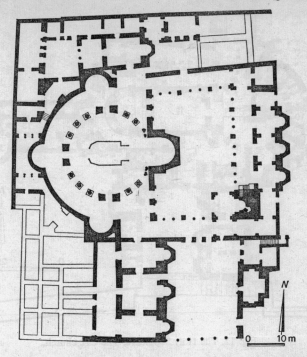

Fig. 11. The Holy Sepulchre. The church as restored by Constantine Monomachus in the C11 (after Couäsnon).

good condition was permitted to remain. Local masons were trained
to trim stone in the style of the C11 for the rotunda, and in that of
the C12 for the church.

Visit (fig. 12). Open 4 a.m.–7 p.m.; no shorts or sleeveless blouses
permitted. The façade [1] is entirely C12; the steps and edicule to the
right [2] were the Crusader entrance to Calvary. After this entrance
was closed in 1187 it became the Chapel of the Franks. The steep
stairs just inside the main door lead up to Calvary [3]. The floor of
the two chapels (Latin and Greek) is level with the summit of the
block of rock left in the old quarry; it can be touched through a hole
beneath the Greek altar. Downstairs, in the Chapel of Adam [4], a
glass plate permits one to see the rock; the crack and the poor

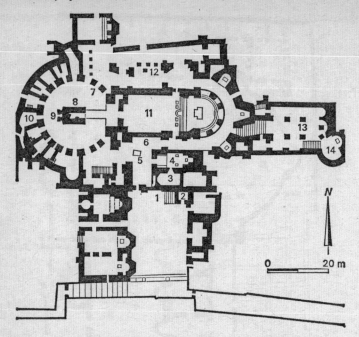

Fig. 12. The Holy Sepulchre. The C12 church.

quality are quite evident. Crusader kings were buried in this chapel;
the effigies of Godfrey de Bouillon and Baldwin I reposed on the
two benches near the door until 1810.

The Stone of Unction [5], commemorating the annointing of Jesus
before burial, appeared first in the C12; the present one dates from
1810. The wall with the paintings [6] has no structural function, and
unnecessarily blocks a fine view across the church. When the fire of
1808 cracked the great arch, a wall was erected to support it, and the
Greeks hung icons on it. The recent restoration of the arch made the
wall unnecessary but the Greeks now had nowhere to hang their
icons, so a new one was built just for this purpose!

The outer walls of the rotunda, for 11 m above ground level, are
C4. The C11 piers and columns, cracked in the fire of 1808, have all
been restored, two exactly as they were found [7]. Note that one has
a rim around the top and the other around the bottom, and that the
taper of the latter is continued in the former. The huge C4 columns

supporting the drum of the dome were simply cut in half and reused to support the upper gallery introduced in the C11.

The tomb monument [8], accurately described as 'a hideous kiosk', dates only from the C19, the fire of 1808 having destroyed the edifice erected in the C11 to replace the rock tomb removed on the orders of Hakim in 1009. On the basis of the representations of the Constantinian tomb embossed on pilgrim flasks of the C6 and on a pre-C10 stone model found in Narbonne, J. Wilkinson has proposed a very probable reconstruction of the C4 tomb of Christ (fig. 13). The polygonal part was the original rock decorated by columns; a canopied masonry structure enshrined the entrance.

A very small section of the original tomb can be seen at the base of the Coptic shrine at the back of the present edicule [9]. The C4 wall and apse are preserved in the adjacent Syrian chapel [10]. Through a dark hole in this wall is a Jewish tomb chamber of the C1 with burial shafts (*kokhim*) in the walls and ossuary pits in the floor; part of the chamber was cut away when Constantine's engineers removed the cliff to isolate the rock tomb of Christ.

The simple dignity of the Crusader church [11] – transitional between Romanesque and Gothic – is marred by the lack of taste displayed in recent Greek Orthodox additions. The upper gallery,

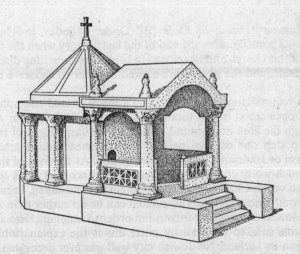

Fig. 13. J. Wilkinson's reconstruction of the C4 Tomb of Christ.

unusual in churches of this period (C12), is due to the corresponding gallery introduced into the rotunda in the previous century.

The curious arrangement of two lines of very different pillars [12] is due to the C12 architect's concern to preserve what remained of the original colonnade on the north side of the Byzantine courtyard in front of the rotunda (see figs. 10 and 11). He placed his weight-bearing pillars inside the Byzantine line which is closest to the present outer wall.

On the walls of the steps down to the crypt of St. Helena [13] note the multitude of crosses carved by pilgrims. This crypt, now in possession of the Armenians, was opened only in the C12, but its north and south walls (left and right when facing the altar) are the foundations of the nave of the C4 basilica. From this church a narrow stairway probably led down to the cistern [14] in which St. Helena is reputed to have discovered the True Cross, but the tradition is first recorded 16 years after the church was completed.

Hidden Parts of the Constantinian Holy Sepulchre

The church of the C4 was much bigger than the present one, and very interesting traces of it are to be found hidden in other buildings in the immediate vicinity. The capital letters refer to the location in fig. 9.

The Russian Mission in Exile [B]. Open: Monday to Thursday: 9 a.m. – 3 p.m. Towards the end of the last century when the foundations of this church and hospice were being dug surprising discoveries were made, and the plans were altered in order to conserve them in place.

The visitors' area is dominated by a much altered triumphal arch which once stood in the forum that Hadrian built here in AD 135. Through the arch and around to the left is a large flight of steps. In the top step one can see part of the pavement which graced the platform of Hadrian's temple to Aphrodite. At the foot of the steps is a much-worn door-sill. The veneration accorded it as the gate through which Christ went out to Golgotha is mistaken, because the heavy wall with which it is associated can be no earlier than AD 135.

The lowest course is set forward in order to accommodate a veneer of marble held to the wall by pins; this is the explanation of the pitting in its surface. No Jewish city wall was ever decorated in this way. Hence, it can only be the retaining wall of Hadrian's temple platform whose veneer of marble is mentioned by Eusebius (*c*.338). Constantine used it as the façade of the atrium ([1] in fig. 10) of his church by simply cutting out three doors. The one visible is the south door; the columns in the recess opposite belonged to the C4 portico. The purpose of the door-sill in Hadrian's plan is unclear; in the C4 it gave access to a cloister running along the south side of the church.

Zalatimo's Shop [C]. At the foot of the steps leading up to the Coptic Patriarchate is a small bakery. The owner will generally give one permission to visit his storeroom where one can see the continuation of the Hadrianic and Constantinian wall noted in the Russian Mission. Here one can inspect the inner surface and the jambs of the massive central door of the C4 Holy Sepulchre ([1] in fig. 10). In [B] and [C], therefore, one can see half the façade of the original church.

Ethiopian Monastery [D]. At the end of the passage reached by the stairs beside the bakery a small door opens into a cluster of mud huts. These poor dwellings are occupied by Ethiopian religious forced from their building by the Copts. Silent and inward looking, the immense dignity of the tall slender men generates the atmosphere of contemplation so desperately lacking in the church. They live among the ruins of a medieval cloister which the Crusaders erected in the space once occupied by Constantine's great basilica. The cupola in the middle of the courtyard admits light to the crypt of St. Helena below ([13] in fig. 12).

Two Mosques [E and F]

North of the Holy Sepulchre is the *Khanqah Salahiyya* [E], a convent of Soufi mystics founded by Saladin between 1187 and 1189 on the site of the palace of the Crusader Patriarch of Jerusalem. During the restoration of 1417 a minaret was erected on the roof.

South of the Holy Sepulchre the *Mosque of Omar* [F] commemorates the prayer of the caliph in AD 638 in the courtyard of the church. The mosque was built in 1193 and restored in the middle of the C13, but the minaret in the courtyard was erected only between 1458 and 1465.

The tops of the two minarets are identical in structure and in the quality of the light stone which contrasts with the darker lower sections of both. This hint that they were intended to be a pair is reinforced by the observation that, despite the difference in ground level, a line joining their summits is absolutely horizontal. A. Walls has further shown that the mid-point of a line drawn between the minarets falls approximately at the entrance of the tomb of Christ in the Holy Sepulchre.

There can be no doubt that this arrangement was intentional, but its purpose remains obscure. The Mamelukes may have desired to 'nullify' the Holy Sepulchre which is the one site associated with Christ that Muslims do not accept.

The Mauristan

This name is given to the square area south of the Holy Sepulchre, one corner being marked by the newest church in the Old City, the Lutheran Church of the Redeemer [G], and the other, diagonally opposite, by the oldest intact church in Jerusalem, the Church of St. John the Baptist [H]. Mauristan is a Persian word meaning 'hospital/hospice' and recalls a tradition going back to the friendship between Charlemagne and the caliph Harun er-Rashid at the beginning of the C9 AD.

In 870 Bernard the Monk wrote of his visit to Jerusalem, 'We stayed in the hospice of the Most Glorious Emperor Charles. All who come to Jerusalem for reasons of devotion and speak the Roman language [i.e. Latin] are given hospitality there. Beside it there is a church in honour of St. Mary, and thanks to the Emperor it has a splendid library. . . . In front of this hospice is the forum, and anyone who does his business there pays the person in charge an annual fee of two guineas.' Damaged, if not destroyed, by the caliph Hakim in 1009, these edifices were restored by a group who had a particular interest in this part of the city, the merchants of Amalfi.

From 1063 these traders combined piety and profit by erecting three churches with their attendant hospitals/hospices; for men, St. Mary la Latine (whose site is now occupied by the Redeemer Church); for women, St. Mary la Petite (whose location is marked by the grotesque fountain in the middle of the 1901 wholesale market); and, for the poor, St. John the Baptist. Overall charge was entrusted to Benedictine monks and nuns.

On the evening of 15 July 1099 the warden of St. John's took in a number of knights wounded in the assault on the city. Some stayed on to serve at his side, and ten years later committed themselves to serving the sick and protecting pilgrims as the Knights of St. John of the Hospital. In a short time they became the military order of the Hospitallers, but they kept the little church of St. John unchanged to remind them of their origins in the midst of great power and wealth.

After the fall of Jerusalem in October 1187 Saladin permitted ten Hospitallers to remain for a year to nurse those still in the hospital. He then used part of their great establishment for different purposes, but his nephew, Shihab ed-Din, continued the tradition of service by claiming part of it as a hospital/hospice in 1219; the name Mauristan dates from this period. As late as the C15 the building was capable of receiving 400 pilgrims, even though it was falling into decay. The end came in the C16 when the masons of Suliman the Magnificent used the huge ruins as a quarry of dressed stones to rebuild the walls of Jerusalem.

Church of the Redeemer [G]. The gallery at the top of the tower (open: 9 a.m.–1 p.m., 2–5 p.m.; Friday 9 a.m.–1 p.m.) provides a magnificent bird's-eye view of the whole area. More specifically, from this vantage point it is possible to correlate visually the scattered remains of the Constantinian Holy Sepulchre.

The present church (erected in 1898) preserves the outlines of the C11 church of St. Mary la Latine; the porch of the north entrance is medieval and is decorated with the signs of the zodiac and the symbols of the months. In the hospice adjoining the church on the south is a magnificent two-tier cloister, part of which dates from the C11 and part from an Ayyubid restoration in the C13; enter by the main door of the hospice.

Recent excavations beneath the centre of the church disclosed a heavy wall which is considered to be the southern retaining wall of Hadrian's forum (AD 135).

Church of St. John the Baptist [H]. The oldest church in Jerusalem is not only located in a hidden section of the Mauristan, but has been buried by the gradual raising of street levels. The entrance from Christian Quarter Road is clearly signposted; it gives access to the courtyard of a modern Greek Orthodox monastery whose priest (when present) will open the church.

The present façade with its two small bell-towers is a modern addition to the C11 church of the merchants of Amalfi which became the cradle of the Knights Hospitallers. As foundations they used the walls of a much earlier church, built about the middle of the C5 and restored by John the Almoner after its destruction by the Persians in 614. Some alterations were made in order to ensure the stability of the superstructure but it is still possible to detect the original plan (fig. 14).

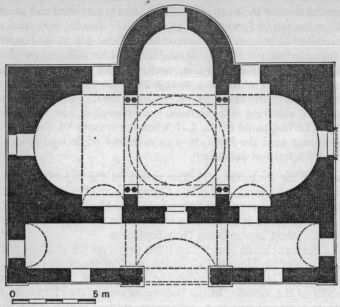

0   5 m

Fig. 14. The C5 church of St. John the Baptist.

The tradition that this was the house of Zebedee, father of the apostles James and John, is first attested in the C14, and must have arisen through confusion between John the Evangelist and John the Baptist.

Pool of the Patriarch's Bath [J]

This great reservoir entirely surrounded by buildings is accessible only through the Coptic Khan [I]. Once a typical caravanserai, the buildings around the courtyard are now used as workshops. If approached properly the owners will sometimes permit visitors to peer through the back windows overlooking the pool. A much-needed restoration project is on the drawing-boards because at present the dry pool is used as a rubbish dump by the dwellings on all sides.

Since the pool has never been investigated by archaeologists, information is sparse. It is thought to date from the Herodian period when it was fed by an aqueduct (still in existence) coming from the Mamilla Pool, and the suggestion has been made that it began as the quarry from which stones were cut for the undated Second Wall.

Josephus mentions it in order to locate one of the points where the Romans attempted to break through in AD 70 (*War* 5: 468). He gives it the name Amygdalon (= almond tree) which is probably a deformation of the Hebrew *migdal* meaning 'tower', the reference being to the renowned towers of Herod's palace nearby (WALLS AND GATES: CITADEL). In the Middle Ages the pool supplied water to baths near the Holy Sepulchre, whence its present name.

Roman Column [K]

A circle at the intersection of four covered streets is lit by a lamppost standing on a column with a Roman inscription which reads, 'M(arco) Iunio Maximo leg(ato) Aug(ustorum) Leg(ionis) X Fr (etensis) – Antoninianae – C. Dom(itius) Serg(ius) Honoratus str(ator) eius.'

The inscription honours Marcus Iunius Maximus, Prefect of Judaea and Legate of the Tenth Legion, and the column was erected at the beginning of the C3 AD by one of his aides, C. Domitius Sergius Honoratus. After participating in the capture of Jerusalem in AD 70, the Tenth Legion was based in the city for over 250 years, occupying the area that is now the Armenian Quarter.

THE ARMENIAN QUARTER

This quarter (fig. 2) takes its name from its central feature, the great compound of the Armenian Convent, which is in fact a city in miniature with its own schools, library, seminary, and residential quarters, all arranged around the Cathedral of St. James. Much of the area was once covered by the palace of Herod the Great (WALLS AND GATES: CITADEL).

Armenia was the first nation to embrace Christianity officially at the beginning of the C4. The church there was subject to the jurisdiction of the Metropolitan of Caesarea, and Armenians were represented in Jerusalem during the Byzantine period. The disappearance of the kingdom of Armenia at the end of the C4 inaugurated a period of persecution and exile which culminated in the massacre of almost two million Armenians in the first part of the C20. As an exiled people their unity is founded on their language and culture, both of which are rooted in their church; two great saints of the early C5, Isaac and Mesrob, are credited with the creation of a national

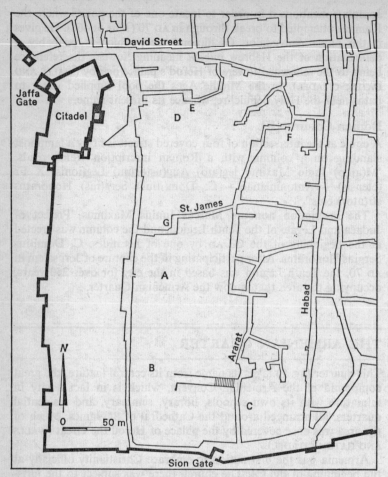

Fig. 15. Armenian Quarter of Jerusalem.

identity which has survived centuries of dispersal. The letters below refer to the locations in fig. 15.

Cathedral of Saint James [A]

In sharp contrast to the sombre weariness of the Holy Sepulchre, this church reflects the life and vigour of a colourful and unified people. On the tessellated floor magnificent carpets glow softly in the reflected light of the innumerable lamps which hang in the air like stars. The altar has been well described as 'a golden conflagration of icons and monstrances' (C. Thubron). Fact and legend are juxtaposed as casually as are artistic creations of different talents and periods.

The first sanctuary on this site was an oratory dedicated to St. Menas, an Egyptian martyr, by the patrician lady Bassa, who came to Jerusalem with the empress Eudokia in AD 444, settling nearby as superior of a convent of women. This foundation was absorbed by the Georgians in the C11; they were the first to erect a church in honour of St. James the Great, possibly because of the close parallel between the legends surrounding the deaths of James and Menas. In the C12 circumstances forced the Georgians to cede their property to the Armenians who were high in favour with the Crusaders. There were many intermarriages and the beauty and intelligence of Armenian women won for a number the dignity of Queen of Jerusalem.

The Crusaders co-operated enthusiastically in the reconstruction of the church of St. James whose authenticity was now established by possession of the head of the apostle and of the hand of St. Stephen. A common devotion to St. James drew Spaniards and Armenians together, and donations from Spain kept the Armenian community alive in the C15. In the following century the Armenians extended their domain by acquiring the adjoining property; it was needed to house the many pilgrims who flocked to Jerusalem.

Visit (fig. 16). The church and compound are open to visitors only by appointment; phone the Patriarchate (282-331). It is possible to visit the church during the afternoon service which starts at 3 p.m.; 2.30 p.m. on Saturdays and Sundays.

The porch [1] was added in the C17 when the entrance was changed to this side of the building; note the pierced brass grilles and the strange pieces of wood and bronze which came into use when Christians were forbidden the use of bells in the C9. Virtually all the structural elements inside the church date from the Middle Ages, but the rib vaulting of the central cupola is typically Armenian, suggesting that the C12 restoration amounted to no more than the consolidation of a building of the C10–C11. The four piers were squared in the C17 to take tile decoration.

The small door in the north-west corner [2] gives access to a stepped passage in the thickness of the wall which leads to an upper

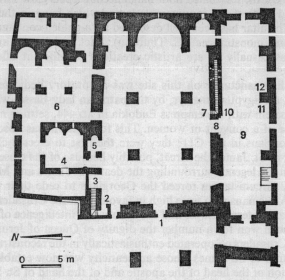

Fig. 16. Armenian Cathedral of St. James.

oratory. There is a similar secret passage in the south wall leading to chapels above the two lateral apses [7]; an inlaid panel set amidst the painted tiles hides a magnificent carved wooden door, dated 1356. Between the chapels commemorating St. Macarius [3], bishop of Jerusalem under Constantine, and St. James [5] is the entrance of the C5 chapel of St. Menas [4].

Unfortunately access to this, the oldest part of the church, is absolutely forbidden; it now houses a collection of croziers.

The C10–C11 chapel of St. Stephen [6] serves as both sacristy and baptistry. Another baptismal font is found in the chapel of Echmiadzin [9] which was the narthex of the medieval church. The elaborate decoration of the door [8] shows it to have been the principal entrance; the pilasters in the south wall were originally free-standing pillars. The arches were walled up in the C17 by the patriarch Eleazar who also gave the chapel its name. It is said that he aspired to be Catholicos, i.e. supreme spiritual leader of the Armenians; this office is as closely tied to the city of Echmiadzin in Soviet Armenia as the Papacy is to Rome and in order to get round this difficulty he created his own Echmiadzin in Jerusalem. To increase the sanctity of the chapel he constructed an altar [12] enshrining stones from Mount Sinai, Mount Tabor, the Holy Sepulchre, and the Jordan. Note in particular the pictorial tiles [10 and 11] made at Kutahia in Turkey in 1729; traces of Persian and even Chinese influence are easily detected.

Convent of the Olive Tree [C]

One feature alone makes it worthwhile visiting the little chapel of Deir el-Zeitouneh. Built into its outer wall is a relic which immediately arouses suspicion but which no one can ever prove false, namely, the stone which would have cried out had the disciples not praised God (Luke 19: 40)!

From the Cathedral of St. James go through the compound towards the Gulbenkian Library [B] and the Mardigian Museum (open: 10 a.m.–4 p.m.; there is also an entrance from Armenian Patriarchate Road) down the flight of steps into a narrow street and through a low square gateway in the far wall. The best time to visit is 8–9 a.m. but until about noon an Armenian nun from the adjoining convent can normally be found to open the chapel.

The chapel, built about 1300, is a fine example of classical Armenian architecture; the unusually large vestibule may be a later addition. An oblique passage to the right of the apse leads to a small oratory where there is a beautifully carved wooden door (dated to 1649 by its inscription) which once belonged to the chapel of St. Menas in the Cathedral of St. James.

The chapel was identified only in the late C14 as the house of the high priest Annas, the father-in-law of Caiphas (John 18: 13). A niche in the north wall became the prison of Christ, and from the C15 an olive tree just outside the chapel on the north was pointed out as the one to which Jesus was tied during the scourging. A step away, built into the north-east external corner of the chapel, is the famous stone; it has a trimmed margin and a cavity in the centre.

Medieval Chapels

Scattered throughout the quarter are three small one-apse churches dating from the Middle Ages. They are of no special historical or architectural interest and only one still functions as a church.

[E] *St. James the Cut-Up.* Located just behind Christ Church [D], the first Anglican church built in the Holy Land (1849), is a little mosque whose name, Yaqubieh, still preserves its medieval dedication to St. James of Persia who was martyred by being cut into small pieces.

[G] *St. Thomas.* Possession of this ruined church has long been a bone of contention between Muslims and Armenians.

[F] *St. Mark.* Open: 9 a.m. – 12 p.m.; closed Sundays. This church is the centre of the Syrian Orthodox community, one of the most interesting of the Eastern Churches and one in which Syriac is still a living language. Its most prized possession is a painting on leather of the Virgin and Child attributed to St. Luke, a tradition which Raphael immortalized in a famous painting showing Mary and Jesus posing for the evangelist. The painting is in fact very old but does not antedate the Byzantine period.

The little building is the focus of an extraordinary number of traditions. It is supposed to cover the house of Mary, the mother of St. Mark, to which Peter went when an angel released him from prison (Acts 12: 12). A little baptistry is reputed to be the one in which the Virgin Mary was baptized. The Last Supper was eaten here where Peter founded the first church. All these legends give a sense of identity and pride to one of the smallest Christian communities in Jerusalem.

THE JEWISH QUARTER

Located in the south-east sector of the city (fig. 2), the Jewish quarter was badly damaged and looted during the birth of the state of Israel in 1948. Restoration began immediately after the conquest of the Old City in 1967 and has not yet been completed. The fine clean stone and surprising vistas make it an entrancing area to stroll through.

The historical monuments above ground are few, one Crusader complex and a number of C16 synagogues, but the archaeological survey, which preceded reconstruction, brought to light several elements which illuminate the Old Testament city. Some of these will be open to the public when the buildings above and around them have been completed. Capital letters below give the location on the map in fig. 17.

The Western Wall area will be treated in the section on Excavations West and South of the Haram esh-Sharif (p. 69).

The First Wall [A]

From the corner of Pelugat Kotel and Shone Halakhot Streets a

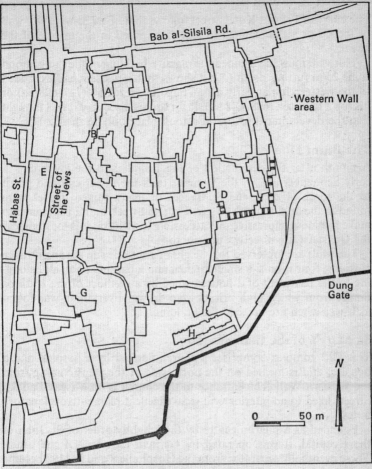

Fig. 17. Jewish Quarter of Jerusalem.

flight of steps leads down to an underground area (not yet open to the public) where archaeologists discovered the 'first wall' mentioned by Josephus (*War* 5: 144). A 9 m-square tower, dated to the first half of the C1 BC, was built against the north-east corner of a massive building of the C8–C7 BC; its walls are 4·5 m thick and stand to a height of 8 m. A burnt layer containing numerous arrowheads recalls the fierce fighting when Jerusalem fell to the Babylonians in 586 BC.

The Iron Age Wall [B]

The curve of Pelugat Kotel Street follows that of a 7 m-wide city wall of the C7 BC; it is planned to leave it exposed in the middle of the street.

This wall must have joined the massive building of the same period some 25 m further north [A]; it shows that Jerusalem had expanded to the western hill as early as the reign of Hezekiah (727–698 BC) or his son Manasseh (698–642 BC). Prior to this discovery it was thought that the development to the west took place only in the C2 BC.

The Burnt House [C]

A month after the destruction of the Temple and the lower city in early September AD 70, the Romans took the upper city and put it to the torch (*War* 6: 403–8). Traces of many ruined houses were found in the area around Misgav Ladakh Street, and it is planned to make the most impressive one accessible to visitors; it is located near the Quarter Café directly opposite to [D].

The walls are preserved to a height of 1 m; one can see an entrance corridor, four rooms, a small kitchen and a bathing pool, all belonging to the basement of a house owned by a member of the Kathros family from which high priests were drawn. Everything was found as it was when fire invaded the building.

St. Mary's of the Germans [D]

This C12 complex comprises a church flanked by a hospital and a hospice, and is located on the north side of the steps coming from the Western Wall. The entrance to the church is on Misgav Ladakh Street; fixed to an interior wall is an excellent plan with explanatory notes.

Founded as a pilgrim centre by the knightly order of St. John of the Hospital, it was operated by German members of the order. These eventually separated from the Hospitallers and in 1190 became an independent military order, the Teutonic Knights. Their first headquarters were at MONTFORT; after the fall of AKKO they moved to eastern Europe and carved out immense territories in Prussia.

The Byzantine Cardo Maximus [E]

A section of the main street of Byzantine Jerusalem, shown on the C6 Madaba Map (fig. 23), can be seen under a row of six arches on the west side of the Street of the Jews (Jewish Quarter Road) 50m north of the minaret (see [F]). Bounded on the west by a heavy wall and on the east by a row of pillars, the 8 m-wide street (two columns are in place) was flanked by porticos 7 m wide. It cut the Iron Age Wall [A] at the junction with Pelugat Kotel Street, and terminated at a gate in the old wall of Aelia Capitolina ([1] in fig. 4).

Hurva and Ramban Synagogues [F]

Both these synagogues rest on the ruins of the Crusader church of St. Martin. The Ramban was founded in the C13 by Rabbi Moshe Nachmanides, a celebrated scholar of the Middle Ages who settled in Jerusalem in 1267. He found only two Jews in the city, both dyers, and a letter written to his family describing the miserable condition of the community has been preserved; a copy is displayed in the synagogue whose massive pillars belonged to St. Martin's church.

Outside the Ramban synagogue is the only minaret in the Jewish Quarter. It was built in the C15 by the mother of one of the members of the community who was converted to Islam after a quarrel with his neighbours.

The first group of organized Ashkenazi (European) Jewish immigrants to Jerusalem arrived in 1700. They acquired land to build a synagogue, but it was never completed; the community split, Muslims burnt the scrolls and held the plot for non-payment of debt. Known as the Hurva, meaning 'ruin', it was restored to the Ashkenazi community by Ibrahim Pasha in 1836; a great synagogue was completed some 20 years later only to be destroyed in 1948.

The Four Synagogues [G]

This sunken complex (open: 9 a.m.–4 p.m.; Fridays to 2 p.m.; Saturdays during services) was the spiritual centre of Sephardi (Oriental) Jews from the C17 AD. The four independent prayer halls were destroyed in 1948 but have now been restored, using elements which survived the wreckage of Italian synagogues during World War II.

Apse of the Nea [H]

The south apse of the Nea, the 'New Church' built by Justinian in AD 543, projects outside the city wall (WALLS AND GATES: SOUTH WALL). An apse is preserved in the basement of a building near the Rothschild House. With your back to the two-level arcaded front of that building, take the steps down to the right, turn left at the bottom, and look through one of a series of small grilled windows;

the curve of the apse is clearly visible in the thick ancient wall to the right.

HARAM ESH-SHARIF (TEMPLE MOUNT)

The jewel of Jerusalem architecture, the Dome of the Rock, graces a vast esplanade whose quiet spaciousness is the antithesis of the congested bustle of the surrounding narrow streets. Muslims call it 'The Noble Sanctuary' and no name could be more appropriate.

The site had a long history as a holy place before the day in AD 638 when Omar, Commander of the Faithful, walked into the city because it was his servant's turn to ride. A little eminence north of the City of David caught the winnowing wind. David bought the threshing-floor there from Arauna to erect an altar (2 Sam. 24: 18–25). About 960 BC, in order to provide a more fitting shrine for the Ark of the Covenant, Solomon erected the first temple on the spot; his palace to the south linked it to the city of his father (1 Kgs. 5: 5–8). No trace has ever been found of this temple which Zorobabel rebuilt *c.*520 BC after its destruction by the Babylonians in 587 BC. Any elements that may remain are buried under the huge platform erected by Herod.

Josephus offers a comprehensive account of the building of the second temple (*Antiquities* 15: 380–425). Herod's grandiose project so frightened the Jews that he had to promise that he would have all the materials ready before touching a stone of the old edifice. In order to obtain a flat surface he surrounded the crest of the hill with immense retaining walls on the west, south, and east; fill and arched supports brought the surface up to the required level. The strength of this platform has enabled it to withstand all the vicissitudes of history, so the dimensions of the present esplanade are Herodian (20–12 BC). All his buildings have disappeared, any which might have survived the destruction wrought by Titus (AD 70) having been swep away by Hadrian (AD 135). Information provided by Josephus and the tractate 'Middoth' in the *Mishnah* enable us to reconstruct them (fig. 18).

Covered galleries ran along all four sides, the Royal Stoa [6] being twice as wide as the others; ramps from the doors at the base of the south wall passed beneath it to emerge in the courtyard [5]. There were also monumental staircases at either end [7]. The Antonia

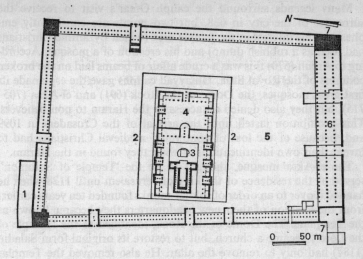

Fig. 18. Reconstruction of the Temple built by Herod the Great.

fortress [1] and a huge reservoir adjoined the north wall. A fence almost 2 m high [2] separated the specifically religious area from the rest; at each of the 13 gates a notice in Latin or Greek proclaimed: 'No Gentile to enter the fence and barrier around the Temple. Anyone caught is answerable to himself for the ensuing death'; this is the wall of partition mentioned by Paul in Eph. 2:14. Such intolerance was to be continued by Christians and Muslims. The Temple proper was at the west end; the altar of sacrifice stood in the Court of the Priests [3]; at the other side of the Beautiful Gate was the Court of the Women [4]. The rock now enshrined in the Dome of the Rock must have been the foundation of the Holy of Holies (the innermost part of the temple building) or of the altar of sacrifice.

On the ruins, Hadrian built a temple to Jupiter. Jews were forbidden entry save for one day in the year when they were permitted to come to anoint 'a pierced rock' (Bordeaux pilgrim, AD 333). Julian the Apostate (361–3) encouraged them to rebuild the temple, but work was immediately stopped by his successor. In general, Byzantine Christians avoided the area as a place accursed (Mark 13:2); if they visited it at all it was as casual tourists.

Many legends surround the caliph Omar's visit to receive the surrender of the city in 638, but two points are consistently emphasized, his interest in the temple area (which Byzantine Christians had used as a rubbish dump) and his erection of a mosque. According to Arculf (670) this was a crude affair of beams laid on the broken columns of the Royal Stoa. Umayyad caliphs gave the esplanade its first great mosques, the Dome of the Rock (691) and el-Aksa (705–715), but they also denied all access to the Haram to non-believers. This prohibition lasted until the arrival of the Crusaders in 1099 and, because of the loss of continuity, medieval Christians had to invent their own identifications of what they found in the Haram.

The el-Aksa mosque, thought to be the 'Temple of Solomon', served as the residence of the king of Jerusalem until 1128 when he handed it over to an order of soldier-monks founded ten years earlier; from the location of their new headquarters they became known as the Templars. The Dome of the Rock, identified as the 'Temple of the Lord', became a church, but to restore its original form Saladin (1187) had only to remove the altar. He also removed the Templar cloister west of el-Aksa. A few small edicules were added in this period, but the Haram was given its present form in the C14–C15 by the Mamelukes who are responsible for most of the buildings along the west wall. The Haram Wall was renewed by Suliman the Magnificent in the C16.

Visit (fig. 19). One may leave the Haram by any gate but non-Muslims must enter by one of the following: Bab el-Ghawanima, Bab en-Nazir, Bab el-Qattanin, Gate of the Chain, or Moors' Gate. Entrance to the Haram is free, but tickets for the Dome of the Rock and el-Aksa mosque should be bought at the ticket offices near Bab en-Nazir and Moors' Gate. Open: 8 a.m.–4 p.m.; closed Fridays. The mosques are closed during the midday prayer hours which vary slightly with the season.

The Haram contains a multitude of small monuments whose history is normally much less interesting than the legends which have become attached to them. Most of these have never been systematically collected and anyone interested in learning more about them should endeavour to find a knowledgeable local Muslim. Only the important monuments can be dealt with here.

Dome of the Rock

The Dome of the Rock, begun in AD 688 and finished in 691, is the

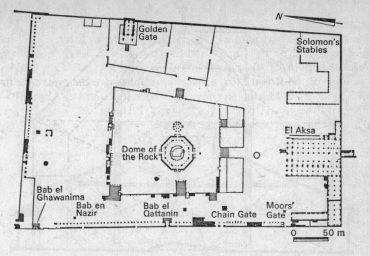

Fig. 19. The Haram esh-Sharif (Temple Mount).

first major sanctuary built by Islam. It is also the only one to have survived essentially intact. The external decoration dates only from 1963 but the mosacis within are the originals.

The extraordinary impression produced by this building is in part due to the mathematical rhythm of its proportions (fig. 20). All the critical dimensions are related to the centre circle circumscribing the rock. The plan has its closest parallel in the Mausoleum of Dio-cletian (AD 303) in Split, Yugoslavia, but the same principles were used in the construction of C6 churches at Ravenna and in Syria. In none of these, however, do we find the integration of plan and elevation that is evident here.

According to current Arab tradition, the purpose of the Umayyad caliph Abd al-Malik in building the Dome of the Rock was to commemorate Muhammad's ascension into heaven, but were this in fact the case there would have been no need to erect the later Dome of the Ascension (Qubbat el-Miraj) nearby! Abd al-Malik's purpose was more complex and subtle. By erecting a beautiful building he intended to instil a sense of pride in Muslims overawed by the majestic churches of Christendom, tours of which were organized by the clever Byzantines for simple desert Arabs who tended to equate splendour and power. In addition Abd al-Malik intended to

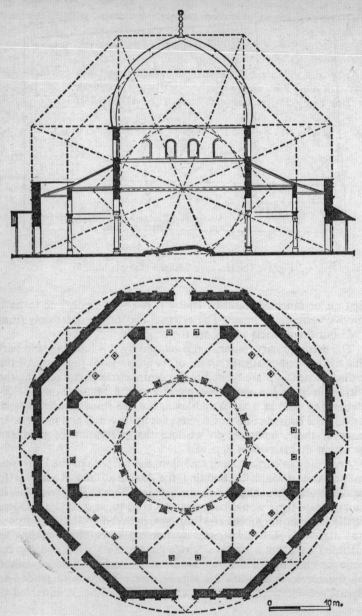

Fig. 20. Dome of the Rock. Mathematical rhythm of structural proportions in plan and elevation (after Creswell and Wilkinson).

make a symbolic statement to both Jews and Christians, the two religions that Islam considered its imperfect predecessors. His building spoke to Jews by its location, to Christians by its interior decoration.

In addition to the memory of its association with the Temple, Jewish legend had endowed the rock with a complex mythology centring round the figures of Abraham and Isaac. By building above it, Abd al-Malik appropriated the rock and its Abrahamic resonances for Islam. The message to Jews was that their faith had been superseded.

The message to Christians was no less clear. The diadems and breastplates represented in the mosaic decoration are the imperial jewels of Byzantine rulers and are the ornaments worn by Christ, the Virgin and saints in Byzantine religious art. These symbols of holiness and power are in the sanctuary of an alien faith because they are the spoils of the victor. Lest the hint be missed it is formally underlined in the founding inscription, part of which reads, 'O you People of the Book, overstep not bounds in your religion, and of God speak only the truth. The Messiah, Jesus, son of Mary, is only an apostle of God, and his Word which he conveyed into Mary, and a Spirit proceeding from him. Believe therefore in God and his apostles, and say not Three. It will be better for you. God is only one God. Far be it from his glory that he should have a son.' An invitation to abandon belief in the Trinity and in the divine Sonship of Christ could hardly be put more clearly.

Visit. The mosaic artists were Syrian Christians but Muslim law forbade the representation of living beings; hence the profusion of vegetation both realistic and stylized. The mosaics of the drum were restored in 1027, but it seems that the original designs were retained. The gold cubes of the background are tilted forward 30 degrees, and so appear brighter than the motifs. The contrary is found on the inner face of the inner octagon: the cubes of the background are vertical but those of the motifs are tilted forward. The result is that the motifs stand out much more clearly, and it is precisely in this register that the significant jewels appear. As a rule of thumb, crowns curve upwards while breastplates and necklaces curve downwards.

The founding inscription is a single line of Kufic script running along the top of both sides of the inner octagon, 240 m in all! It gives credit for the construction of the building to the Abbasid caliph al-Mamun in the year 72 of the Hegeira. However, 72H = AD 691 and al-Mamun reigned from 813 to 833. This maladroit effort to claim credit for the achievement of a member of the previous dynasty is of a piece with the claim of the Abbasid historian Yaqubi (*c.* AD 874) that Abd al-Malik built the Dome of the Rock in order to replace the Kabah at Mecca as the place of pilgrimage. He was trying to discredit the caliph by accusing him of heresy, the pilgrimage to Mecca being one of the foundations of the faith of Islam.

The columns supporting the inner octagon and those in the centre-circle are all of different sizes; the crosses on some show them to have been borrowed from churches. None of the windows antedates the reconstruction of the exterior by Suliman the Magnificent in 1522; the light coming through the pieces of coloured glass set in carved plaster has already been filtered by panes of green glass set inside the pierced tiles of the exterior.

The carved ceilings on either side of the inner octagon were not part of the original design: they first appeared in the C13 and have been renewed since; the Mameluke star is the dominant motif.

The high reliquary beside the rock contains a hair of Muhammad's beard. Muslims call the cavity beneath the rock Bir el-Arwah, 'the Well of Souls'; the voices of the dead mingle with the falling waters of the still lower rivers of paradise as they drop into eternity. In days gone by those who prayed here, after having walked round the rock, were given a certificate entitling them to admission to paradise; it was to be buried with them. The hole in the ceiling is that seen by the Bordeaux pilgrim (AD 333) and is the basis of the suggestion that the rock was the altar of sacrifice in Herod's temple; its purpose would have been to drain away the blood.

According to an Arab writer of the C14, 'Externally the building is covered up to a height of 7 cubits [= 3 m] with white veined marble, and above 7 cubits up to the gutters with mosaics depicting various forms of vegetation.' Suliman the Magnificent removed the remains of this mosaic in 1552 and replaced it with tiles which were completely renewed in 1963.

Dome of the Chain

The Dome of the Chain is simply a small dome supported on 17 columns all of which can be seen from any point. One's immediate reaction is to wonder why such a building exists. One answer is that it was the model for the Dome of the Rock (whose contemporary it in fact is), but this does not stand up to any critical comparison between the two edifices; it is a legend that appears for the first time at the end of the C15. Another answer, based on parallels in other great Islamic sanctuaries, is that it was the Treasury of the Haram. This may well be correct, but is impossible to verify. The earliest description (AD 903) gives it 20 columns, showing that its original form has been radically modified, probably by the Mameluke sultan Baybars in the C13. It owes its name to the legend that Solomon hung a chain from the roof; those who swore falsely while holding it were struck by lightning. Such legends would tend to confirm the hypothesis that it was a treasury, superstitious fear of the place being its best protection. It is unclear whether any significance should be given to the fact that the Dome of the Chain stands at the precise centre of the Haram area.

Scales

The graceful arcade at the top of each of the eight stairways leading to the platform of the Dome of the Rock is known in Arabic as *mawazin*, 'scales', because of the belief that on the Last Day the scales of judgement will be suspended there to weigh the hearts of men against truth. They were not all built at the same time. Three are dated to the C10 and the last was added in the C15. The two oldest are on the south end of the platform. Beside the one in line with el-Aksa and the Dome of the Rock is the stepped pulpit of the judge Burhan ed-Din, erected in 1388 re-using Byzantine and Crusader elements. It is especially associated with prayer for rain.

Fountain of Sultan Qaytbay

After the Dome of the Rock the most beautiful edifice in the Haram is the *sabil* (a public fountain founded as a charitable act pleasing to God) donated by Sultan Qaytbay in 1482. Unfortunately, it is often ignored because the attention of the visitor is dominated by the vivid colouring of the nearby Dome of the Rock, but it is a superb example of Mameluke decorative architecture (fig. 21). The interior is executed with the same care. Both repay close examination.

The ornate inscription running round all four sides provides three items of historical interest in addition to quotations from the Koran: the existence of an earlier Mameluke domed building, the name and date of the existing *sabil*, and mention of a restoration in 1883. Apart from the inscription, the restoration made no significant changes, except in the window lintels. The original star-pattern strapwork is preserved inside, but the joggled external lintel, typically Mameluke in form, is the work of an Ottoman!

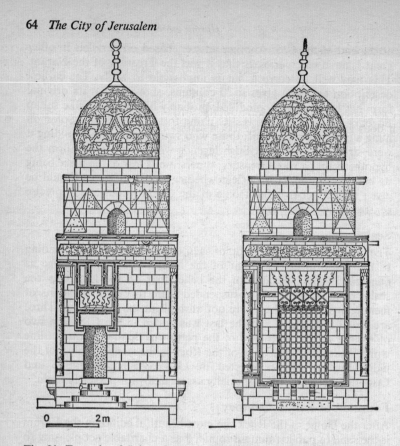

Fig. 21. Fountain of Sultan Qaytbay. East (left) and south (right) elevations (after Burgoyne).

The building was erected by Egyptian craftsmen under the direction of a Christian master-builder, and the unique form of the fountain is due to the fact that, being experts in funerary architecture, they had given a simple fountain the prominence normally reserved for tombs. The relief decoration of the dome, found elsewhere only in Cairo, is achieved by cutting back the stone blocks.

The well-shaft is beside the door inside; from it water was poured into troughs beneath each window; cups chained to a bronze ring fitted into the two holes in the window sill.

Madrasa Ashrafiyya

Just beside the Sabil Qaytbay a building projects into the Haram area interrupting the covered porch. When new (1482) this college had the reputation of being the third finest edifice in the Haram, and even though the square porch on the south is now rather delapidated it does give a very clear idea of its former glory. Note particularly the red and white fan ceiling with the blunt Mameluke star in the centre, and the very intricate black and white joggling of the relieving lintel.

It was built, on the orders of the sultan Qaytbay (one of whose names was al-Ashraf), by the same team of Egyptian craftsmen who constructed the fountain. Visiting Jerusalem in 1474, he was disappointed at the college which he had inherited and royally endowed, so he ordered it to be torn down and a new one built.

Bab el-Mathara

Just north of Madrasa Ashrafiyya an unpretentious gate, euphemistically called the Ablutions Gate, gives access to what are probably the oldest public latrines in the world still in use. They were built in 1193, shortly after the Crusaders lost Jerusalem, by Saladin's brother Malik Adil Abu Bakr.

Immediately outside the gate, at the head of the passage leading to the latrines, are two fine Mameluke buildings. The Madrasa Uthmaniyya on the left (south) was built by an Asiatic princess, Isfahanshah, in 1437; the college is called by her family name which shows her to have been related to the Ottoman dynasty. On the other side of the passage is the Ribat Zamani, a pilgrim hospice erected in 1476 by one of the close advisers of the sultan Qaytbay; note in particular the very intricate centre joggle over the window.

Bab el-Qattanin

This ornate gate, built by the emir Tankiz in 1336, was but one of his many contributions to the beautification of Jerusalem; see the note on Suq el-Qattanin in the section MUSLIM QUARTER: MAMELUKE BUILDINGS. He is also responsible for the covered porch (1307) running along the west wall of the Haram.

Golden Gate

The Golden Gate is the focus of many traditions, but there is little certitude regarding its true history. According to the *Mishnah* (Middoth 1:3) the Temple had an eastern gate facing the Mount of Olives, and Herodian elements have been detected in the present structure. The Piacenza pilgrim (AD 570) mentions its ruin as a curiosity noted in passing from the Mount to the city gate which was 'next to the Gate Beautiful which was part of the Temple, and its threshold and entablature are still in position there'. It is significant that he does not relate it to Peter's cure of the lame man at the Gate Beautiful (Acts 3:1–10), because it has been thought that the empress Eudokia built the present edifice in the mid-C5 to commemorate the miracle. Further evidence of lack of Christian interest in the site is provided by Theodosius (before 518) who claims that Jesus entered the city by the Gate of Benjamin (north of the Temple) on Palm Sunday.

The architecture suggests a date at the very end of the Byzantine period and it is possible that Modestus built a ceremonial gate to receive the emperor Heraclius in 631 when he returned the Cross taken by the Persians in 614. It was probably closed by the Muslims later in the century when they denied access to the Haram to all non-believers, thus giving rise to the legend (first mentioned about 830) that when the emperor appeared in his magnificent robes 'suddenly the stones of the gate descended and closed together to make a solid wall'; when he humbled himself the gate opened again. This story gained tremendous popularity in the Middle Ages when the gate was unblocked twice a year, on Palm Sunday and on the feast of the Exaltation of the Cross. The present name also took firm root at this period, though attested in the C7; the Greek *horaia*, 'beautiful', was confused with the Latin *aurea*, 'golden'.

After the departure of the Crusaders the gate remained closed. The reasons presumably were practical, but the fact fostered a more theological explanation which combined Ezek. 44:1–3 and Jesus' triumphal entry on Palm Sunday. The gate was shut because the God of Israel had entered by it, and will open again only when Jesus returns in judgement. Muslims still call one part the Gate of Mercy and the other the Gate of Penance; through these the just will enter with their Judge.

El-Aksa Mosque

The name el-Aksa first applied to the whole Haram area, and dates from the time (C10 AD?) when it was firmly accepted that Jerusalem was the *masjid el-aksa*, 'the furthermost sanctuary', whither Muhammad was transported on his famous Night Journey. Its use was eventually restricted to the great prayer mosque.

34182

The first impression on entering is of a forest of glacial marble columns (donated by Mussolini) and a garish painted ceiling (a gift of King Farouk); they belong to the last restoration (1938–42). Virtually nothing (except perhaps the general proportions) remains of the first mosque built by the caliph al-Walid (AD 709–15), twice destroyed by earthquakes in the first 60 years of its existence. As restored by the caliph al-Mahdi in 780 it had fifteen aisles, but these were reduced to the present seven when the caliph az-Zahir rebuilt it after the earthquake of 1033.

The oldest visible element in the mosque is the mosaic decoration of the drum supporting the dome and of the façade of the arch dominating the centre aisle; an inscription dates these mosaics to 1035. The artistic quality is clearly inferior to those in the Dome of the Rock, but there are certain similarities in the motifs; it is suggested that the Byzantine master-craftsman was instructed to copy an earlier Umayyad mosaic.

After the capture of Jerusalem in 1099 the mosque became first the royal residence and then the headquarters of the Templars. They left their mark on the building by adding the three central bays of the porch (restored 1217). Saladin contributed the decoration of the *mihrab* in 1187 and a magnificent carved wood pulpit that unfortunately was destroyed in the fire of 1969 (started by an insane Christian tourist who believed that the Messiah would not come until abominations had been cleared from the Temple Mount). Saladin tore down the Templar constructions west of the mosque with the exception of the present Women's Mosque (along the south wall and formerly the refectory of the knights) and the Islamic Museum (along the west wall).

Mameluke sultans restored both sides of the mosque and added two bays to either side of the Crusader porch (1345–50). Their work is visible only on the west side of the interior, because the nave and east side were torn down and rebuilt in 1938–42.

Just outside the main entrance a flight of 16 steps leads down to a green door. This is the entrance to an underground area which for centuries took the overflow from the mosque above on great feasts. It is not normally open to visitors, but those with sufficient charm and persistence can sometimes prevail on the officials of the Supreme Muslim Council (whose offices are at G in fig. 8) to send someone with the key. Inside, a long vaulted passage leads to the blocked-up Double Gate; it was by a ramp such as this that visitors entered Herod's temple from the south.

The vestibule just inside the Double Gate is characterized by a single column supporting two pairs of domes. This column and the two others beside the steps belonged to the original Herodian entrance. Other elements, particularly the structure of the domes, have close parallels in the Golden Gate and must be dated to a reconstruction in the early C7 AD. Still later the monolithic lintels of the doors cracked and were shored up by marble columns at either side; these repairs must be related to the building of the mosque above (C8 AD) or to one of its early reconstructions.

Solomon's Stables

This great underground area has nothing to do with Solomon. The outer walls are Herodian, and the twelve rows of pillars support the esplanade above. Since the ground sloped steeply, substructures were necessary to create a flat surface above. This fact explains why el-Aksa has suffered so much from earthquakes: this end of the Haram shakes much more than the bedrock on which the Dome of the Rock is built. To gain entrance, follow the same procedure as noted above for the underground part of el-Aksa.

Archaeologists have never been permitted to investigate this area and, in consequence, precise information is lacking. Many blocks in the pillars are of Herodian cut; they may have stood continuously or may have been relaid during the repair work undertaken in the C8 and C12 AD. The beginning of a great arch in one of the walls belonged to the pre-Herodian temple; it probably supported one of the terraces stepping down to the City of David. At one time it was possible to go through to the far end to see the interior of the Triple Gate, but this is now blocked off; nothing now remains but it must have been substantially identical with the Double Gate described above, and served the same purpose in Herod's temple.

During the Crusader period the Templars used this area to stable their specially bred war-horses which were remarkable for their size and power. The holes in the pillars to which they were tied can still be seen. Medieval piety identified the shell decoration of a Roman building as the cradle of Jesus which is shown at the bottom of the entrance steps.

EXCAVATIONS WEST AND SOUTH OF THE HARAM ESH-SHARIF

The excavations around the Haram esh-Sharif (fig. 22) can be divided into three sections: the Western Wall [A], the area around the south-west corner of the Haram inside the city wall [B], the area outside the Double and Triple Gates [C].

The Western Wall [A]

For centuries this section was called the Wailing Wall; Jews from the adjoining Jewish Quarter came there to pray and to lament the destruction of the Temple. Prior to 1967 houses came to within four metres of the wall, but after they were razed to create the present piazza the name was changed to something less evocative of a sad past.

The great stones of the lower part of the wall reveal characteristically Herodian workmanship. They formed part of the retaining

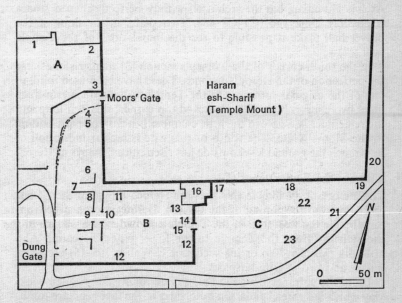

Fig. 22. Excavated areas west and south of the Haram esh-Sharif (Temple Mount).

wall built by Herod the Great in 20 BC to support the esplanade of
the Temple. The top of the wall is obviously different; in AD 70 the
Romans pushed out the part of the wall projecting above floor-level
inside and it was rebuilt by the Muslims. The original wall at this
level was constructed of the same beautiful stones as the lower section but had pilasters at regular intervals; evidence from the excavations is confirmed by the perfectly preserved Herodian wall of the
Tomb of the Patriarchs at HEBRON.

Elements at both ends merit close inspection. On the north a great
arch [2] was discovered by Charles Wilson in 1868 and Dr Barclay
was the first to notice a gate in the south corner [3].

Wilson's Arch [2] carries the Street of the Chain across the
Tyropoeon valley to the Temple. Open: 8.30 a.m.–3 p.m. Sunday,
Tuesday, Wednesday; 12.30–3 p.m. Monday, Thursday; closed
Saturday. The entrance [1] leads to a series of long vaulted chambers
of uncertain date. At one point a grilled window on the right permits
inspection of the so-called Masonic Hall at a lower level; this finely
constructed chamber is at least Herodian and possibly Hasmonaean
(150–40 BC); its original function is unknown. The pier of Wilson's
Arch is Herodian, but the arch itself with its perfectly shaped stones
is possibly Umayyad (C7–C8 AD). Two shafts in the floor of the
prayer hall make it possible to see the foundations of the Temple
wall.

In the south corner of the women's section [3] smaller stones mar
the perfection of the Herodian stones. These have been used to fill in
one of the original entrances to the Temple. Above them is a huge
lintel two courses high with a notched top corner; it is 7 m long and
the remainder is visible in the little chamber beneath the path leading
to the Moors' Gate. The width of this gate is a clear indication of
how much the ground level outside has risen since the days of Herod.

The South-West Corner [B]

The important remains in this area are Herodian (end of the C1 BC)
and Umayyad (beginning of the C8 AD). Herod paved a street running beside the west wall of the Temple and under an arch carrying
the stairway from the Temple to the lower city. The caliph Abd
al-Malik (AD 685–705) or his successor el-Walid (705–15) erected a
palace and two pilgrim hospices.

From the entrance near the Dung Gate follow the wooden walkway which has three bends. On both sides of the first bend are tombs
of the C9–C8 BC; these were cleared during the preparations for the

erection of Herod's temple and transformed into baths and cisterns. Diagonally across are the ruins of a Byzantine house [8].

The second bend comes at a point where the walkway crosses a heavy wall. A couple of steps forward and you are between [7] the two Umayyad hospices; their corners and that of the palace created a crossroads at the south-west corner of the Haram which is still visible. In the middle of the trench is a wall from the Herodian period with the beginning of an arch on each side. Since the one on the left (north) side is much higher than that on the right it can only have been the pier of a ramp. Prior to this discovery it was thought that Robinson's arch (whose beginning is visible half-way up the temple wall) was part of a bridge to the upper city. It is now clear that the pathway from the Royal Stoa (HARAM ESH-SHARIF, fig. 18) turned south on the square pier [6] on which the arch rested and continued down a stepped ramp.

Four small openings in a line were shops in the side of the pier [6] facing the Herodian street beneath the arch. The pier also contained other chambers reached by a flight of steps along the north side. Just to the left (north) is another flight of steps with a small pier; this was the route to the upper city.

A large Byzantine bath-house lies on both sides of the wooden walkway at the third bend. The paved area at the end of the walkway is Umayyad as is the rectangular bath [5] with rounded steps in two corners. At the bottom of the deep trench [4] the magnificent slabs of the Herodian street are exposed with just the edge of a raised pavement on the west side.

The two horizontal cuts in the Herodian temple wall were probably designed to take ceramic pipes which carried water to the Umayyad buildings.

Continuing to the south beside the temple wall one can see on the right first, the steps to the upper city; second, the steps to the chambers in the square pier [6]; third, the front of the four little shops with the pavement of the Herodian street which is again visible at the very corner of the temple.

A plastic screen on the wall of the temple protects a Hebrew inscription; it is a quotation from Isa. 66: 14, 'You shall see, and your heart shall rejoice; your bones shall flourish like the grass.' It was probably cut during the brief reign of the emperor Julian the Apostate (AD 361–3) who tried to restore the Jewish Temple.

Return to the beginning of the wooden walkway and turn left down the beaten earth ramp used by the excavators. The gate [9] of the southern Umayyad hospice is clear on the left; steps lead up to the courtyard. Directly opposite is the gate [10] of the Umayyad palace; note on either side the flattened columns from Herod's temple used as foundations.

The paved area inside the gate [10] is the Umayyad floor level; it led to a courtyard in the middle of the palace which covered the whole area between the walls. The present C16 wall [12] is built on the Umayyad wall which reuses blocks from Herod's temple.

Walk directly towards the double gate [14] in the east wall. The first trench on the left [11] exposes part of the Herodian plaza leading to the hippodrome lower down the Tyropoeon valley. In the trenches [13 and 15] at both sides of the path near the gate are Byzantine houses with mosaic floors.

Little is known about the building [16] projecting out from the el-Aksa mosque. It probably originated as a Crusader tower and was later transformed by Saladin (inscription of 1191) and by the Mamelukes at the end of the C15.

Outside the Double and Triple Gates [C]

The difference between Umayyad and Ottoman construction is clear in the wall on both sides of the gate [14]. Just outside the gate one can see in the wall reused Byzantine lintels which may have come from the Nea, the great church built by Justinian in 543 (WALLS AND GATES: SOUTH WALL). The rock cuttings between the gate and the road were cisterns and cellars of Herodian houses.

The steps on the left lead up to the Double Gate [17], one of the original entrances to Herod's temple. Some of the steps have been restored; the remaining ancient stones are perfectly smooth. Only a small portion of the Double Gate remains visible; the ornate cornice is probably Umayyad. Note in the third course above the cornice part of a Roman inscription upside-down; it belonged to one of the statues placed in the temple by Hadrian in AD 135. For the interior of the Double Gate see HARAM ESH-SHARIF: EL-AKSA.

At the end of the steps, before the Triple Gate [18] and to the right of the restored pavement, the rock was cut to create a series of ritual baths of the Herodian period. Originally these must have been covered by a building.

Some 30 m outside the Triple Gate and a little to the east a 3 m-high block of masonry is just beside a magnificent Byzantine split-level house [22]. The upper storey has disappeared but the two lower floors are very well preserved, as are the connecting stairways. Some of the rooms are floored with stone slabs, others with plain mosaic. On the north and south the house is bordered by parallel paved streets.

The wall running out from the south-east corner of the Haram [19] was built by the empress Eudokia in the middle of the C5 AD to enclose the City of David and Mount Sion. Note that this wall is simply juxtaposed to the Herodian blocks; the seam is perfectly clear.

Another seam [20] is visible some 30 m north of the corner; the Herodian blocks of the southern part of the temple are carefully fitted to an older wall which may have belonged to the Syrian Akra, the fortress which played such a critical role in the Maccabean wars (1 Macc. 4: 41; 10: 9; 11: 20–44; 13: 49–52). Note in the Herodian section the springing of an arch similar to Robinson's arch on the western side; presumably there was also a monumental staircase on this side.

The wall of Eudokia leads to a deep trench [21] opposite the fourth lamp standard on the road counting from the corner of the Haram. Here one can see the base of a tower of the C8 BC incorporated into the Herodian and Byzantine city wall which followed the crest of the Ophel ridge to the south.

Opposite the fifth lamp standard is a huge excavated area [23]. The dominant feature is a massive wall which makes an angle to encircle a series of masonry piers. These were the foundations of an Umayyad building; beneath them one can see Iron Age walls running at a different angle.

There are two building complexes between the massive wall and the road. On the left (east) are the basements of a palace of the Herodian period; this may have been the residence of Queen Helena of Adiabene (NEW CITY – NORTHERN SECTION: TOMB OF QUEEN HELENA OF ADIABENE). The western side is overlaid by a Byzantine complex of houses and courtyards.

MOUNT SION

Today Mount Sion designates the part of the western hill projecting out beyond the south wall of the Old City in the area of Sion Gate; it is bordered on the west and south by the Hinnom valley and on the east by the Tyropoeon valley. In the Old Testament period Sion was the eastern hill; David 'captured the stronghold of Sion, and it is now known as the City of David' (2 Sam. 5: 7). The name changed in the C4, presumably on the basis of such passages as Mic. 3: 12: 'Sion shall be ploughed as a field, Jerusalem shall become a heap of ruins, and the Mountain of the Lord [i.e. the Temple Mount] a wooded hill.' The prophet intended to say the same thing in three different ways but Christians, such as the Bordeaux pilgrim (333) who quotes the text, took it as a description of the two hills on which Jerusalem is built; if the eastern hill was the Temple Mount, Sion had to be the western hill.

This area was first brought inside the city walls in the C2 BC. The present south wall probably represents the southern limit of Aelia Capitolina (AD 135), Titus having dismantled the earlier walls in AD 70. The empress Eudokia rebuilt the ancient walls surrounding Mount Sion between 444 and 460. Her walls survived until 975 when the caliph el-Aziz had them torn down because they enclosed an area too great to defend effectively. Saladin extended the Crusader wall to include the Tomb of David.

The C6 AD Madaba map (fig. 23) gives a surprisingly detailed picture of Mount Sion as it was in the Byzantine period. From the city gate [4] the wall runs past the Tower of David [5] to the south, enclosing the church of Sion [6] and the church of Siloam [2]. The colonnaded street passes in front of the church of New St. Mary, the Nea [1], and terminates at a gate [3] in the old wall of Aelia Capitolina.

The Cenacle and the Tomb of David

Both these monuments are located in the same building (fig. 24); it has a minaret and small cupola and stands in the shadow of the great round church of the Dormition (built 1900). To reach the Cenacle from the little alley [1] outside Sion Gate, enter the doorway [2] and, after climbing the stairs [3], pass through a room and across the roof to the vaulted chamber above [5]. To reach the Tomb of David [4], enter the covered passageway [6] and take the first turn to the left.

David, of course, was buried in his city on the eastern hill (1 Kgs. 2: 10) and, even though the Byzantines regarded the western hill as Sion, no one thought of locating his tomb there until the very end of the C10 AD. It won little favour among the Crusaders, and both Jews and Muslims remained highly sceptical until the C15 when the legend of treasures buried with the king gripped the imagination; then it became important to get the Franciscans out of the building which they had restored in the early C14.

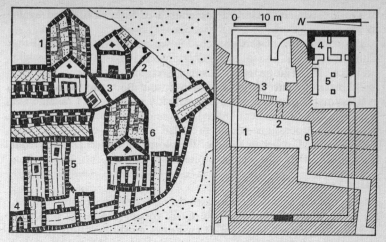

Fig. 23. The southern part of Jerusalem in the mosaic map on the floor of a church in Madaba (Jordan).

Fig. 24. Reconstruction of the Church of Mount Sion (after Wilkinson). The solid black indicates the remains of ancient walls.

The tradition concerning the Cenacle is also unreliable. It is first attested in the early C5 AD and appears to be a derivation from the better supported tradition which located on Mount Sion the descent of the Spirit on the apostles at Pentecost (Cyril of Jerusalem, before 348). This latter event took place in an 'upper room' (Acts 1: 13; 2: 1), and it was natural to assume it to be the same one in which the Last Supper was celebrated (Mark 14: 15).

The Bordeaux pilgrim (333) mentions no gospel event apropos of Mount Sion. Yet Egeria (384) implies that there was a building associated with Pentecost because she says, 'it has now been altered into a church'. Had the Christian community in Jerusalem preserved some relationship to the synagogue which, according to the Bordeaux pilgrim, was the only one remaining of the seven which had once stood there? It is impossible to say, but some scholars have identified the 'Tomb of David' [4] as an ancient synagogue on account of the niche in the north wall. This suggestion must be regarded with caution because the typological dating of synagogues is still an open question. The stones of the niche are cracked, perhaps by the heat of the fires which consumed the church of Sion in 614 and again in 965.

The restoration of this church, known as the 'Mother of all the Churches', in fig. 24 (following Wilkinson) is based on very slight evidence. In addition to two small sections of ancient masonry (solid black) we have only a sketch by Arculf (670) and C9 and medieval estimates of the dimensions. Already in ruins and outside the walls when the Crusaders arrived, it was one of the stations on the penitential procession which preceded the final assault in July 1099. Restored, it became one of the glories of Jerusalem, but from the mid-C13 the ruins were exploited as a quarry.

Saint Peter in Gallicantu

Another modern church dominates the eastern slope of Mount Sion, St. Peter at the Crowing of the Cock (open: 8 a.m.–12 p.m. and 2–5.30 p.m.; closed Sundays). It enshrines most interesting rock-cut structures, cellars, cisterns, stables, dating to the Herodian period (37 BC–AD 70). Beside it runs the ancient stepped way from the top of the hill to Siloam; from the balcony of the church there is a magnificent view of the CITY OF DAVID and of the three valleys which shaped Jerusalem.

Some Christians venerate the site as the house of the high priest Caiphas to which Jesus was taken after his arrest (Mark 14: 53) and where Peter denied him (Mark 14: 66–72). Enough traces have been found to demonstrate the existence of a monastic church of the C6 which a very late document (c.675) identifies as the place where Peter wept after his betrayal; 'he went out and wept bitterly' (Matt. 26: 75). The same text places Jesus' confrontation with Caiphas and Peter's denial in the immediate vicinity of the church of Sion. It is much more likely that the house of the high priest was at the top of the hill; luxurious houses of the Herodian period have been found in the Armenian property (just beside the Dormition Abbey) where another house of Caiphas is exhibited. However, in the late Byzantine period the piety of pilgrims was no longer content with the key events of the life of Jesus venerated in the major sanctuaries and sought to localize every detail mentioned in the gospels. Inevitably new identifications proliferated and are devoid of all historical credibility.

Aceldama

From the viewpoint at St. Peter in Gallicantu one can see, in the Hinnom valley. the Monastery of St. Onuphrius, an Egyptian hermit famous for the length of his beard which was his only garment! To its right is the ruin of a vaulted medieval charnel house near a series of *kokhim* graves cut into the low cliff. From the time of Eusebius (AD 330) this site has been identified as the 'Field of Blood', so called either because the chief priests bought it with the 30 pieces of blood-money as a burial-place for strangers (Matt. 27: 7–10), or because Judas, who had bought the field, committed suicide there (Acts 1: 18–19). This contradiction within the New Testament led some Byzantine pilgrims to distinguish two sites. The burial-place for strangers was always fixed in the Hinnom valley, but the tree on which Judas hanged himself moved all over the city.

THE CITY OF DAVID AND THE KIDRON VALLEY

The oldest part of Jerusalem lies on the Ophel ridge running south from the Haram esh-Sharif (Temple Mount). It is a long triangle created by the Tyropoeon ('Cheesemakers') valley on the west and the Kidron valley on the east; these are marked by the two converging roads in fig. 25. In order to get a clear impression of the whole area, go to the Maison d'Abraham on the south end of the Mount of Olives ([9] in fig. 29).

Though mentioned in Egyptian texts of the C20 BC, the little Jebusite city on the ridge was too insignificant to attract Joshua's murderous attention during the Conquest. Thus it did not belong

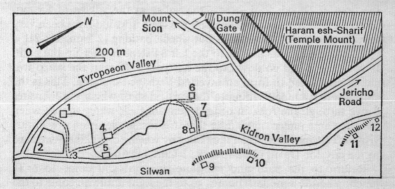

Fig. 25. The City of David.

to any tribe and in 997 BC, when David needed a capital independent of the tribal structure, he took it (2 Sam. 5: 6–9; 1 Chr. 11: 4–7). By bringing the Ark of the Covenant, the religious symbol which united the Israelites, into the city (2 Sam. 6), he made Jerusalem the effective centre of his people; politics and religion have been inextricably mixed in the history of Jerusalem ever since. Inevitably the seat of power moved as the city grew to the north and then to the west, but the Ophel ridge was within the city walls during the Herodian and Byzantine periods.

The Kenyon Excavations

The spring of Gihon [8] is on the left side of a school playground separated from the road by a wire fence; from the right side a stepped path climbs the hill. At the 77th step from the bottom there is an opening to the right. A few steps along the edge of the trench (now used as a rubbish pit by the local residents) brings one face to face with the C18 BC Jebusite wall [7]. It is built of very big untrimmed stones and runs the width of the trench; the angle with a gutter suggests that this part was one of the towers of the city gate which the inhabitants used in order to draw water from the spring. It surprised everybody to find the wall so far down the side of the hill; the Jebusite city was bigger than expected. David retained this wall, and it remained in use until the C8 BC when another wall was built just inside it. This later wall is in the centre and its rough construction clearly distinguishes it from the modern retaining walls built by the archaeologists; it served until the Babylonian invasion of 586 BC. In order to visualize what the terraced city might have looked like in the time of David, look across the valley at the village of Silwan. Since the palace must have been on the crest it would have been very easy for the king to have seen Bathsheba bathing (2 Sam. 11: 2)!

A little track branches off to the left 44 steps further up the path. If you take it and go down to the left you will see in the scarp two cut stones placed to form an inverted V-shaped opening. This is the entrance to a tunnel leading to the vertical shaft which the Jebusites drove through the rock in order to ensure their water supply when the city came under siege; note that it is inside the defence wall just visited. This may have been the *sinnor* by which Joab gained entrance to the city for David (2 Sam. 5: 8; 1 Chr. 11: 6).

Return to the path and continue up until you come to a T-junction beside a modern house; go to the right until you come to the middle of another excavated area [6]. Facing uphill and reading from left to right there is a large tower, a sloping construction, and a smaller tower. The small tower is dated to the C5 BC; the other elements were added in the C2 BC to strengthen the city wall constructed by Nehemiah *c.* 445 BC; the dramatic narrative of his night inspection and successful completion of the work despite SAMARITAN and Ammonite opposition is worth reading (Neh. 2: 11–4: 23). He abandoned the older line further down the hill both because he did not need the space (many had remained in Babylon) and because a line near the crest made better military sense. A small section of his wall is still visible to the right of the small tower.

At the foot of the fortifications are houses of the C7 BC. They deteriorate as each year passes, but on the right one can see a few steps and the squared stone pillars which supported the roof. The stones are untrimmed and the workmanship poor but it was from little homes such as these that the inhabitants of Jerusalem were dragged off to exile in Babylon in 586 BC.

The Royal Tombs

Go back to the T-junction and continue straight ahead between the houses. Eventually you will come to a point where you can look down on an area where the rock has been laid bare [4]. To get down is not always easy but it is worth the effort.

The irregular shaping of the rock shows that it was worked as a quarry, probably by the Romans in AD 135 when they razed Jerusalem and erected the new city of Aelia Capitolina on its site. To extract stones they cut a trench around three sides of the block and then drove in wedges to break it free; such grooves can be seen throughout the area. It did not concern them that they cut into two great shafts running into the hill; it is generally assumed that these were the tombs in which David (1 Kgs. 2: 10) and his successors were buried. The shaft on the left looking in is the most impressive. At the far end a regular depression in the floor suggests the emplacement of a massive sarcophagus. The floor at the front was cut down to create a lower tomb, but an artificial floor permitted continued access to the far end; note that the groove on both sides is angled so as to take a shallow arch which supported the floor above.

Nearby the excavators found a Greek inscription, dated in the Herodian period (37 BC–AD 70), which commemorated the foundation several generations earlier of a synagogue and hostel 'for the accommodation of those who, coming from abroad, have need of them'. Acts 6: 9 attests the presence in Jerusalem of a 'Synagogue of the Freedmen' whose members came from North Africa and Asia.

Looking over the edge near the road one can see another tomb cut in the rock face and, below, the foundations of a round tower which may date from the C2 BC. Jesus mentions a tower at Siloam which fell killing 18 people (Luke 13:4). New excavations have just been begun in this area.

It is possible to continue down the hill between the houses to emerge at the confluence of the Tyropoeon and Kidron valleys. Rock-cut steps once visible at this point were identified with those mentioned in Neh. 3:25; 12:37.

Gihon and Hezekiah's Tunnel

The reason why the Jebusites settled on the low Ophel ridge was the presence of a perennial spring [8] in the Kidron valley. It is first called Gihon in the dramatic account of the rush to get Solomon anointed king before his older half-brother Adonijah could usurp the title (1 Kgs. 1). The name means 'gushing' and it is perfectly justified because the spring is a siphon which pours out a tremendous quantity of water for some 30 minutes and then almost dries up for between 4 and 10 hours. By itself it could support a population of about 2,500.

In order to ensure a better water supply for his expanding city Solomon (965–928 BC) drove a tunnel along the bottom of the hill, part of which can be seen at [5]. It had sluice gates at intervals, permitting surplus water to be used to irrigate the fields in the bottom of the Kidron valley, and terminated in a great pool [2] at the end of the Tyropoeon valley, today called Birket el-Hamra and planted with fig trees; the tunnel cut through the tip of the Ophel ridge is visible on both sides [3]. This tunnel shows clear evidence of two stages of development, the original floor having been cut down to reverse the direction of flow.

The stability of Solomon's reign meant that this tunnel was no risk, but later it became a liability. 'Realizing that Sennacherib's advance was the preliminary to an attack on Jerusalem, Hezekiah [727–698 BC] and his officers and champions decided to cut off the water supply from the springs situated outside the city. A great many people were gathered and they stopped all the springs and the brook that flowed through the land [the Solomonic tunnel with its sluices], saying, Why should the kings of Assyria come and find much water?' (2 Chr. 32:2–4). Having thus camouflaged the source of the city's water supply, Hezekiah 'constructed the pool and the tunnel to bring water into the city' (2 Kgs. 20: 20); 'he directed the waters of Gihon down to the west side of the city of David' (2 Chr. 32: 30). We know exactly how he did it because of a Hebrew inscription placed by the proud engineer inside the tunnel near the pool of Siloam [1] which reads:

Behold the tunnel. This is the story of its cutting. While the miners swung their picks, one towards the other, and when there remained only 3 cubits to cut, the voice of one calling his fellow was heard – for there was a resonance in the rock coming from both north and south. So the day they broke through the miners struck, one against the other, pick against pick, and the water flowed from the spring towards the pool, 1200 cubits. The height of the rock above the head of the miners was 100 cubits.

The inscription (now in the Istanbul Museum) does not have Hezekiah's name but its authenticity is guaranteed by the archaic script.

It is possible to walk through the 512 m-long tunnel; for a consideration the guardian will open the metal gate at Gihon and provide candles. The passage is narrow and low in parts, but perfectly safe. If the water suddenly starts to rise, think yourself fortunate to see the siphon effect; it will rise only 15–20 cm. The steps to the water level are medieval, the ground in the valley having risen. Some 20 m into the tunnel, at a point where it makes a right-angled bend to the left, there is a chest-high wall blocking another channel; this leads to the vertical Jebusite shaft whose surface entrance can be seen between the two sections of the Kenyon excavations [6 and 7]. Towards the middle of the tunnel one can see the false starts which the miners made as they tried to work out where the other team was. Once the roof starts to rise the pool of Siloam is close; the miners started too high at the southern end and had to lower the floor in order to get the water to flow. The inscription was found 10 m before the end of the tunnel on the left-hand wall.

Pool of Siloam

The original form of the pool [1] has been lost for ever. It is likely that Herod introduced alterations during his vast building programme in Jerusalem, but these can hardly have survived the sack of the City of David by the Romans, who 'burnt the whole place as far as Siloam' (*War* 6: 363). The Bordeaux pilgrim's description (333) of the pool as having four porches probably refers to Hadrian's reconstruction in AD 135; it has been confirmed archaeologically (C in fig. 26). Christians were attracted to the pool because of its association with Jesus' miraculous cure of the man born blind (John 9), but the first church there was built by the Empress Eudokia *c*.450. Excavations have borne out the description of the Piacenza pilgrim (570), 'You descend by many steps to Siloam, and above Siloam is a hanging basilica beneath which the water of Siloam rises' (A in fig. 26). The relationship of the pool to Gihon had long been forgotten; Josephus in fact always speaks of Siloam as a spring.

The church was destroyed by the Persians in 614, but the tradition of the curative powers of the waters, mentioned by Byzantine pilgrims, continued among the Arabs; the colonnade around the pool is mentioned as late as the C15. What happened thereafter is a mystery. Possibly debris from higher up the valley washed down into the pool and was sporadically cleared to the sides by Silwan villagers who needed the water; drawings and descriptions of early C19 travellers show the pool to have acquired its present form (B in fig. 26) by that period. The mosque was built in the 1890s.

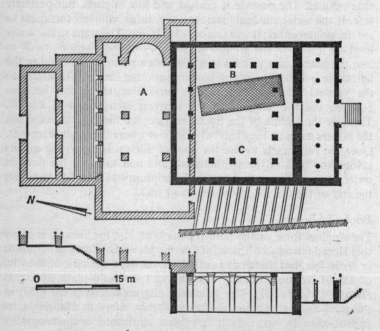

Fig. 26. The C5 church and pool of Siloam (after Vincent).

The overhang of the scarp of the City of David on the far side of the path running beside Birket el-Hamra [2] was at one time part of Hezekiah's tunnel carrying the overflow from the pool to the gardens in the Kidron valley. The tunnel at this point was half destroyed by Roman quarrying operations in the C2 AD. In the Byzantine period the overflow went into the Birket el-Hamra which, according to the Piacenza pilgrim (570), was used as the city laundry. Were this an ancient custom it would explain the naming of the Fuller's Field nearby where King Ahaz (733–727 BC) met the prophet Isaiah and his son (Isa. 7: 3).

Tombs in the Kidron Valley

The entire east side of the Kidron valley is a vast cemetery with a number of structures of unusual interest. Inevitably they have been given popular names which have changed over the centuries and which, in most cases, have little to do with reality. Three free-standing rock monuments catch the eye from the modern road running round the south-east corner of the Haram esh-Sharif (Temple Mount), the 'Tomb of Absalom' [12], the 'Tomb of Zachariah' [11], and the 'Tomb of the Pharaoh's Daughter' [10].

The 'Tomb of Absalom' (fig. 27) is dated to the C1 AD. It is rock up to the corniche; the bottle-shaped top is masonry. It in fact contains a tomb, but the position of the door (above the corniche on the south side) shows that the tomb had been cut in the cliff before the decision to free the monolith was taken. The structure was designed to serve as a funerary monument or *nephesh* for the eight-chambered catacomb cut in the cliff behind; the entrance is surmounted by a fine pediment.

Some 50 m further south the pyramid-roofed 'Tomb of Zachariah' serves as the funerary monument of another catacomb (fig. 28) which a Hebrew inscription on the architrave above the two Doric columns identifies as belonging to the priestly family of the Bene Hezir. The complex is dated to the second half of the C2 BC.

The 'Tomb of the Pharaoh's Daughter' [10] sits on the very edge of a small escarpment still further south. At first sight it looks like one of the small houses of Silwan which surround it but it has no windows. When cut in the C9–C7 BC it was surmounted by a pyramid like that of the 'Tomb of Zachariah'; traces on the present rock roof show that the pyramid was quarried for stone in the Roman period. Other changes were effected by the Byzantine hermit who made it his home some time in the C4–C6 AD; in enlarging the entrance he

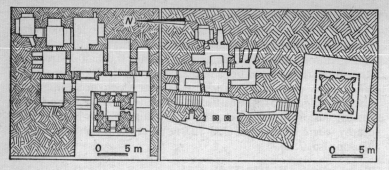

Fig. 27. The 'Tomb of Ab-
salom' (after Vincent).

Fig. 28. The 'Tomb of Zachariah' (after
Vincent).

cut through a Hebrew inscription, two letters of which are visible
near the upper left-hand corner. Two other tombs of the same type
have been found incorporated into houses in the main street of
Silwan.

Still further south [9] a series of square openings appear in the cliff
below the houses. These are the entrances to rock-cut rooms with
gabled ceilings. On one side are places for one or two burials, the
husband's resting place being slightly higher than that of his wife!
These are also dated in the C9–C7 BC.

THE MOUNT OF OLIVES

From Jerusalem the view to the east is blocked by the Mount of
Olives (fig. 29) rising some 100 m above the city. A road [1] runs
along the top of the ridge; at various points there are magnificent
views over the Old City and out across the Judaean desert to the
Jordan valley and the mountains of Moab.

In the time of David (1004–965 BC), who escaped that way when
confronted by Absalom's treachery, there was a Jewish sanctuary
(Nob?) on the summit (2 Sam. 15: 30–2). In the next generation other
sanctuaries appeared; Solomon built temples for the gods of his
foreign wives on the southern spur (2 Kgs. 23: 13) near the present
Maison d'Abraham [9] from whose wall there is a dominant view
encompassing the whole of the CITY OF DAVID. After the establish-

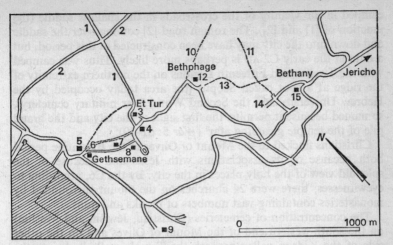

Fig. 29. The Mount of Olives.

ment of the Temple in Jerusalem the ritual of the Red Heifer (Num. 19: 1–10) was celebrated on the Mount of Olives; leaving the Temple by the East Gate, the procession led by the High Priest crossed the Kidron valley on a special causeway and climbed to the summit where the animal was sacrificed (*Mishnah*, tractate 'Parah').

Jesus' familiarity with the Mount of Olives stemmed from the fact that, when in the Jerusalem area, he stayed with his friends at Bethany (Luke 10: 38; Mark 11: 11); each day he walked over the hill to the city and returned at nightfall (Luke 21: 37). The lie of the land permits only one route if the traveller wants to avoid climbing in and out of wadis: from Gethsemane straight up the hill to et-Tur and along the ridge to Bethphage (roughly the modern road), then along another ridge to Bethany. One evening, seated on the slope opposite the Temple, Jesus spoke to his disciples of the fate of the city (Mark 13: 3) whose lack of faith had driven him to tears (Luke 19: 37, 41–4). Amid waving palms he rode down towards Jerusalem in triumph (Mark 11: 1–10), passing the garden of Gethsemane where he was arrested a few days later (Mark 14: 26–52). Luke locates the Ascension on the Mount of Olives (Acts 1: 6–12).

As the Roman legions gathered for the siege of Jerusalem in AD 70, the Tenth Legion came up the east side of the Mount of Olives and camped in the vicinity of the crossroads in the shallow saddle (the junction of [1] and [2]). The roman road [2] coming over the saddle and down into the city may have been constructed at this period, but a date in the early C2 AD is perhaps more likely. Titus was camped with the Twelfth and Fifteenth Legions on the northern extremity of the ridge at a spot called Scopus (the area today occupied by the Hebrew University and the Second World War military cemetery), so named because it permits 'the first sight of the city and the grand pile of the temple gleaming afar' (*War* 5: 67–70).

Christians flocked to the Mount of Olives in the Byzantine period both because of its associations with Jesus and because of the splendid view of the holy places in the city. By the C6, according to eyewitnesses, there were 24 churches on the mount surrounded by monasteries containing vast numbers of monks and nuns.

The concentration of cemeteries (Christian, Jewish, and Muslim) on the south-western end of the Mount of Olives and on the other side of the Kidron valley beneath the Temple walls is due to the belief that the Kidron is the Valley of Jehoshaphat where humanity will assemble to be judged by God. The identification results from the combination of Joel 3: 2 with Zech. 14: 4, and was first recorded by the Bordeaux pilgrim (333).

Gethsemane

Having eaten the Paschal meal somewhere in the city (Luke 22: 10), Jesus 'went forth with his disciples across the Kidron valley, where there was a garden' (John 18: 1) on the Mount of Olives called Gethsemane (Mark 14: 26, 32). The place was known to Judas, 'for Jesus often met there with his disciples' (John 18: 2), perhaps to take a rest (while reflecting on the experiences of the day) before starting the climb up the steep slope en route to Bethany. Jesus knew his life to be in danger (John 11: 8, 16); he suspected Judas of treachery (Mark 14: 17–21); on his way up the Kidron valley he could not have avoided seeing the tombs in the bright moonlight. Awareness of the imminence of death struck him with great force; he had to stop and be alone for a moment because a decision had to be made. His enemies would come from the city, but ten minutes' fast walking would bring him to the top of the Mount of Olives with the open desert before him. Escape would be easy; he could postpone the inevitable. Only in prayer could he find the answer to the agonizing question of whether to stand or retreat.

The Church of All Nations

This church ([6] in fig. 29), built in 1924, is located on the traditional site of the garden in which Jesus prayed, which has a strong claim to authenticity. No one can be sure of the exact spot on which Jesus knelt, but this limited area must have been very close to the route leading from the Temple to the summit of the Mount of Olives. A flight of ancient rock-cut steps was discovered in the property of the Russian church further up the hill, and until the introduction of earth-moving equipment in this century an established route was never changed.

The present edifice (shaded area, fig. 30) is the latest in a series of three churches. It covers 'the elegant church' (Egeria) built between AD 379 and 384 (solid black line)) on the site where the pre-Constantinian Jerusalem community commemorated the prayer of Christ. Willibald, in 724–5, is the last pilgrim to mention this church; it was destroyed by an earthquake some 20 years later. The Crusaders first built an oratory in the ruins which they later (*c*.1170) replaced by a church (double line); they gave it a slightly different orientation

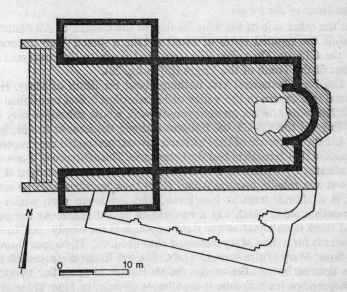

Fig. 30. The three churches at Gethsemane, C4 (solid black), C12 (white), and C20 (shaded).

in order to have a piece of rock in each apse – a rather material interpretation of the triple prayer of Christ. The fate of this building is unknown; still functioning in 1323, it was abandoned in 1345.

Visit. Open: 8.30 a.m. – 12 p.m. and 2–5 p.m. (Nov.-March) or 3–7 p.m. (April-Oct.). The olive trees in the garden, though extremely ancient, are unlikely to have been in existence in the time of Christ; the wooded slopes of the Mount of Olives must have been a prime source for the vast quantities of timber required for the Roman siege in AD 70 (*War* 5: 264).

The rock in the nave was also the central feature of the C4 church whose outline and columns are traced in black marble on the floor; glass panels protect sections of the Byzantine mosaic floor. Part of the present south wall is solid rock. This was the centrepiece of the Crusader church; on the top (about eye level) note a levelled surface and a cut hole suggesting the emplacement of an altar. The reconstructed trace of the Crusader edifice can be seen outside the south wall. Leave the church by the main door and turn left.

The Tomb of the Virgin

On the other side of the alley leading to the Church of All Nations stands the reputed tomb of Mujir al-Din, a famed Arab historian of the C15 AD. On either side steps lead down to the courtyard in front of the Tomb of the Virgin ([5] in fig. 29).

The New Testament says nothing about the death of Mary. Her burial in a cavern in the Valley of Jehoshaphat is first mentioned in the *Transitus Mariae*, an anonymous work whose substance may be as early as the C2–C3 AD. Ephesus claimed the honour in 431, but in 451 the eloquence of the Patriarch Juvenal persuaded the Emperor Marcian that Jerusalem had the better case. The existence of a church is attested by writers of the late C6. If the Persians destroyed it in 614 it was rebuilt, because Arculf (670) thus describes what he saw: 'It is a church built at two levels, and the lower part, which is beneath a stone vault, has a remarkable round shape. At the east end there is an altar, on the right of which is the empty rock tomb in which for a time Mary remained entombed. . . . The upper church of Saint Mary is also round.' The Crusaders found the ruins left by the destructive passage of the caliph Hakim in 1009, but by 1130 the Benedictines had rebuilt the double church; in 1178 Theodoric noted that there were as many steps down to the crypt as there were up to the church. In 1187 Saladin destroyed the superstructure and used the stones to repair the city wall, but removed only the decoration of the crypt.

Visit (fig. 31). Open: 6–11.30 a.m. and 2–5 p.m.; closed Sundays. The façade and the monumental stairway are early C12. On the right [1] is the tomb of Queen Melisande (d. 1161), the daughter and wife of Crusader kings of Jerusalem; other members of the family of Baldwin II were buried in the niche opposite [2]. An arch protruding above the modern door [3] betrays the Byzantine entrance; there was another on the far side of the apse [4]. About the middle of the steps the architectural style changes, the pointed arches giving way to round vaults.

The crypt [5] is Byzantine, in part constructed (solid black) and in part cut out of the rock. The rising passage [6] disturbs the cruciform symmetry of the Byzantine crypt; it is in fact a much older entrance to an underground cemetery – there are good parallels further up the hill in the DOMINUS FLEVIT and in the TOMBS OF THE PROPHETS. A grille high in the side of the niche [9] covers part of a tomb [10] whose type is compatible with a C1 AD date. Its entrance disappeared when the rock was cut away to isolate another tomb [8] which tradition considers to be that of the Virgin Mary. Glass

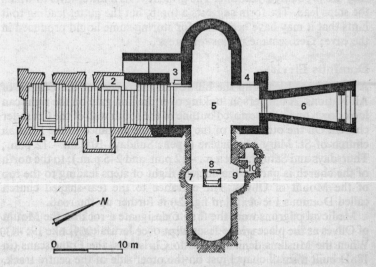

Fig. 31. The Tomb of the Virgin at Gethsemane (after Bagatti).

plates reveal the living rock on three sides; the rock bench, on which the body was laid, has suffered from the piety of pilgrims. Originally there was only one entrance; the lintel over the secondary door facing the niche [9] is medieval. The idea of isolating the tomb in the middle of the crypt was suggested by the Holy Sepulchre where, a century earlier, Constantine's engineers had cut away the rock around the tomb of Christ in order to bring it within the church.

The curved *mihrab* [7] gives the direction of Mecca; the site is holy to Muslims because, according to Mujir al-Din (C15 AD), Muhammad saw a light over the tomb of his 'sister Mary' on his night journey to Jerusalem (details in HARAM ESH-SHARIF: DOME OF THE ROCK).

The Cave of Gethsemane

From the façade of the Virgin's Tomb a narrow passage leads to a cave which Byzantine Christians regarded as the place where the disciples rested while Jesus prayed a stone's-throw away (Luke 22: 41); it was there that Judas saluted him with the traitor's kiss.

Visit. Open: as Church of All Nations. The original form of the cave is problematic; it has been restored several times. Traces of two levels of mosaic floors are preserved in the corner on the right as one enters; they are probably Byzantine. The grille reveals a lower level to which the steps lead. The form suggests a tomb, but the gutter leading to it hints that it may have been used for storing some liquid produced in the cave; Gethsemane means 'oil press'.

Dominus Flevit

A tarmac road leads up the hill round the corner of the Church of All Nations. A tall person looking over the first gate on the right can look down on to the restored outline of the south wall of the Crusader church. On the other side of the road is the entrance to the Russian church of St. Mary Magdalene (open: Sundays 10 a.m. – 12 p.m.; Thursdays and Saturdays 9 a.m. – 12 p.m. and 2–5 p.m.); to the north of the church is part of the ancient flight of steps leading to the top of the Mount of Olives. The entrance to the tear-shaped church called Dominus Flevit ([7] in fig. 29) is further up the road.

Medieval pilgrims were the first to designate a rock on the Mount of Olives as the place where Jesus wept over Jerusalem (Luke 19: 41). When the Muslims denied access to Christians, the Franciscans (in 1881) built a small chapel just on the other side of the centre track. In 1954 excavations in the southern part of their property brought

to light a monastery of the C5 AD and an immense cemetery, first used
*c.*1600–1300 BC and again later in two main periods, 100 BC–AD 135
and AD 200–400.

Visit. Open: 7 a.m. – 12 p.m. and 3–5 p.m. (Nov.-March) or 3–6 p.m.
(April–Oct.); toilets. The cemetery has been covered in again but
examples of the two types of tombs have been left visible. The first
two on the right (counting from the entrance gate) are typical *kokhim*
graves of the period 100 BC–AD 135; the dead were buried in oven-
shaped shafts and later their bones were collected in beautifully made
stone boxes (ossuaries) in order to make room for others. Such
burials ceased here in 135 when Hadrian forbade Jerusalem to Jews;
BET SHEARIM was adopted as an alternative. The XP (Chi-Rho) sign
on one ossuary does not mean that the person was a Christian; it is
attested as an abbreviation for 'sealed'.

The third tomb is quite different; the bodies were laid in arched
niches (arcosolia); it is dated in the C3–C4 AD. The fourth tomb is of
the earlier period; two fine sarcophagi are displayed. So little remained of the 'Jebusite' (pre-Israelite inhabitants of the town on the
Ophel ridge) tomb that nothing could be preserved; it was located
in the area now occupied by the toilets.

The new church (1955) preserves the outline of the Byzantine
chapel whose apse is preserved to a considerable height; the emplacement of the altar and that of the chancel screen are still visible, as are
portions of the mosaic floor. The Greek inscription in the mosaic
floor outside reads, 'Simeon, friend of Christ, made and decorated
this oratory and offered it to Christ Our Lord in expiation of his sins
and for the repose of his brothers, the hygumenos Georgios and the
friend of Christ Dometios.' The present open space was the monastic
courtyard; in the corner diagonally opposite the entrance to the
church is a mosaic-floored wine tank. This monastery was but one
of the many which proliferated on the Mount of Olives in the C4–C6
and was not associated with any particular event in the life of Christ.

Tombs of the Prophets

The sign at the entrance ([8] in fig. 29) claims that this catacomb
contains the tombs of the prophets Haggai, Zechariah, and Malachi
who lived in the C6–C5 BC. This medieval Jewish tradition is contradicted by the form of the graves; *kokhim* shafts came into use only
in the C1 BC. The catacomb was part of the pre-AD 135 Jewish
cemetery on the Mount of Olives. The only unusual feature is the fan

shape (fig. 32). Open: 9 a.m. – 3.30 p.m. weekdays only; bring a torch.

Mosque of the Ascension

Luke is the only evangelist to mention the Ascension of Jesus. At the end of his gospel he says, 'He led them out as far as towards Bethany, and lifting up his hands he blessed them. And it came to pass that as he blessed them, he parted from them and was carried up into heaven' (Luke 24: 50–2). Reading the whole of ch. 24 one has the impression that the event occurred on Easter Sunday; the place is not precisely located. According to Luke's second work, the Acts of the Apostles, the Ascension (1: 9) took place 40 days after the Resurrection (1: 3), somewhere on the Mount of Olives, a Sabbath day's journey (= 2,000 paces) from the city (1: 12). The inconsistency of the two accounts is real, but Luke could accept it because he was aware that he was not recording an historical event; from his point of view the Ascension was much more a literary way of drawing a line between the terrestrial mission of Jesus and that of the apostles.

In the pre-Constantinian period Jerusalem Christians venerated the Ascension in a cave on the Mount of Olives, probably because it was safer to congregate in a hidden place. When Egeria participated in the liturgical celebration of the Ascension in 384 it took place on the nearby open hillock. Poimenia, a member of the imperial family, built the first church on the site ([3] in fig. 29) before 392; the proposed reconstruction (fig. 33) is based on the descriptions of Byzantine pilgrims, a drawing by Arculf (670), and archaeological investigations. Nothing visible remains of this church whose centre was open to the sky. In the Crusader reconstruction an octagon replaced the original circular shape, and the shrine was surrounded by a fortified monastery. In the Middle Ages great veneration was accorded to the mark of Jesus' feet in the stone floor of the edicule; in the Byzantine period the footprints were 'plainly and clearly impressed in the dust' which pilgrims were permitted to take away (Arculf)!

Saladin conveyed the site by deed to two of his followers in 1198 and it has remained in Muslim possession ever since. The Muslim restoration of 1200 preserved much of the Crusader edicule but added a roof and a *mihrab*; though not mentioned in the Koran, Islam believes that Jesus ascended into heaven.

Visit: If the guardian is not present ask any Arab in the vicinity to find him. He can also procure admission to the gallery above the

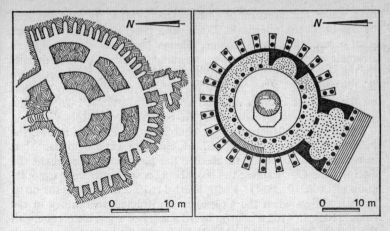

Fig. 32. The Tombs of the Prophets on the Mount of Olives.

Fig. 33. J. Wilkinson's reconstruction of the C4 Church of the Ascension.

mosque which is the best viewpoint in the area; to the west the Old City is laid out like a model and to the east one can see the Jordan valley and the Dead Sea.

From the gallery it is immediately evident that the much repaired medieval octagon surround-wall has been truncated on the east. From the hooks set into this wall the various Christian communities stretch awnings to provide a temporary roof for the celebration of the feast of the Ascension. Inside the edicule a small rectangle surrounds the mark of Jesus' right foot; the section bearing the imprint of the left foot was taken to the el-Aksa mosque in the Middle Ages. To its left is another stone in which holes have been bored; at one time they may have held a protective grating. The eccentric position of the supposed footprint highlights the secondary character of the edifice.

Church of the Pater Noster

The apocryphal Acts of John (C3 AD) attests the existence of a particular cave on the Mount of Olives associated with the teaching of Jesus (ch. 97). According to Eusebius (260–340), Constantine's building programme in Palestine focused on the three caves linked to the key mysteries of the faith, the birth cave in Bethlehem, the rock-cut tomb near Golgotha, and the cave on the Mount of Olives with which the Ascension was also linked. The church built over this cave, under the direction of Queen Helena ([4] in fig. 29), was seen by the Bordeaux pilgrim in 333; Egeria (384) is the first to record what became the common name, 'Eleona' (Jerusalemites attached an Aramaic *a* to the Greek *elaion*, meaning 'of olives'). After the site for the commemoration of the Ascension had been moved further up the hill, the cave was exclusively associated with the teaching of Jesus on the ultimate conflict of good and evil (Matt. 24: 1–26: 2 – the gospel Egeria heard read in the cave on Tuesday of Holy Week).

Despite the destruction of the church by the Persians in 614, the memory of Jesus' teaching remained, but there was a significant shift in its content. It tended to become the place where he taught the disciples the Our Father; the basis being a sophisticated harmonization of Luke 10: 38–11: 4 with Mark 11: 12–25. This was the dominant tradition when the Crusaders constructed an oratory in the ruins (1106). In 1102 a pilgrim heard a story of a marble plaque with the Lord's Prayer inscribed in Hebrew; another saw one in Greek placed beneath the altar (1170); an inscribed Latin version was found in the excavations.

This tradition has been revived in the decoration of the cloister erected after the Byzantine foundations were brought to light in 1910; tiled panels give the Lord's Prayer in 62 languages.

Visit. Open: 8.30–11.50 a.m. and 3–4.30 p.m. After passing through the iron gate go left and then right. The tomb is that of the Princesse de la Tour d'Auvergne who bought the property in 1868 and built the Carmelite convent. To reach the cave go round the cloister to the left, down a short flight of stairs, and enter the first door to the right.

The cave acquired its present shape under the chisels of the C4 builders. There were two entrances, one opposite the other; the cutting near the apse may have been the original entrance. In preparing the cave the builders broke through into a C1 AD *kokhim* tomb. They blocked the hole with masonry which has now been removed; the tomb can be entered via the steps at the end opposite the apse. It seems unlikely that the venerated cave was originally a tomb; had the builders cut away *kokhim* graves it would have been much wider.

The half-reconstructed church gives a good idea of the Byzantine building whose raised sanctuary covered the cave. It has the same dimensions, and the garden outside the three doors outlines the area of the atrium.

Bethphage

Bethphage is mentioned in the Gospels as the starting-place of Jesus' triumphal entrance into Jerusalem amid waving palms, but the texts are not as clear as one would wish. According to Mark, Jesus was *in the vicinity of* 'Bethphage and Bethany, at the Mount of Olives' when he sent the disciples into the village opposite to fetch the ass (11: 1–2), but for Matthew, Jesus had *entered* Bethphage before sending the disciples on their mission (21: 1–2). Inevitably, the location of Bethphage is uncertain. Everything depends on the route that Jesus took coming from Jericho. The ancient road lay in the long wadi Umm esh-Shid continuing due east from [2] in fig. 29; once one got to the back of the Mount of Olives there were different options, the best two of which are numbered 10 and 11 in fig. 29. Bethphage could have been on the ridge between the two. The present site ([12] in fig. 29) has a reasonable chance of being in the vicinity; the chapel is the starting-point for the Palm Sunday procession.

Visit. Ring the bell for admission. From the courtyard it is obvious that the lower part of the church walls are older than the rest. The present church was built in 1883 on the ruins of a medieval church which enshrined a stone that the Crusaders regarded as the mounting-stone of Christ, forgetting that a Palestinian donkey was in no way comparable to their huge battle chargers. The medieval paintings on the stone are beautiful, and have not been damaged by the 1950 restoration. One records the meeting of Lazarus's sisters with Jesus (John 11: 20–30). In 384 Egeria noted, 'About half a mile before you get to the Lazarium [= Bethany] from Jerusalem there is a church by the road. It is the spot where Lazarus's sister Mary met the Lord.' The original purpose of the stone is unknown.

It is sometimes possible to get permission to go behind the church into the Franciscan property. Numerous cisterns, tombs (one closed by a rolling stone), and a mosaic-paved winepress witness to continued occupation from the C2 BC to the C8 AD.

To walk to Bethany from Bethphage go left on leaving the church and follow the path beside the high wall of the monastery ([13] in fig. 29). Some 50 yards after the wall swings away to follow the side of a small wadi, the path divides: take the rougher track to the right and the churches of Bethany soon come into sight.

For those who prefer to drive, it is best to go straight through the crossroads and turn left on the main Jericho road; it is possible to go left at the crossroads but the road is very narrow and steep.

Bethany

Bethany was the village in which Jesus' friends Martha, Mary, and Lazarus lived; from its cemetery he raised Lazarus from the dead (John 11). There is no problem about its identification. A village ([15] in fig. 29) on the main Jericho road fits the distance from Jerusalem given in John 11: 18, and its Arabic name el-Azariyeh preserves the Greek *Lazarion*, 'the place of Lazarus', by which it was known to Eusebius (330) and all subsequent Byzantine and medieval pilgrims.

The present village is built round the tomb of Lazarus as the result of a development parallel to that which occurred in HEBRON. In the C1 AD the area was a cemetery; tombs of this period have been found a short distance north of the church. The village of (Bet) Ananiah inhabited by Benjaminites after the Exile (Neh. 11: 32) was located further up the hill ([14] in fig. 29). The site is not accessible to visitors; excavations prove it to have been occupied from the C6 BC to the C14 AD.

Jerome records the existence of a church in 390. After its destruction by an earthquake, a second one was built in the C5. It has the same width as its predecessor, but the apse was moved 13 m further east. The extra space was necessary because Egeria (381), who knew the first church, says, 'so many people have collected that they fill not only the Lazarium itself, but all the fields around.' From the atrium of both these churches a rock-cut passage gave access to the tomb of Lazarus. The Crusaders shored up the Byzantine edifice by adding buttresses and doubling the size of the pillars. They also built a new church directly over the tomb; it appears to have served as a chapel for the Benedictine convent founded by Queen Melisande in 1138. By the end of the C14 both churches were in ruins, and the original entrance to the tomb had been turned into a mosque. The Muslims also venerated the raising of Lazarus and at first permitted Christians to continue their liturgical visits. When this became progressively more difficult the Franciscans cut the present entrance to the tomb between 1566 and 1575. They erected the new church and the adjoining monastery in 1954. The Greek Orthodox church (begun in 1965) on the other side of the tomb incorporates part of the north wall of the medieval Benedictine chapel.

Visit (fig. 34). Open: 7 a.m.–12 p.m. and 2–5.30 p.m. Just inside the entrance of the modern cruciform church (shaded) trapdoors on both sides expose the masonry of the apse of the C4 church. The mosaic

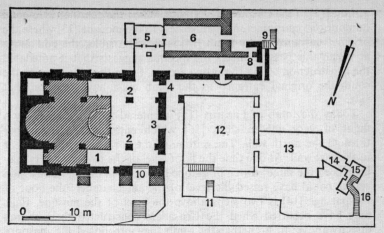

Fig. 34. Superimposed churches at Bethany (after Saller): C5 (solid black), C12 (cross hatching), C20 (shaded area).

beneath the grille is that of the C5 church (solid black lines) whose apse is outlined in white marble on both sides of the main altar.

In the courtyard one can see part of the masonry of the C4 church [1] whose mosaic floor once covered the entire area; the preserved portions are now covered by metal plates; those nearest the C5 façade [3] with its three doors show how this wall cuts across the original design. On the side of the centre pillars [2] fragments of mosaic about 30 cm above ground level belong to the floor of the C5 church; a few centimetres above them another fragment of mosaic betrays the floor laid during the Crusader restoration in the C12. Just outside the C5 south door [4] is a pillar of the atrium, and two medieval graves; the mosaic floor is C4–C5 and can be seen again at the door [7] which connected the atrium with a long room on its south side. Toilet facilities are available off the pilgrims' dining room [5] just beside a room of the medieval monastery [6] containing a mill and oil press. Immediately inside the small door [8] one can see the turn of the C5 wall. The staircase [9] leads to the extensive upper section of the Crusader monastery.

When climbing the stairway [10] to the street note the medieval reinforcement (cross hatching) of the C5 church wall. From the entrance [11] of the Mosque el-Ozir one can look down into the atrium [12] of the C4 and C5 churches. When the guardian is in good humour one can sometimes gain access to the mosque [13] where the original entrance to the tomb [14] is clearly visible; the odd angle at which this passage meets the mosque suggests that it antedated the construction of the Byzantine atrium. Since the hill slopes to the south the original entrance to the tomb must have been on that side.

Today the tomb of Lazarus [15] is entered from the street by a flight of very uneven steps [16] which enters the antechamber through the north wall. The outline of the earlier entrance is clear in the east wall. At one time the floor level of the two chambers may have been the same; rotten limestone falling from the unusually high ceiling could have raised the level of the antechamber; the floor of the passage [14] is two steps above the level of the mosque. Falls may have occurred when the Crusaders constructed their church directly above; to strengthen the tomb they introduced the masonry which still obscures the original rock except for a few holes in the inner chamber.

Walking up the street from the present entrance [16] one passes the new Greek Orthodox church before coming to a four-way crossroads. To the left are the ruins of a medieval watch-tower; the track to the right leads to Bethphage. The path winds up between the houses. At the top one can look down into a shallow wadi which carried the ancient road from Bethany to Jericho; keep left along the high wall of the Franciscan property to get to Bethphage.

NEW CITY

New suburbs were first built outside the walled city in 1860. The impetus to expand did not come from within the Old City. Three centuries of Ottoman rule had reduced its inhabitants to a state of torpid misery. Arbitrary taxation penalized any initiative, and foul cisterns, the only source of drinking water, meant that 50 per cent of the small population suffered from endemic malaria; the rubbish of centuries clogged the streets.

The authorities of Czarist Russia, responsible for 12,000 pilgrims each year, were not prepared to permit them to live in such dangerous and unsanitary conditions, and built a series of great hostels on a hill outside the north-west corner of the Old City. Its centrepiece, a many-domed church near Jaffa Road, is still a Jerusalem landmark, but the defensive wall has disappeared. Such protection was necessary because the Turkish authorities were neither capable nor willing to provide protection outside the walled city; they had only 120 troops in Palestine and these were themselves no more than licensed brigands; to recruit new members they simply shanghaied peasants.

Encouraged by the Russian initiative, an English philanthropist, Sir Moses Montefiore, went ahead with his project to house residents of the Jewish Quarter west of the city at Mishkenoth Shaananim ('Abode of Tranquillity'); its symbol is the windmill which he had erected in 1857 to grind flour for the city.

The success of these two efforts had its impact on inhabitants of the walled city only in 1869 when, attracted by the commercial opportunities offered by the presence of so many Russian pilgrims, seven Jewish families moved out to the area near the present Sion Square.

As the century progressed Christian and Jewish immigration consolidated these gains. Jewish immigrants concentrated in the north-western and western sectors. German Christians founded a farming village in the south-west, the Refaim valley, while American and European Christians spearheaded expansion north of the Old City. The architecture of all these developments still betrays the concern for security. Housing areas were so designed that the backs of contiguous houses formed a wall and gates at the end of streets could be locked; institutions were surrounded by forbidding walls.

This situation changed only in 1918 when Palestine came under the Mandatory Government. The great contribution of the British was the provision of an efficient police force; security permitted free expansion, but ripening tensions between Jews and Arabs fostered the development of homogeneous neighbourhoods. The population of Jerusalem grew continuously under British administration, increasing 162 per cent between 1922 (62,700) and 1946 (164,000). The contribution of Jews and Arabs to this growth was almost equal.

The bitter fighting which followed the departure of the British and the creation of the State of Israel resulted in the partition of Jerusalem. Arabs retained possession of the Old City, whose Jewish population had decreased steadily during the British Mandate, and the area along the ridge to the north. Fortunately subsequent growth in this sector was slow because lack of planning permitted linear development along the Nablus road. Growth in the western sector was intense because of the need to absorb Jewish immigrants from

Europe and Arab countries; the population increased from 82,900 in 1948 to 197,750 in 1967.

No development outside the walled city was ever intended to consecrate a site of historical or archaeological interest, but scattered throughout the urban area are a number of sites which reflect the history of Jerusalem. Most are in fact tombs, some of them unusually interesting. The two sketch maps (figs. 35 and 39), which locate sites in the northern and western sectors, should be used in conjunction with a detailed map of the city; the best is 'Jerusalem' (1: 14,000) produced by the Survey of Israel.

NEW CITY: NORTHERN SECTION

One salient feature of the landscape north of the Old City is the amount of unused land; it has not been built on, neither is it developed as a park. This was the No-Man's Land during the 20 years when the city was divided between Jordanians and Israelis. One triangle narrows as it runs north from Damascus Gate; where it comes to a point at the junction of Shmuel Ha-Navi and St. George another triangle immediately begins to broaden out (fig. 35). This crossroads was the famous 'Mandelbaum Gate'. No gate ever existed here; it was the only point where visitors could cross from one side of the city to the other.

By the C1 AD the low hills surrounding Jerusalem on the north and east had become a vast cemetery. A great number of tombs have

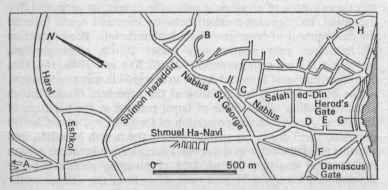

Fig. 35. New City – Northern Section.

been discovered and many excavated, one containing the body of a young man crucified by the prefect Varus in AD 6. It is possible to mention only those of exceptional interest. Capital letters refer to the location in fig. 35.

Sanhedrin Tombs [A]

Located in a garden at the end of Sanhedrin Street, the cave containing these tombs is notable for its magnificent carved pediment, the finest in Jerusalem. Pomegranates and other fruits are scattered among the stylized acanthus leaves; the workmanship is typically C1 AD.

The entrance to the tomb chamber has a smaller pediment. The great chamber immediately inside is unique in that it has two rows of shaft graves (*kokhim*) one above the other; arcosolia group those of the upper level in pairs. There are two other chambers on the same level, and others below reached by stairs.

The number of burials that the tomb can accommodate is responsible for its popular name; it approximates to the membership (70) of the Jewish Sanhedrin.

Tomb of Simon the Just [B]

Popularly identified as the tomb of the high priest Simon who said, 'By three things is the world sustained: by the Law, by the Temple-service, and by deeds of loving-kindness' (Aboth 1: 2), this tomb in fact belong to the Roman matron Julia Sabine, as an inscription proves.

Its interest lies less in its architectural style, which is negligible, than in the fact that it illustrates an ancient Jewish custom; it is a place of pilgrimage for Oriental Jews who offer prayers of petition. The custom of praying at the graves of revered religious leaders is attested for the C1 AD by a work called *The Lives of the Prophets*. The disciples of Jesus did the same; texts such as Mark 16: 6 take on their full meaning when spoken during prayer services at the tomb. It is not surprising, therefore, that the location of the tomb of Christ should have been indelibly fixed in the memories of Jerusalem Christians (CHRISTIAN QUARTER: HOLY SEPULCHRE).

Tomb of Queen Helena of Adiabene [C]

The majestic façade of this tomb complex (fig. 36) convinced the first archaeologist to explore it that the graves belonged to the kings of Judah, whence the popular name Tombs of the Kings. His intuition regarding royal origin was correct, but the founder was a queen of

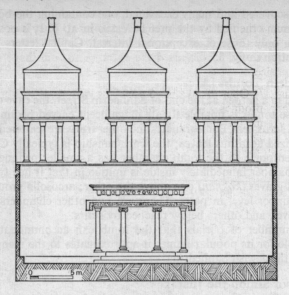

Fig. 36. L.-H. Vincent's reconstruction of the façade of the Tomb of Queen Helena of Adiabene.

Adiabene in northern Mesopotamia, about whom Josephus tells us much (*Antiquities* 20: 17–96).

Early in the C1 AD Helena, dowager queen of Adiabene, and her son Izates, were converted to Judaism by proselytizing Jewish merchants. She arrived in Jerusalem on pilgrimage during the great famine (Acts 11: 27–30) which occurred between 46 and 48, and immediately set about procuring food from as far away as Egypt and Cyprus. Deciding to stay in Jerusalem, she built a palace in the Lower City (*War* 5: 253) where she lived for some 20 years. The death of King Izates brought her back to Adiabene in 64–5, but she did not outlive him long; 'Monobazus [another son] sent her bones, as well as those of Izates, his brother, to Jerusalem, and gave order that they should be buried at the pyramids which their mother had erected; they were three in number, and distant more than three furlongs from the city of Jerusalem' (*Antiquities* 20: 95).

Robbers looted the tomb but they did not find the sarcophagus of the queen; it bore her Aramaic name 'Saddan' and is now in the Louvre. Her suite decided not to place the sarcophagus in the main chamber designed for it; the First Revolt was on the point of exploding and the risk would have been too great. They had to knock off the corners of the sarcophagus lid in order to get it into one of the lower chambers, and disguised the entrance so well that it escaped casual notice.

Visit (fig. 37). Open: 8.30 a.m.–5 p.m. The vast courtyard originated as a quarry producing beautiful *malaky* stone; the staircase developed from the ramp up which blocks were hauled. Winter rains cascading down the steps are caught in two gutters which direct the water into channels in the side which terminate in cisterns at the landing level.

Both outside [1] and inside the vestibule [2] are basins which were used for purifications for the dead. The cuts around the small entrance closed by a rolling stone [3] were to take heavy slabs designed to hide the entrance completely. From the antechamber [4] doors lead into three burial chambers [5, 6, 8]; note the unusual double shaft-graves (*kokhim*) with ossuaries at the side or far end. Further development was planned, but these chambers [9, 10] were never finished. The chamber containing Queen Helena's sarcophagus was entered by a secret stairway below the floor of *kokh* grave [7].

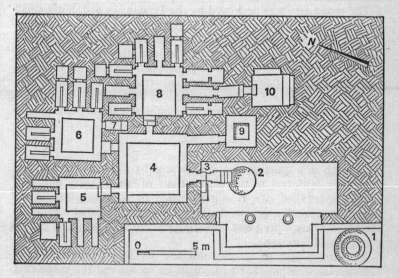

Fig. 37. Tomb of Queen Helena of Adiabene (after Vincent).

St. Stephen's Church [D]

A squat tower and a high gable roof set back from the high wall fronting Nablus Road marks the site of a church built by the empress Eudokia in 460 to receive the relics of St. Stephen, the first Christian martyr (Acts 6: 8–7: 60). The new basilica (dedicated in 1900) is part of the complex of the École Biblique et Archéologique Française founded in 1890 by French Dominicans as the first graduate school for biblical and archaeological studies in the Holy Land.

Excavations revealed the complete plan of the Byzantine church; it was retained when the new church was built, and the rugs on the floor protect large sections of the original mosaic floor. Nothing remains of the vast complex of buildings, which in 516 served as the meeting place for 10,000 monks, save the cistern system and a number of tombs. These are marked by metal covers in the cloister of the atrium; the pavement around the well is Byzantine. One of the tombs was closed by a stone door, the other by a rolling stone. Standing in a niche beside the former is the tombstone which originally sealed the flight of steps; the inscription reads, 'Tomb of the deacon Nonnus Onesimus of the Holy Sepulchre of Christ and of this monastery.'

The monastery was destroyed by the Persians in 614, but a small chapel was built before 638 by the patriarch Sophronius. Already in the C6 the place where St. Stephen's relics were kept had become confused with the place where he was stoned; this belief became the dominant tradition in the Middle Ages when the Knights Hospitallers (CHRISTIAN QUARTER: MAURISTAN) restored the chapel and erected stables beside it. They tore down this complex in the late summer of 1187 in order to deprive Saladin of a strongpoint so near the walls.

Garden Tomb [E]

This tomb in a quiet garden is venerated by many as the tomb of Christ; it conforms to the expectations of simple piety and it is outside the walled city. It is much easier to pray here than in the Holy Sepulchre. Unfortunately there is no possibility that it is in fact the place where Christ was buried. Open: 8 a.m.–1 p.m. and 3–5.30 p.m.; closed Sundays.

The first visitor to identify this site as Golgotha was General Charles Gordon in 1883; he thought he recognized the shape of a skull in the hill behind the tomb, and argued thus:

The morning after my arrival at Jerusalem I went to the Skull Hill, and felt convinced that it must be north of the Altar. Leviticus i, 11 says that the victims are to be slain on the side of the Altar northwards (literally to be slain slantwise or askew on the north of the Altar); if a particular direction was given by God about where the types were to be slain, it is a sure deduction that the prototype would be slain in some [*sic!*] position as to the Altar: this Skull Hill fulfils. . . . The Latin Holy Sepulchre is west of the Altar, and therefore, unless the types are wrong, it should never have been taken as the site. . . .

And I will come to the more fanciful view, that the mention of the place of Skull in each four gospels is a call to attention. Wherever a mention of any particular is made frequently, we may rely there is something in it; if the skull is mentioned four times, one naturally looks for the body, and if you take Warren's or others' contours with the earth or rubbish removed showing the natural state of the land, you cannot help seeing that there is a body, that Schick's conduit is the oesophagus, that the quarries are the chest, and if you are venturesome you will carry out the analogy further. (*Palestine Exploration Fund Quarterly Statement*, 1885, pp. 79–80.)

The words fail to hide an unbalanced scriptural mysticism, and the value of the argument in the last paragraph is best perceived graphically (fig. 38).

The excavation of the nearby Church of St. Stephen, and in particular the discovery of the tombstone of the deacon Nonnus which mentioned the Holy Sepulchre, quickly convinced Protestants desirous of having a Holy Place of their very own that this was the

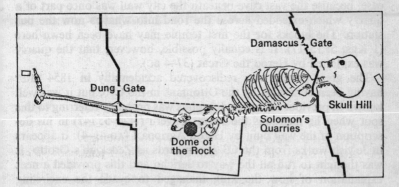

Fig. 38. General Gordon's argument for locating Golgotha at the Garden Tomb (after Wilson).

place where the Byzantines located Calvary and the Tomb. Despite
the protestations of those best qualified to judge, the Anglican Church
committed itself to the identification, and what had been known
scornfully as 'Gordon's Tomb' suddenly became the 'Garden Tomb'.
Sanity eventually prevailed, and the Anglican Church withdrew its
formal support, but in Jerusalem the prudence of reason has little
chance against the certitude of piety.

The tomb dates at least from the C1 AD and may even be older,
but was reworked in the Byzantine period, presumably as part of the
great monastic complex of St. Stephen's.

Armenian Mosaic [F]

Perfectly preserved, this mosaic floor is perhaps the most beautiful
in the country; still brilliant colours depict many species of birds in
the branches of a vine. An Armenian inscription at the far end, just
where the apse should begin, reads, 'For the memory and salvation
of the souls of all Armenians whose names are known to God alone.'
When the mosaic floor was laid down in the C5–C6 AD this was a
mortuary chapel; many tombs were found in the immediate vicinity.

The building is clearly indicated by a sign proclaiming the recent
dedication to St. Polyeuctus in a cul-de-sac just beside the Jerusalem
Student House in Prophet Street. Open: 7 a.m.–5.30 p.m.

Solomon's Quarries [G]

So great is the reputation of Solomon that Jerusalem Arabs tend to
attribute anything grandiose to him. They may be correct in this
case, because the vast cave beneath the city wall was once part of a
quarry which extended across the road into what is now the bus
station. The blocks for the first temple may have been hewn here
(1 Kgs. 5: 15–17). It is equally possible, however, that the quarry
was exploited by Herod the Great (37–4 BC).

The great cavern was rediscovered accidentally in 1854 after
having been concealed by the Ottomans in the C16, but it was well
known in previous centuries. Josephus was probably referring to this
spot when he mentions the Royal Cavern (*War* 5: 147) in his description of the wall built by Herod Agrippa I (AD 41–4). It appears
in Jewish works from the C3 AD onwards as Zedekiah's Grotto; it
was thought to run all the way to Jericho and this provided a neat
explanation of how the king managed to evade the encircling
Babylonian army in 586 BC (2 Kgs. 25: 4–5; Jer. 52: 7–8). This legend
was accepted by the famous Arab geographer al-Muqadassi in 985.

Visit. Open: 8.30 a.m.–5 p.m.; tickets for Saturday must be bought in advance. The entrance is signposted in the garden across from the bus station on Suleiman Street. The cave runs under the city for about 200 m. There is little to see save the traces of ancient quarry working. Stones were released by cutting a trench around three sides and then driving in wedges to break blocks free. Pieces of wood were wedged in the triangular niches to support oil-lamps. Note the different types of limestone, in particular the prized *malaky*, the hard white limestone that Herod used so much; the cave probably originated because of a bank of this stone.

Rockefeller Museum [H]

Open: 10 a.m.–6 p.m.; Fridays and Saturdays to 2 p.m. Established in 1927, this museum is exclusively archaeological. The exhibits, running from the Stone Age to the C18, are arranged chronologically.

NEW CITY: WESTERN SECTION

The historical monuments are concentrated in a band running between the Old City and the campus of the Hebrew University at Givat Ram (fig. 39). Capital letters refer to the location on the map

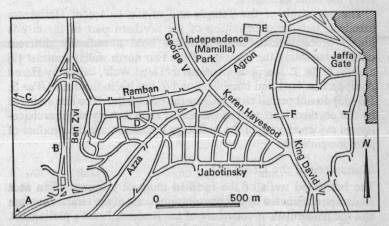

Fig. 39. New City – Western Section.

Model of Herodian Jerusalem [A]

In the grounds of the Holyland Hotel there is a 1 : 50 scale model of Jerusalem as it was at the beginning of the First Revolt in AD 66. Covering several hundred square metres, it offers a unique oppor-tunity to visualize the city of Herod the Great. The hotel lies between Herzog Street and Herzl Avenue; the access road, Uziel Street, is clearly signposted on both. Open: 9 a.m.–5 p.m.; 4 p.m. on Fridays; admission tickets for Saturday must be bought during the week.

The model, based on data supplied by Prof. M. Avi-Yonah, reflects what is known of the C1 AD city both from archaeological excavations and from texts, the New Testament, Josephus, the *Mishnah*, the *Tosephtha*, and the Talmuds. The topographical in-formation provided by the New Testament is incidental, and never detailed. Josephus furnishes many details, but his enthusiasm some-times led him to exaggerate, and he does not always give a precise location for the buildings he mentions. The information in other Jewish works was recorded after Hadrian had radically changed the appearance of the city in AD 135, and occasionally contradicts what is found in Josephus.

In order to construct the model many arbitrary decisions had to be made, and imagination often supplied what the texts or archaeo-logist's trowel could not provide. The model, therefore, is a hypoth-esis, a vision of the city as it might have been, and not all elements carry the same guarantee.

The portrayals of the Temple and of the Palace of Herod are excellent, but the presentation of the northern part of the city is highly problematical. Other scholars hold a radically different opinion regarding the position of the two north walls; contrast [7] and [8] in fig. 1. Josephus mentions a 'Third Wall', begun by Herod Agrippa I in 41–4 and completed in 66, but his indications (*War* 5: 147–55) do not permit us to redraw the precise line. The line assumed by the northernmost wall of the model rests on very slight archaeo-logical evidence, and all the buildings it encloses are the product of pure imagination.

Monastery of the Cross [B]

The buttressed walls of the fortified monastery appear alien in a landscape dominated by the graceful silhouette of the Israeli Museum and the modernistic architecture of the Knesset, Israel's parliament. The new divided highway, Ben-Zvi Avenue, which runs alongside, makes it seem even more out of place, a relic of the days when this valley was the vineyard of the Crusader kings of Jerusalem.

The monastery was founded by King Bagrat of Georgia between 1039 and 1056 on the site of a C5 church, and derives its name from the legend that the tree from which the cross of Jesus was made grew here. The church is substantially C11 but various additions were made throughout the centuries to other parts of the complex. The Georgians enjoyed excellent relations with the Mamelukes because they came from the same part of the world, and though they lost the monastery in 1300 because of the welcome they gave the Tartars (also neighbours) it was restored in 1305. Their numbers decreased consistently in succeeding centuries, and eventually they were obliged to sell the monastery to the Greek Orthodox in 1685.

Open: 8 a.m.–12 p.m.; closed Sunday; afternoons by appointment (tel. 284–917).

Israel Museum [C]

Open: 10 a.m.–6 p.m.; Fridays and Saturdays to 2 p.m.; Tuesdays 4–10 p.m. only. This museum has exhibits of all facets of Jewish history. In addition to the magnificent displays in the Bronfman Archaeological Museum, there is the Shrine of the Book (whose roof represents the cover of a Qumran scroll jar) housing some of the Dead Sea Scrolls and other manuscripts found in the Judaean desert; a number of the manuscripts exhibited are only photographic reproductions.

The museum is located in Ruppin Street opposite the Knesset building.

Jason's Tomb [D]

A small stone pyramid in a quiet residential road, Alfasi Street, reveals the presence of what is perhaps the most interesting tomb in Jerusalem. Not only is it a beautiful monument, but its history is known in detail.

It was built, during his lifetime, by Jason the senior member of a wealthy Jerusalem family towards the beginning of the C1 BC. After his death two or three generations of his family were buried there; the unity of the family was thus prolonged beyond the grave. A curious form of belief in the afterlife is attested by the fact that cooking pots with food were placed in the individual graves as well as lamps to light the way in the nether-world. Some were also provided with dice for recreation. Drawings in the porch represent a warship pursuing two other ships; Jason or one of his sons must have been a naval officer. Sea power was used in the Maccabean struggle for Jewish independence; Simon carved ships on the tomb of his brother Jonathan at Modein (1 Macc. 13: 29).

The tomb was robbed before it was finally destroyed by the great earthquake of 31 BC, the same catastrophe which forced the Essenes to abandon QUMRAN. The excavator relates this sacrilege to the slaughter of supporters of the Hasmonaean dynasty (which Jason had served) when Herod the Great entered Jerusalem in 37 BC. One final burial took place in the ruined tomb in AD 30, the year in which Jesus Christ was also buried elsewhere in the city.

Visit. The pyramid over the porch (supported by a single central column) has been reconstructed; it is preceded by three courts, the one immediately before the porch being entered by a vaulted gate. The ship drawings and the inscription identifying Jason were all drawn in charcoal on the walls of the porch. Looking in through the protective iron grille, the burial chamber with 8 shaft graves (*kokhim*) is through the small opening on the left. When space was needed for later burials the bones were transferred to the charnel chamber, the small opening directly in front.

Zawiya Kubakiyya [E]

In the Muslim cemetery at the eastern end of Independence (Mamilla) Park stands a square one-room building surmounted by a dome. An inscription over the door identifies it as the tomb of the emir Aidughdi Kubaki, buried there in AD 1289. Having started life as a slave in Syria, he rose to be governor of Safed and of Aleppo before falling foul of a new Mameluke sultan, who first imprisoned him and then exiled him to Jerusalem. He was 60 when he died, a very good age for a Mameluke.

Crusader materials are reused; note the elbow columns supporting the porch. The relieving arches above the door and windows are in fact monoliths cut to simulate joggled voussoirs.

Nearby is the Mamilla Pool connected by a channel to the POOL OF THE PATRIARCH'S BATH in the Christian Quarter of the Old City. Its exact date is unknown but it may be Herodian.

Herod's Family Tomb [F]

Towards the end of a cul-de-sac, Abu Sikhra Street, just south of the King David Hotel, a great round stone signals the entrance to the family tomb of Herod the Great (37–4 BC). A narrow passage leads to four chambers, three square and one rectangular, disposed on each side of a much smaller room; all are beautifully faced with cut stone. Little was found inside because tomb robbers got there before the archaeologists.

The existence of a family tomb in Jerusalem belonging to Herod is attested by Josephus; the king brought his youngest brother there for burial in 5 BC (*War* 1: 581). The tomb may have been cut for the interment of his father Antipater in 43 BC (*War* 1: 228). We know it was located west of the city because Josephus uses the monument as a reference point in his description of the Roman circumvallation wall in AD 70 (*War* 5: 108 and 507); the nearby 'Serpent's Pool' is probably to be identified with the present Birket es-Sultan in the upper part of the Hinnom valley. Herod himself was buried at the HERODION.

INDEX OF PLACES IN PART 1
NOT LISTED IN THE CONTENTS

PART 2
The Land

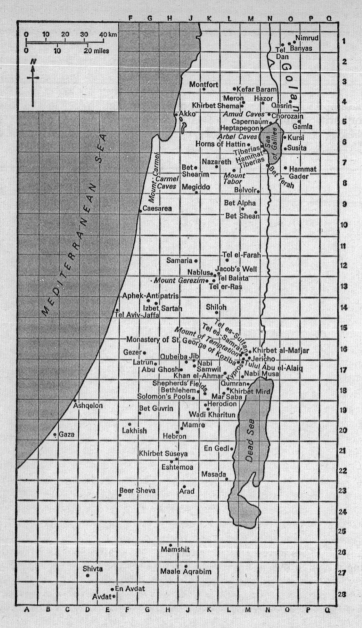

ABU GHOSH (J17)

Abu Ghosh is a village to the north of the Tel Aviv–Jerusalem highway 15 km from the Holy City. In the early C19 AD it was the encampment of a brigand chief powerful enough to defy the Turkish authorities but not sufficiently ambitious to pose a serious threat to their rule. As a result they permitted him to levy tribute on travellers, and his name replaced the traditional name of the village, Qaryet el-Enab, which is simply the Arabic version of Qiryat Yearim.

Qiryat Yearim is mentioned frequently in the Old Testament as a mountain village on the border between the territories of the tribes of Judah and Benjamin. What makes it unique is that it was the resting place of the Ark of the Covenant for the 20 years between its restoration by the Philistines (1 Sam. 6: 21–7: 2) and its removal to Jerusalem by David (2 Sam. 6). The village of this period is located on the height of Deir el-Azhar, today crowned by the great statue of the Virgin and Child. The modern sanctuary of Notre-Dame de l'Arche d'Alliance is built on the ruins of a C5 AD church, sections of whose mosaic floor are still visible.

It is not clear when the village moved down the hill to the valley. It can only have happened during a period when strong control assured peace, and when there was sufficient traffic on the road to make the move worthwhile. Thus it may have happened as early as the C2 AD when a detachment of the Tenth Legion was stationed there and built a reservoir over the spring. This reservoir was incorporated into an Arab caravanserai in the mid-C9 AD when the road formed part of the Byzantine road system renewed by the Umayyad caliphs; two milestones of Abd el-Malik (685–705), the builder of the Dome of the Rock, were found in the vicinity of Abu Ghosh.

The Byzantine tradition which located the Emmaus where the Risen Christ made himself known to two disciples (Luke 24: 13–35) at LATRUN was apparently unknown to the Crusaders. The event was too important to be neglected so they simply measured 60 stadia (11·5 km) from Jerusalem and identified the nearest village, Qaryet el-Enab, as Emmaus. Since the reservoir was the obvious spot for any travellers to rest, the Hospitallers consecrated the site by erecting a church over it some time after 1141. They also respected the caravanserai which, in their eyes, was the place where the meal took place.

After the defeat of the Latin Kingdom at the Battle of the HORNS

OF HATTIN in 1187 Qaryet el-Enab lost all its importance, principally because travellers took another route to Jerusalem. One consequence of this change was the transfer of the dignity of Emmaus to QUBEIBA. When the Mamelukes restored the caravanserai between 1350 and 1400 they left the church intact, contenting themselves with adding a mosque.

Visit. The Crusader church is the largest building in the village; from the Jerusalem side it is hidden by trees but the minaret of the nearby mosque is clearly visible. Ring the bell in the top left-hand corner of the door for admission; closed Sunday.

The simple strength and serenity of the church's proportions are paralleled only at St. Anne's in Jerusalem. The peeling frescoes give it a slightly tragic air but they are precious relics of the short period when Frankish and Byzantine artists complemented each other (BETHLEHEM). The crypt is entirely medieval save for the outer walls which are those of the Roman reservoir; beside the entrance in the north wall is an inscription reading *Vexillatio leg(ionis) X Fre(tensis)*. The two original stairways leading into the reservoir still exist on either side of the medieval staircase at the west end of the church. In order to take the reservoir out of service the medieval engineers lowered the level of the spring and cut a new channel which can be seen through the grating on the steps between the two pillars. The low altar over the spring is out of alignment with the crypt; it is oriented due east and the Crusaders probably intended this to correct the slightly false orientation of the church.

On the far side of the Benedictine monastery are the remains of the caravanserai. The large vaulted chamber was built in the C12 over a reservoir of the C9; facing the entrance was a bread oven.

AKKO (ACRE) (H5)

The Crusades account for only about one twentieth of the long history of the walled port of Akko, but the imprint of their passage is more enduring than that of any other occupant. Beneath a thin veneer of modernity, often no more than a coat of whitewash, it is still a medieval city. The logic of the Crusaders' planning commanded respect, while the strength of their constructions made other options unviable.

Egyptian execration texts of the C19 BC are the first to mention

Akko; it was then located on a mound, Tel el-Fukhar, 1·5 km north-east of the present wall. When the Israelites acquired control of the interior in the C13 BC (Judg. 1: 31), Akko remained in the hands of the Phoenicians; no longer a market, it continued to serve as a coastal station because it was one of the best harbours on the eastern littoral of the Mediterranean. Its strategic importance, both military and commercial, became progressively more evident and in the C4 BC it assumed the primacy that Tyre and Sidon had once enjoyed. To some extent this was due to the favour accorded it by Alexander the Great; in 333 BC he established a mint which functioned for 600 years.

In the struggle for power among Alexander's generals which followed his death, Akko became the possession of the Ptolemies of Egypt, and its name was changed to Ptolemais. They lost it in 200 BC to their rivals, the Seleucids of Syria, who held it with great difficulty until Pompey brought it under Roman control in 63 BC; for over two centuries the city counted its years from the visit of Julius Caesar in 47 BC.

As CAESAREA, founded by Herod the Great in 10 BC, developed, the importance of Akko decreased. Christianity quickly won adherents among the foreign population; Paul spent a day there during his third voyage (Acts 21: 7) and its first known bishop was Clarus (190). By the time of the Arab conquest in 636 the artificial harbour of Caesarea had become badly silted up, and Akko regained its position as the premier port of Palestine. Arab development of the port facilities made it inevitable that it should become the main link between the Latin Kingdom and Europe after its conquest by Baldwin I in 1104.

The development of the city was determined by the maritime powers of Europe, the city-states of Genoa, Pisa, Venice, and Amalfi; recruits, pilgrims, and supplies travelled in their ships. Each nation governed and maintained its own self-sufficient quarter. The military orders of the Temple and the Hospital also had their own territories and they provided facilities for pilgrims on landing and departure and guaranteed the security of the route to Jerusalem. Such divisions did not matter as long as the Latin Kingdom remained secure, but they contained the seed of the city's destruction.

Akko surrendered to Saladin without a battle in 1187. The Crusader presence in the Holy Land was reduced to Tyre, but reinforcements arrived in 1191 under Richard the Lionheart of England and Philip of France. These enabled the Crusaders to pursue the siege and still hold off Saladin's counterattacks; for a year he had pinned the army of Tyre against the walls of the city. Victory came quickly and the city became the Latin Kingdom for just 100 years. The space within the original wall (just inside the present wall) soon proved to be insufficient and new walls were built enclosing an area three times as great as the walled city of today.

These were the days of Akko's glory, but for every Francis of Assisi who came on pilgrimage or Marco Polo who used it as a staging-point there were three merchants. As Akko developed as the centre of east–west trade, the merchant colonies began to interfere more and more in politics. Since the king was the source of the privileges on which profits depended, disputes over the succession became progressively more bitter, eventually erupting into open war between the fortified quarters. Venice and Genoa fought sea battles in sight of the city when it was threatened by the Mongols in 1259 and by the Mamelukes of Egypt in 1265.

The arrival of Henry II of Cyprus in 1285 established his claim to the crown. His concern for the common good brought about a concerted effort to improve the defences, but it was already too late. The Mamelukes had committed themselves to the conquest of Akko. The attack began in April 1291 with the defenders outnumbered ten to one. They held out for two months, time for some of the population of between 30,000 and 40,000 to escape to Cyprus, but the end was inevitable.

Akko lay in ruins for the next 450 years until a local Arab sheikh, Daher el-Omar, exploited the weakness of the central Ottoman administration to create a virtually independent fiefdom in Galilee. He encouraged trade and developed Akko as the port for Syrian exports from 1749 until his assassination in 1775. His place was taken by the Albanian soldier of fortune Ahmed Pasha, known as el-Jazzar, 'the Butcher', because of his cruelty. He continued the restoration of the town and its fortifications and with the aid of a British fleet successfully defended the city against Napoleon in 1799; the siege lasted 60 days. Napoleon was moving north after his conquest of Egypt in order to open a route to India; his failure here forced him to retreat to Egypt and changed the course of history.

In 1832 Ibrahim Pasha with an Egyptian army took Akko from the Turks; he ruled Palestine and Syria from the city until 1840 when British intervention forced him to retire to Egypt. The walls, damaged by the bombardment, were repaired and Akko resumed its place as the principal port for exporting grain from the southern Golan.

Visit (fig. 40). Three roads permit cars to enter the walled city: Rehov Ha-Hagana [A] with parking near the lighthouse at the southern tip; Rehov Weizmann [B] and Rehov Jonathan Ha-

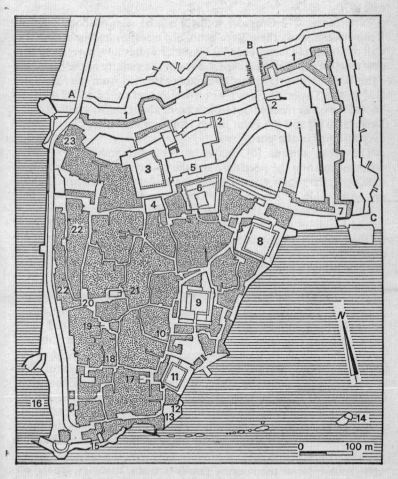

Fig. 40. Street plan of the walled city of Akko (Acre).

Hashmonai [C] with parking near the tall minaret of the Mosque of el-Jazzar [6].

The present broad wall [1] with its ditch and counterscarp was built by Ahmed Pasha el-Jazzar after Napoleon's retreat in 1799. He also refaced the whole of the sea wall, in part with stones from the Crusader castle at Atlit. Only two of the gates are original, the Land Gate [7] and the Sea Gate [12] which is now part of the Abu Christo café [13].

Parts of the C12 Crusader wall [2] can be seen on both sides of Rehov Weizmann; these were probably incorporated into the C18 wall of Daher el-Omar. The C13 Crusader wall is now covered by the new city; on the east it reached the sea in the vicinity of the high-rise Palm Beach Hotel. One medieval mole extended from the Sea Gate [12] to the Tower of Flies [14] on which there used to be a lighthouse; the other reached out from a point about halfway between the Land Gate [7] and the Palm Beach Hotel; in 1172 a pilgrim counted over 80 ships in the port.

The great mosque [6] was erected by el-Jazzar in 1781. The columns creating the porch around the courtyard were looted from CAESAREA; the rooms were intended for students and pilgrims. Below are large vaults, the basement of the Crusader church of St. John.

This area was in fact the quarter of the Knights Hospitallers whose ruined buildings were resurrected by Muslim rulers of the C18–C19 as their citadel [3]; it is now the central prison and inaccessible except for a large underground area, the street level in this part of the city being 7–8 m above the Crusader level.

The entrance [5] to the subterranean city is just across from the Mosque of el-Jazzar [6]; open: 9 a.m. – 4.30 p.m.; Fridays to 1 p.m. An excellent detailed explanatory leaflet is obtainable at the ticket office. Nothing in these magnificent vaulted halls has changed since the C12–C13. The massive round piers supporting the fan vaulting in the refectory of the Knights Hospitallers hint at the weight of the structures above, and the secret passage to the advance-guard post dramatically highlights the danger of the times. Just outside the exit is the Municipal Museum [4] located in public baths built by el-Jazzar.

Khan esh-Shawarda [8] dates only from the time of Daher el-Omar or el-Jazzar. Like the other khans (inns) it served the great camel caravans which brought the grain of the southern Golan to the ships. The tower in its south-east corner is the only C13 tower still standing; note the masons' marks (crosses, triangles, letters) on the bossed stones.

Khan el-Faranj [9] owes its name, 'Inn of the Franks', to the French merchants who established themselves there in 1516. In the C13 it was the centre of the Venetian quarter and Crusader materials are recognizable in the foundations and columns of the present building. At the north-east corner is the C18 church of the Franciscans.

A square clock-tower erected by the Ottoman sultan Abdul Hamid II in 1906 stands over the entrance to the picturesque Khan el-Umdan [11], 'Inn of the Columns', restored by el-Jazzar. This was the inn of the Genoese quarter which fronted on to a large empty square (reaching as far as Khan el-Faranj [9]) used for loading and unloading from the port. The Genoese quarter was the oldest and biggest merchant commune and enjoyed special privileges because the Genoese fleet played a crucial role in Baldwin I's capture of Akko in 1104. It ran due north through the centre of the city from the gate [10] which once opened directly on to the main port square. The street level in this sector is the same as that of the Crusader period and the alley running towards the church of St. George [21] has Crusader buildings on both sides.

There are two exits from the Khan el-Umdan [11]. The one in the centre of the south side leads into the heart of the Pisan quarter; all the buildings on both sides are Crusader. The cafe Abu Christo [13] is on the site of the Pisan port; the Sea Gate [12] and its wall are medieval.

The street parallel to the tip of the peninsula leads into the Templar Quarter. The Franciscan church of St. John [15] built in 1737 rests on vaults corresponding to the position of the Crusader church of St. Andrew. The fortress of the knights, famed for its beauty and strength, must have stood where the sea has eroded into the town [16]. It was undermined by the Mamelukes in 1291 and its stones later used for other buildings; not a trace remains.

Directly opposite the south-west exit from Khan el-Umdan [11] is Khan esh-Shuna, once the Inn of the Pisans [17]. Follow the street which borders it on the north to the four-way cross [18] which was the junction of several quarters, Pisan on the south, Templar on the west, Genoese on the north; a strong Templar tower controlled this critical point. The street to the right (north) has interesting Crusader residences on the left; it leads to a square [19] which follows Crusader building lines. Such open spaces were a feature of the C12–C13 city but buildings have encroached on many of the others.

The square beside the white Bahai Temple [20] also preserves its medieval dimensions, and was the junction of several quarters. The street leading to the C17 Greek Orthodox church of St. George [21] was the fortified gate of the Genoese quarter. The little street behind the Bahai Temple cuts through the middle of the Rectangular quarter whose two long strips [22] make it the best-defined of all the medieval units; the street to the right (east) was a neutral street dividing this quarter from the Genoese.

The inner street is Crusader on both sides, but the houses on the left (west) are worth close examination for they have been well preserved on the ground floor. The street has a sharp turn at both ends; otherwise attackers would have had a clear field of fire. Some houses were deliberately set forward to provide enfilading fire; this occurs regularly at intervals of about 50 m. The same mode of defence was used in the small central square where the well of the quarter and a public building were probably located.

The Museum of Heroism [23] is a monument to Jewish resistance fighters during the British Mandate. Open: 8.30 a.m.–5.30 p.m.; Fridays to 12.30 p.m.

AMUD CAVES (MEARAT AMIRA) (M5)

The plain of Ginnosar is divided into three by two wadis, Nahal Zalmon and Nahal Ammud, which terminate in the Sea of Galilee. Nahal Ammud contains two easily accessible prehistoric caves. At the north end of the plain of Ginnosar take the turn-off signposted 'Huqoq'; from there it is 2·6 km to the bridge crossing the wadi. The Cave of the Column is located 400 m north of the bridge on the left (west) side of the wadi, near the spring, and beside the natural limestone pillar which gives the wadi its name. The Cave of the Gipsy Woman lies about the same distance south of the bridge on the left side of the wadi going towards the lake. The first is 25 m and the second 45 m above the bed of the wadi which floods in winter and spring.

Both caves were occupied during the Middle Palaeolithic period (80,000–35,000 BC), and both yielded human bones. The skull fragments found in the Cave of the Gipsy Woman are known as Galilee Man but there is some reason to think that they belong to a woman. Among the animal bones were those of a bear and a hippopotamus. In the Cave of the Column the excavators found the complete skeleton of a young man who had been buried lying on his left side with his knees drawn up; he was 1.8 m tall and about 25 years old.

Nearby were fragments of the bones of another adult male and of two children aged between 3 and 4.

APHEK (ANTIPATRIS) (G14)

The jagged outline of a C16 Turkish fort at the top of a green slope marks the site of a town as old as trade between Egypt and Mesopotamia. It lies at the source of the River Yarkon (whence the name of the township Rosh ha-Ain = the head of the spring); the foothills of the Judaean mountains begin 3 km to the east. The great trade route, the Way of the Sea, had to pass through this gap which shade and water made an attractive resting-place. Today a beautiful park offers the same sense of ease that weary traders of the past experienced.

A walled city stood here *c*.3000 BC; its name is mentioned in Egyptian texts of the C19 and C15 BC. Joshua took the city from the Canaanites (Josh. 12: 18) whose ruler had a monumental palace on the summit of the mound. In the C12 BC with the advent of the Philistines, or even earlier, the Israelites were forced to move back to the hills and the city marked the northern border of Philistia. Here the Philistines assembled for two great battles against Israel a century later; in the first, when the Israelites gathered at Eben-ezer which is identified with IZBET SARTAH (fig. 41), they captured the Ark of the Covenant (1 Sam. 4: 1–11) and struck through to SHILOH; in the second they slaughtered Saul and Jonathan at Mount Gilboa and hung their bodies on the walls of BET SHEAN (1 Sam. 29–31). Thereafter the city is not mentioned in the Bible, but Assyrian and Babylonian texts show it to have been an important stronghold in the C7.

In the Hellenistic period (332–37 BC) the city was known as Pegae (= the springs); Herod the Great (37–4 BC) changed the name again to commemorate his father, 'choosing a site in the loveliest plain in his kingdom with an abundance of rivers and trees, and naming it Antipatris' (*War* 1: 417). After the foundation of CAESAREA the city lay on the route between the principal port and Jerusalem; from being a staging-point on the north-south route it had become a major crossroads. Paul spent the night there on his way under guard from Jerusalem to Caesarea (Acts 23: 23–35). The early southern battles of the First Revolt (AD 66–70) were fought in this area (*War* 2: 513–555).

To the Crusaders of the C12 the tel was known as Le Toron aux fontaines sourdes (= the tower of the silent springs); they had a fortress nearby at Mirabel (Migdal Aphek). An edict of the Ottoman sultan in 1571 ordered the reconstruction of the ruined Mameluke fort; it was allowed to fall into decay some two centuries later.

Visit (fig. 42). The Turkish fort is clearly visible to the left (north) of the road from Petah Tiqwa to Rosh ha-Ain. At present the turn-off is signposted 'Railway Station'; from this point the Crusader castle of Mirabel (Migdal Aphek) can be seen at the edge of the hills to the south-east. Follow the road around the park fence to the entrance. The development of the park is not complete, and excavations are still in progress.

From the north wall of the fort one can look down on to the stone foundation [1] of the Bronze Age city wall. Just inside the angled gate of the fort a significant portion of a Canaanite monumental building (1550–1200 BC) has been exposed [2]. The one immediately recognizable element is a flight of six steps leading from a paved court into a tower with a U-shaped chamber; east of the court, and

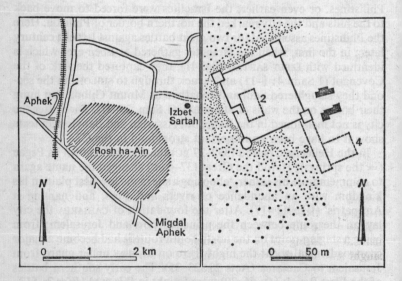

Fig. 41. Map showing relationship between Aphek and Izbet Sartah.

Fig. 42. Excavation areas at Aphek-Antipatris.

perpendicular to it, is a 4 m-wide passage, probably a street. This complex was burnt after a vicious battle; arrowheads were found driven into the walls. The destruction date (*c.*1200) would fit with the campaign of Joshua, but internecine warfare was endemic among the Canaanite city-states.

The eastern wall of the fort lies above an Herodian street which continues to the south [3]. Many of the flagstones, laid diagonally, are still in place and the camber is obvious; the street was flanked by shops with circular pits cut into the raised pavement in front. Originally considered to have been display bins, some of these have now proved to be ovens which may be associated with the nitrate industry for which Antipatris was known. To the east of the street (which continued in use for seven centuries) are the ruins of an impressive house [4] dated between the C2 and C4 AD. From the street, to the south, one can see a drinking-fountain; from it a path leads round the hillock on the left to the heavily overgrown area hiding the beautifully built arches which constituted the elevated podium of a great public building.

ARAD (J23)

Some 2 km north of the highway and 8 km to the west of the new city of Arad a square fortress squats on the highest of a group of low hills. Known as Tel Arad, this site offers the best example in the country of an Early Bronze Age city. The excavated area covers several acres and the street plan is perfectly clear. Excellent restorations (everything above a heavy line of plaster), signs identifying the purpose of each building, and an explanatory leaflet facilitate a visit. Open: 8 a.m.–4 p.m.; Fridays to 3 p.m.

Lower City. In contrast to the surrounding area the rock formation here is impervious to water. This feature explains why the first squatters settled here, and why, when they built their city, it was not limited to the ridge. The horseshoe-shape acted as a natural catchment area during the winter rains; the bottom of the little valley caught and held the run-off from the surrounding slopes. The wide city wall, strengthened by frequent semicircular towers, is sited on bedrock and follows the exact line of the crest; it is 1200 m long and encloses an area of 22 acres.

The city flourished between 2900 and 2700 BC. The inhabitants cultivated the plain and pastured their flocks there, but the city was also a trade centre. Some of the local pottery is made of sand found only in the Araba (the valley linking the Dead Sea with the Gulf of Aqaba) and in the mountains of southern Sinai. This was only one import; Egyptian vessels attest contact with more distant lands. The city was destroyed twice. The first time it recovered, but after the second its life came to an abrupt halt, and the site lay desolate for 1,500 years.

The layout of the city shows evidence of deliberate planning: public buildings are located in the centre with private dwellings on the periphery. The principal public edifice is a double temple, two rectangular halls entered from the east. A similar twin temple of the same period is visible at MEGIDDO. Just on the other side of the street to the south is a large building which may have been a palace.

A walk through the narrow streets quickly reveals that all the houses were built to the same basic design: one large living room, a kitchen or storeroom, and a courtyard. The living room is characterized by a stone bench running round all four walls. All the doors open to the left, as the position of the hollowed stone door socket shows. The level of the street or courtyard is normally higher than the room floor, a curious feature in an area which gets quite a lot of rain. The houses had no windows, and the light roof was supported by a wooden pillar resting on a stone base. One of these, together with a carved stone mortar, appears in most houses.

Just inside the postern gate in the city wall the archaeologists have cleverly preserved two levels in the one building. The corner of a later room overlaps the upper part of an earlier one. Both are of the same type, showing ethnic continuity, but the overlap reveals that the earlier building had been destroyed.

Citadel. When the site was resettled in the C11 BC occupation was concentrated in the highest part of the ancient city, because for the Israelites its importance was primarily strategic. A fortress there commanded the frontier road to Edom and Elath. A series of fortresses was built on the ruins of those destroyed by enemy attacks; the last is dated to the end of the C1 AD.

The visible remains are all from the Israelite period. There is a splendid view from the walkway on top of the reconstructed C8–C7 BC wall. To the north one can see very clearly where the Judaean mountains stop and the Negev begins. The most interesting building within the citadel is an Israelite temple with a small Holy of Holies and a brick and rubble (Exod. 20: 25) altar of sacrifice. The dating of some elements in the citadel area is the subject of controversy.

ARBEL CAVES (M6)

The southern end of the fertile plain of Ginnosar is dominated by the sheer cliffs of Mount Arbel. The caves with which they are honeycombed recall dramatic moments in Jewish history. Just north of Magdala take the side road signposted 'Maghar' and then the first left into the Wadi Hammam. The trail to the base of the cliffs begins behind the first group of houses on the left. Those who are unprepared to scramble up can see the caves by driving further into the wadi.

In 160 BC partisans of the Maccabees were slaughtered here by the Syrian general Baccides (1 Macc. 9: 2). The best-documented episode occurred in 38 BC when Herod the Great moved against the supporters of his rival Antigonus who had holed up in the caves now linked by hewn stairways. Josephus reports:

The king, whose men were unable either to climb up from below or creep upon them from above because of the steepness of the hill, had cribs built and lowered these upon them with iron chains as they were suspended by a machine from the summit of the hill. The cribs were filled with armed men holding great grappling hooks, with which they were supposed to draw toward them any of the brigands who opposed them, and kill them by hurling them to the ground. . . . One of the soldiers in irritation at the delay caused by the brigands who dared not come out, girded on his sword, and holding on with both hands to the chain from which the crib was suspended, lowered himself to the entrance of a cave. And when he was opposite an entrance, he first drove back with javelins most of those who were standing there, and then with his grappling hook drew his opponents toward him and pushed them over the precipice (*Antiquities* 14: 423–6).

One of the caves, called Qalaat Ibn Maan, was turned into a fortress by an Emir of Tiberias during Galilean resistance to the Turks in the C18 AD.

ASHQELON (C19)

From the promontory of Mount Carmel the coast descends to the south-west in a smooth line unbroken by any natural harbour. Sand-dunes line the pitiless lee shore. Only the presence of drinking water can explain the choice of any particular spot as the site of a city. Ashqelon has no spring, but it is rich in wells. Inevitably, therefore, it became an important staging-point on the great trade route linking Egypt and Mesopotamia, the Way of the Sea, which continued north through APHEK, MEGIDDO, and HAZOR. Today it is a beautiful National Park combining the pleasures of archaeology and the beach.

By 2000 BC Ashqelon was a city. In subsequent centuries its name appears regularly in Egyptian texts. It is found on the Stele of Merneptah (1230 BC), the only Egyptian text to mention Israel during the Exodus: 'Carried off is Ashqelon; seized upon is Gezer; ... Israel is laid waste, his seed is not.' Not long afterwards it was taken by the Philistines, becoming one of the five city states into which their territory was divided (Josh. 13: 3; 1 Sam. 6: 4). The city lost its independence in the C8 BC, being first controlled by the Assyrians and then in turn by Egypt and Babylon. Under the Persians it belonged to Tyre, but in the C2 BC, when the Jews, having consolidated their position in the mountains, began to eye the fair cities of the plain, Ashqelon put itself under the protection of Rome. Thereafter it flourished as a free city.

According to Josephus, Herod the Great (37–4 BC) endowed Ashqelon with 'baths, magnificent fountains, and colonnaded quadrangles, remarkable for both scale and craftsmanship' (*War* 1: 422). After Herod's death his palace there was given to his sister, Salome, by imperial decree (*War* 2: 98). Herod's munificence may have been motivated by the fact that his grandfather had been hierodoulos of the temple of Apollo in Ashqelon. The loyalty of the city to Rome during the First Revolt (AD 66–70) won for it new privileges which it used to the utmost during the six centuries of peace which followed. It became ever more prosperous and powerful, a centre of learning and religion. A fragment of the C6 Madaba Map shows a great colonnaded piazza inside the massive east gate.

In AD 636 Ashqelon surrendered to the caliph Omar, and suffered badly in a last paroxysm of Byzantine energy. Rebuilt by Abd el-Malik in 685, it grew again to a beautiful city lauded by the Arab chroniclers. Secure on its high walls, with the gates selfishly shut, the inhabitants saw the Frankish charge which destroyed the army of Egypt in August 1099. It remained a Fatimide base until the Crusaders finally took it in 1153. They did not hold it long. Immediately after the Battle of Hattin in 1187 Saladin laid siege to Ashqelon; a Christian fleet could put new forces ashore there. His prisoner, the king of Jerusalem, persuaded the garrison to surrender. In 1191 when Richard the Lionheart looked like reconquering the Holy Land, Saladin ordered Ashqelon to be destroyed. He agonized over the decision to ruin so much beauty but, once committed, he carried it through methodically. Richard could see the flames from his camp at Jaffa, but his desire to march at once was overruled by the council. The Crusader army finally reached Ashqelon several months later; the walls that they, in some fashion, rebuilt were torn down by agreement with the Arabs when Richard left, but Christians remained in possession until the Mameluke sultan Baybars levelled the city in 1270. It never rose again.

Visit (fig. 43). Open 8 a.m.–5 p.m.; Fridays to 4 p.m. The plan shows the main roads in the park; the arrows indicate one-way traffic. There are two parking-lots [5 and 9] from which steps lead to the beach.

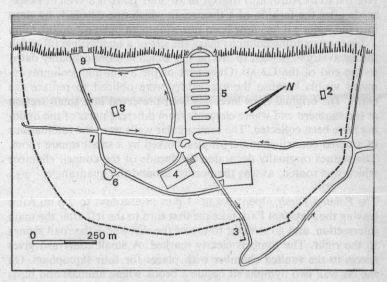

Fig. 43. The ancient city of Ashqelon.

Just inside the park entrance the road passes through the medieval wall (broken line) at the Jaffa Gate [1]. The wall can be traced all the way round the site, but the best part to walk is from the Jerusalem Gate [3] to the southern Sea Gate; on this section the sand which has invaded the city underlines the presence of the desert to the south. The two great bastions in the south-west corner, the Tower of the Virgins and the Tower of Blood, have collapsed on to the beach. Parts of the sea wall are visible at the base of the cliffs; the granite columns used for bonding protrude dramatically from the eroded wall just north of the bastions. Some have thought that the columns in the water were part of a Crusader mole, as at CAESAREA, but it is more likely that they have simply fallen from the wall.

From the beach it is clear that the area between the two parking-lots [5 and 9] is the oldest part of the site; strata from the Middle Bronze Age (beginning *c*.2000 BC) to the Roman period are piled one on top of the other in the eroded cliff-face.

With one significant exception few buildings have been preserved. The two Crusader churches [2 and 7] are very ruined, and the Byzantine church [8] is so overgrown that nothing is visible; none is worth a visit. The circular depression [6] may possibly be the area referred to by Antoninus Martyr in AD 560: 'there is a Well of Peace, made after the fashion of a theatre, in which one descends by steps into the water'; it has now been turned into an open-air auditorium.

Lines of standing columns mark the site of a quadrangle [4] which the excavators assigned to Herod but which is more probably dated to the end of the C2 AD. Only part of the 8·3 m-high columns remains visible because the excavators were obliged to replace the earth. The original floor level has been preserved in a small section at the southern end where elements from different parts of the building have been collected. The semicircular walls were the foundations of a tiered council chamber; it was flanked by a small square room. The statues originally decorated the façade of the council chamber which was roofed, as was the portico around the quadrangle.

The Painted Tomb. Open: 9 a.m.–1 p.m.; Saturdays to 2 p.m. After leaving the National Park take the first turn to the left after the main intersection, and go straight to top of the cliff where the road swings to the right. The tomb is clearly marked. A small courtyard gives access to the vaulted chamber with places for four sarcophagi. On the far wall two nymphs sit beside a brook where animals and birds come to drink. Various mythological figures – Koré/Demeter,

Medusa, Pan – appear among the vine branches on the ceiling. The tomb is dated to the C3 AD.

AVDAT (HORVOT AVEDAT) (E28)

The kibbutzim in the Negev command admiration for the courage and skill that have made the desert bloom, but their achievement pales beside that of the NABATAEANS who created great cities in the same harsh environment. Avdat is the most impressive of these desert cities. The silhouette of the large buildings on the acropolis dominates the plain around the canyon of EN AVDAT with its prehistoric remains. The site is 65 km south of Beer Sheva on the Mizpe Ramon road to Elath.

Coins and pottery betray the existence of a town here in the C2 BC, and attest contacts with Egypt, Greece, and Asia Minor. At this time Avdat was already one of the key points on the trade route linking Petra with the Mediterranean coast. The town died when the Nabataeans lost control of the port of Gaza about 100 BC. It came to life again in the C1 AD when the death of Herod gave them easy access to the Mediterranean. The revival of Avdat received a further stimulus when the deified king Obodas II (30–9 BC) was buried there, and the town became known as Oboda (which in Arabic became Abdah, and in Hebrew Avdat). His son, Aretas IV (9 BC–AD 40), created a flat area on the acropolis by building great retaining walls, and in the north-west corner erected a temple.

The shift of the trade route from Arabia to the Nile valley meant that life became progressively more difficult for Avdat. To support itself the city turned increasingly to agriculture; the evidence for its continued existence in the reign of Rabel II (AD 70–106) comes principally from agricultural installations in the valleys to the south and west.

The decline of Avdat was intensified in the C2 AD when nomads from the south began to move into the cultivated areas where Nabataean installations provided water. These bedouin were responsible for the rock-drawings in the vicinity. When the growing insolence of the nomads made travel dangerous, the Romans, who had annexed the Negev in AD 106, were forced to intervene, and ex-soldiers were settled at Avdat. In return for land grants they patrolled the roads, and provided a reserve force for emergencies. The

Roman camp north-east of the city probably dates from the early part of this period. Fortifications were also erected on the acropolis. The names in inscriptions of the C3 show the population to have been the usual eastern Mediterranean mixture of races. There were temples to Zeus, Obodas, and Aphrodite.

Though the city was badly damaged by an earthquake in the early C5 AD, the transition from the Late Roman to the Byzantine period took place without any interruption in occupation. It seems likely, however, that there was an influx of new inhabitants, because churches were soon built. Virtually all the structures on the acropolis are from the C6 AD. The population in the Byzantine period is estimated at 2,000 to 3,000. This figure is based on the 350–400 dwelling units arranged on terraces on the slope between the acropolis and the main road. These dwellings are unique in that a cave cut in the rock forms an integral unit with the house in front. The caves were used as storerooms or workshops, and some were certainly wine cellars. Grapes were cultivated in addition to barley, wheat, and lentils. A complex system of channels and small dams in the fields below the city extracted the maximum value from the slight annual rainfall and the night dews.

The Persians sacked the city in AD 620; the excavators found the acropolis area covered by a thick layer of ashes. Any hope of restoration was ended by the arrival of the Arabs some years later.

Visit. Open: 8 a.m.–4 p.m.; Fridays to 3 p.m. An explanatory booklet is available at the ticket office.

The roofed building on the same level as the ticket office is the best-preserved Byzantine bath-house in the country; it is built on the classic Roman pattern – cold pool (separate entrance), dressing room, hot room, and warm room – which the Byzantines passed on to the Arabs (KHIRBET EL-MAFJAR). Beside the intermediate parking-lot is a reconstructed Byzantine house; note in particular the square lavatory and the method of roofing. A passage connects the house with the multichambered cave behind; note the projections from the ceiling for hanging vegetables, the bench with two rows of hollows to hold jars, and the rock-cut bins for grain storage. Two other caves of the same type have been cleared further up the slope; one has four capitals carved from the rock. The graffiti in all these caves suggest that they served as places of refuge during and after the Persian invasion.

To the right of the road to the upper parking-lot a sign indicates burial caves. The most important is a big square chamber containing 22 burial places cut into the rock on three sides; note in each the slots to hold the slabs covering the body interred below. At one time thought to be the tomb of Obodas, this complex is now dated to the middle of the C3 AD.

Once at the upper parking-lot it is best to go first to the top of the reconstructed C3 tower (an inscription above the lintel dates it to AD 294). From there, facing the acropolis, one can see the Byzantine winepress (left), the residential quarter of the C3 (below and in front), and the Nabataean pottery workshop (right).

The winepress has a square treading area into which grapes were fed from small storage rooms on three sides. On the fourth side is a round pit into which the grape juice flowed via a channel under the treading floor from a central sump. There are two other winepresses elsewhere in the city.

The pottery workshop was in use in the C1 AD, and is the only such Nabataean installation known. There were three kilns. Near one is a room with a bench on three sides; this served to dry the pottery made on the wheel supported on the adjacent round pedestal. Embedded in the floor of this area are broken sea-shells, apparently from the Red Sea: they may have been used as temper.

The C3 AD Roman camp (visible from the railed viewpoint on the fortress wall) is of the garrison type (as opposed to the siege type found at MASADA). The double walls strengthened by square towers surround eight long barracks separated by passageways 6 m wide with a pavement on either side. In the Byzantine period this camp was used as a source of ready-made cut stones. From the camp the C1 AD Nabataean road can be traced to the south-east for some 12 km. The untrimmed kerb stones (which first appear on the ridge 530 m from the camp) show it to be 5 m wide; it was never paved, but all loose stones were carefully cleared. The first milestones appear at 4·7 km from the camp. This was part of the trade route between Petra and Gaza.

The C6 AD fortress is simply a large open space encircled by a heavy wall with three towers on each side; it could have offered protection to the inhabitants and their flocks only against hit-and-run bedouin raiders. The small chapel was built after the Persian invasion.

The ecclesiastical area to the west of the fortress is supported by Nabataean retaining walls on the north and south; the staircase-tower leading to the terrace overlooking the slope is also Nabataean, but nothing remains of their buildings. Apart from the C3 AD tower behind the apse of the Church of St. Theodore, all the buildings are religious and dated to the C6 AD. The North Church stands alone; the Church of St. Theodore is surrounded by monastic cells, and is distinguished by a series of tombstones ranging in date from 541 to 618.

Desert Agriculture. From the terrace of the acropolis a swathe of green in the arid valley below immediately catches the eye. This is an experimental farm established in 1959 by Israeli scientists in order to rediscover the agricultural techniques which enabled the Negev to support the relatively dense population of the Nabataean and Byzantine periods. The research done here is the source of all reliable information on ancient farming methods in the area and highly successful crops prove the theories correct.

Aerial surveys shows that the whole area (500,000 acres) between MAMSHIT and SHIVTA, including barren slopes, was put to the service of agriculture. The oldest system is also the simplest: low terrace walls were built across the bed of shallow wadis to hold direct rainfall and to ensure some ponding in case of floods. The Nabataeans significantly increased the efficiency of this method by systematic control of the catchment area (fig. 44).

The key to desert agriculture is run-off, i.e. surplus rain which is not absorbed into the soil. The Negev gets mostly light rain (3–10 mm at a time; rarely more than 20 mm in any one day) but the loess soil quickly forms an impermeable crust when dampened and run-off always develops. The Nabataeans divided the catchment area into sections by building low walls [1] at an angle across the sloping side of the wadi. This not only divided the run-off into manageable quantities, but the 15 cm walls served as conduits which directed the run-off into specific fields. They also increased the run-off from light rains by as much as 20–40 per cent by collecting the stones on the slopes into heaps [2]. The net result, since the ratio of catchment area to cultivated area averages 20: 1, was that each field received water equivalent to a rainfall of 300–500 mm per year (the average in the mountains round Jerusalem) even though the average in the Negev is only 100 mm per year.

The cultivated area in the centre of a shallow wadi was walled [3] to ensure even ponding, and was divided into fields by terrace walls projecting some 40 cm above soil level. In the middle of each was a drop structure [4] which permitted surplus water to pass to the field

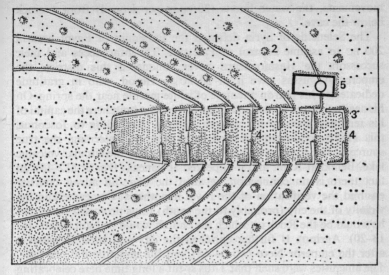

Fig. 44. Schematic drawing to illustrate desert farming techniques.

below. Many of these units had their own farmhouse, each equipped with an internal underground cistern [5] served by its own catchment conduit. A catchment area of half an acre would be more than adequate to create the 20 cubic metres of drinking water per year necessary for a family of six plus a donkey, a couple of camels, and a small flock of sheep and goats.

There are several farms of this type on either side of the road between Avdat and En Avdat (marked on the 1: 100,000 map), but one must be prepared to walk.

BANYAS (O1)

The present name is a corruption of Paneas, signifying a place sacred to the god Pan. The Jordan is by far the most important river in the region, and in antiquity a spring in the large cave was one of its principal sources. Little wonder, therefore, that it became a place where a nature god was venerated. Today, because of seismic movements, the water bursts (20 cu.m per second) from a crack below the cave.

The Seleucids of Syria defeated the Ptolemies of Egypt here in 200 BC to assume control of Palestine. The Maccabees and their successors the Hasmonaeans never conquered this district; the emperor Augustus gave it in 20 BC to Herod, who in gratitude dedicated to his patron a temple of white marble near the spring. On his death, the area passed to his son Philip who built here the capital of his territory, naming it Caesarea Philippi. According to Josephus, this Philip conducted the first experiment to determine the true source of the Jordan: he had chaff thrown into the circular volcanic lake, Berekhat Ram, and it appeared at Paneas (*War* 3: 512–13). In fact there is no connection between the two; an adroit courtier ensured the verification of the royal hypothesis! Somewhere in the vicinity of the city (probably to the south) Jesus promised Peter that he would be the Rock on which the church would be built (Matt. 16: 13–20). Agrippa II further enriched the city and tried to name it after the emperor Nero (AD 54–68), but the new title did not take. The amenities were such that Titus spent a long time here celebrating the capture of Jerusalem (AD 70); 'many of the prisoners perished here, some thrown to wild beasts, others forced to meet each other in full-scale battles' (*War* 7: 24).

In 1126 the fanatical sect of the Assassins obtained possession of Banyas but, in retaliation for the massacre of members of the sect by the authorities in Damascus, handed it over to the Crusaders in 1129. The site was important because it controlled the road between Damascus and Tyre; the Franks gave it strong fortifications and in addition built the great fortress of Subeibe (NIMRUD). The city changed hands several times before definitely falling to Nur-ed-din in 1164. After the failure of the Crusades the site reverted to its original insignificance, and was only a village of some 200 inhabitants when it was taken by the Israelis in 1967.

Visit. The centrepiece is still the Cave of Pan which is clearly visible from the parking-lot. The niches in the cliff face beside it were cut in the Graeco-Roman period to receive statues. Above the cave to the left (north) is the Weli (tomb of a Muslim saint) of el-Khader (St. George), sacred to Muslims and Druze. There have been no systematic excavations but the columns, capitals, and blocks scattered through the area attest the importance of the C1 AD city; north of the source, one room of an Herodian building has been brought to light.

The ruins of the Crusader fortifications are on the far side of the main road, and are so dilapidated as to be hardly worth a visit. The city was built between two streams which gave the defenders certain natural advantages.

BEER SHEVA (BEERSHEBA) (F23)

In the Old Testament, 'from Dan to Beer Sheva' is a stereotyped expression for the limits of the land of Israel (Judg. 20: 1; 1 Sam. 3: 20; 2 Sam. 3: 10; 17: 11; 24: 2; etc.). Although located just beyond the southern edge of the mountainous region where the Israelites were able to maintain effective control, Beer Sheva was important because of its association with the Patriarchs. The name is explained as 'the well of the seven' or 'the well of the oath' in the narrative of Abraham's treaty with Abimelek the Philistine (Gen. 21: 25–33). The dispute centred on the possession of a well (extremely important for nomadic pastors) and flared up again after the death of Abraham. It was settled in the same amicable way, and Isaac built an altar there in memory of the promise of Yahweh (Gen. 26: 15–33). It was at Beer Sheva that Jacob received the vision encouraging him to take his family to Egypt (Gen. 46: 1–7).

The allusions to Philistines in the Patriarchal narratives are anachronistic, and reflect the situation at the time of the Judges (C12 BC), when the area was settled again. Excavations at various sites scattered around the modern town show that the area was occupied during the 4th millennium BC. These people, who had introduced domesticated sheep to the Negev, moved away about 3000 BC; thereafter nomads wandered through the area in seasonal patterns. After the return from Egypt Sheva is listed as part of the territory of Simeon which was eventually absorbed by Judah (Josh. 15: 28; 19: 2); the corrupt sons of Samuel judged there (1 Sam. 8: 2). As a frontier settlement, with the Philistines and Amalekites as threatening neighbours, Beer Sheva cannot have had a very tranquil existence until David (1004–965 BC) strengthened Israelite control over the area.

Excavations at Tel Beer Sheva contribute most to our knowledge of the region from that time on. Late in his reign David built a fortified town on this mound where Saul, his predecessor, had erected a small fort during his campaign against the Amalekites from the south (1 Sam. 14: 48; 15: 2–9). It was destroyed in a tremendous conflagration at the end of the C10, which is plausibly related to the invasion of Israel by the Pharaoh Shishak in 925 BC. The town cannot have been of any great importance because it is not listed among the captured cities inscribed on the wall of the temple at Karnak in Egypt. ARAD, on the contrary, is mentioned. Beer Sheva rose from the ashes, and there is evidence of growing prosperity in the C9–C8 BC. The most significant artefact from this period is a great horned altar (now exhibited in the Israel Museum, Jerusalem, but the Beer Sheva Museum on Derech Haatzmaut has a copy).

The cut stones of this altar do not conform to biblical law which lays down that an altar should be 'of unhewn stones upon which no man has lifted an iron tool' (Deut. 27: 5; Josh. 8: 31). The hint of irregularity in the cult practised at Beer Sheva is confirmed by the condemnation of the C8 prophet Amos (5: 5; 8: 14). The altar was broken up and used as building material during the religious reforms of King Hezekiah (2 Kgs. 18: 4). At the end of the C8 the town was utterly destroyed – by Sennacherib according to the excavators. Some of the survivors made a feeble attempt to rebuild, but soon gave up and moved to the area of the present town. Thereafter the mound was the site of a series of fortresses starting with a Persian one of the C4 BC and ending with a Roman of the C2–C3 AD.

Visit (fig. 45). Excavations are still in progress, but some sections have already been restored and offer the visitor a unique view of the planning of an Iron Age town. The tel is east of modern Beer Sheva, and the turn-off from the main Beer Sheva–Jerusalem road is signposted.

The single gate [8] of the town was built in the early C10 BC. It had three piers of equal width, creating two guardrooms on either side, and was protected by an outer gate [10]. Just outside that is a deep well [11] which the excavators claim is dated to the C12. If this is correct, the well was in use in the period when the Patriarchal narratives (Gen. 21: 25–33; 26: 15–33) were given their present form, and may be the one that the editors had in mind. However, had the well been in existence when the outer gate was built, it is curious that the wall was not sited outside it. When the town was rebuilt after the destruction by Shishak the outer gate was abandoned; the two outer piers of the reconstructed gate [9] were enlarged in compensation. At this period the original solid defence wall was transformed into a casemate wall (parallel walls whose rooms could be filled in time of danger).

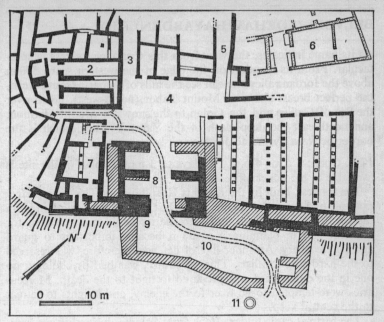

Fig. 45. Tel Beer Sheva. Excavated area around the city gate (after Aharoni).

Inside the gate is a small square [4] from which streets [1, 3, 5] radiate into the town. The circular street [1] passes between two dwellings [2 and 7] and leads to a group of reconstructed four-room houses in the western quarter. These are all of the C9–C8 BC; earlier buildings are visible at a lower level. On the other side of the gate are three storehouses, similar to those found at HAZOR and MEGIDDO; these were an integral part of the taxation system established by Solomon (965–928 BC). Just across the street, but at a higher level, one can see the paved entrance [6] of the Roman fort (C2–C3 AD).

In the deep trench at the north-east corner of the tel (overlooking the archaeologists' camp) one can see the stone glacis of the C8 BC. Beside it, on the slope, is a later glacis of the Roman period.

BELVOIR (KOKHAV HAYARDEN) (M8)

As its name indicates, the view from this Crusader fortress is spectacular. From its location on the edge of the western scarp 500 m above the Jordan valley one can see the hills of Samaria (south-west), the perfect breast shape of Mount Tabor (north-west), north over the Sea of Galilee and the Golan to the snows of Mount Hermon, and north-east the deep slash of the Yarmuk valley which is the border between Syria and Jordan.

Visit. Open: 8 a.m.–4 p.m., Fridays to 3 p.m. A plan of the site is available at the ticket office.

The fortress, built by the Knights Hospitallers in 1168, is a perfect example of a concentric castle. In the last days of the Latin Kingdom the loyalty of auxiliaries and mercenaries could not be taken for granted, and in planning a castle it became important to guard against treachery. An inner line of defence, therefore, was reserved to the hard-core loyalists. This, of course, was bad psychology: no one in the outer ward was prepared to fight to the death. Mercenaries were tempted to go over to the enemy, and knights to retreat to the central keep.

The fortress came under attack from Saladin during his two campaigns in the Beisan valley in 1182–3, but had little difficulty holding out. On 1 July 1187 the impotent defenders saw his 12,000 mounted archers stream down the north edge of the Yarmuk on their way to victory at the HORNS OF HATTIN. Thereafter they were under siege. It lasted until January 1191 when sappers brought down the east tower protecting the switchback entrance ramp. The writing was now on the wall, and the defenders sued for terms. Saladin permitted them to march out to Tyre. His troops tore down the gates, but the castle was systematically destroyed only in the early C13 when there was reason to fear that the Crusaders would return. They did regain possession of Belvoir in 1241, by treaty not by arms, but their stay was too short to permit reconstruction.

BET ALPHA (M9)

A C6 AD synagogue celebrated for the colour and vigour of its mosaic floor. Open: 8 a.m. – 4 p.m.; Fridays to 3 p.m.

Only fragments of walls remain but they show that there was an open courtyard with two doors leading into the vestibule from which three doors gave on to a basilical hall. The apse, which orients the building towards Jerusalem, housed the Ark of the Law and the community safe (a hole in the floor covered with stone slabs). Just inside the entrance to the central aisle are two inscriptions: one, in Greek, mentions the two craftsmen who laid the mosaic floor, Marianos and his son Hanina; the other, in Aramaic, says that the floor was laid during the reign of the Emperor Justin. The inscription is mutilated just at the point where the exact date was given, but there were only two Justins; the first reigned from 518 to 527, and the second from 565 to 578. Since Justin II was notorious for his persecution of Jews, it is assumed that the inscription refers to Justin I. The inscriptions are flanked by a lion and a bull. These have a long history in the ancient Near East as symbols of forces locked in combat, but they were also complementary as the symbols of the god Hadad and his consort Atargatis. Were they intended to remind the Jew of the world he would re-enter on leaving the synagogue?

The world evoked by the three panels of the mosaic floor (fig. 46 – Hebrew lettering omitted) was very different. In the first, Abraham's readiness to sacrifice the willing Isaac symbolizes absolute submission to the divine will (Gen. 22: 1–19). The donkey driver with his whip stands by as his helper prepares to take off the saddle. The ram tethered to a bush and the bound hands of a small, fearful Isaac (apparently suspended from his father's fingertips) are details not found in the Bible; they show that the artists had been listening to the Aramaic paraphrase which made the Hebrew Bible intelligible to the average Jew. The whole scene is dominated by the hand of God and the words 'Do not lay (your hand upon the boy)'. The radiant dark cloud, from which the hand emerges, underlines the paradox of religious truth, a theme reinforced by the contrast between the neatly ordered stylized palm trees of heaven and the rather haphazard vegetation scattered round the figures' feet.

The centre panel elaborates the theme of heaven in a quite different way, drawing on the symbolism of the pagan world. The busts of winged women represent the four seasons (anticlockwise

Fig. 46. Bet Alpha. Mosaic floor of the C6 synagogue.

from the top left-hand corner): *Nisan*, Spring; *Tammuz*, Summer; *Tishri*, Autumn; and *Tebeth*, Winter. In the hub of the zodiac wheel Helios, the sun god, drives his four-horse chariot across a sky studded with moon and stars. The twelve signs start at 3 o'clock and run anticlockwise: *Taleh*, Aries; *Shor*, Taurus; *Teomin*, Gemini; *Sartan*, Cancer; *Aryeh*, Leo; *Betulah*, Virgo; *Meoznayim*, Libra; *Aqrab*, Scorpio; *Kashat*, Sagittarius; *Gedi*, Capricorn; *Deli*, Aquarius; and *Dagim*, Pisces. The twisted cord border underlines the unity of the wheel, but if the intention was to divide the twelve signs into groups of three someone slipped!

This arrangement of the solar chariot, zodiac wheel, and personified seasons is taken directly from paganism, and reflects the Graeco-Roman assimilation of Babylonian astrology. The influence of classical sources is much more evident in the zodiac floor of the C4 AD synagogue found at HAMMAT TIBERIAS. Such pagan beliefs naturally created problems for the rabbis, but the very human desire to look into the future was too strong, and they were forced to find ways to make the zodiac acceptable. The frequency of the number twelve in the Bible (tribes, showbread, jewelled dress of high priest, etc.) furnished an obvious link with received tradition. Such juxtaposition of the sacred and the profane (found also in the synagogue floors at Naaran and HAMMAT TIBERIAS) is much less effective than the solution adopted here where the zodiac is bracketed by two specifically religious panels which reduce it to a purely decorative role. Nowhere else is the zodiac associated with the sacrifice of Isaac whose message implicitly condemns the futility of star-gazing; it is God who guides the course of human life.

The open curtains framing the upper panel invite the believer to enter the realm of mystery by contemplating the symbols which are the traces of God's presence in history, the Temple and the Law. The Temple is suggested by the double menorah, the two square incense shovels, the two shofars (ram's-horn trumpets), and the lulab (bundle of branches) plus ethrog (citrus fruit). These souvenirs of a ritual which no longer existed are relegated to a secondary position by being disposed around the central element, the shrine of the Law. Pilasters support its heavily inlaid doors; a lamp hangs from the apex of the stepped gable adorned with a shell motif. The richness of decoration symbolizes the honour accorded the Law, the focal point of Jewish life. It seems precarious to assign any symbolic value to the five animals.

BET GUVRIN (G19)

The ruins on either side of the main road (Qiryat Gat–Bet Shemesh) passing through Bet Guvrin are Crusader. They are the remnants of one of the three castles – Bet Gibelin, Blanche Garde, and Ibelin – built by Fulk of Anjou (1131–43) in order to blockade ASHQELON; the tactic succeeded only when the capture of Gaza in 1150 closed the circle. The area contains a number of other fascinating remains, but they are all underground; a torch is useful but not indispensable because there is enough light for the eyes to adapt after a few moments.

The turn-off is just beside a huge tree (fig. 47). After a short distance the tarmac road forks; the left-hand branch terminates in a circular parking-lot, from which a well-worn path runs over a slight rise into a sort of great pit [1]. On all sides are entrances to vast bell-shaped caves; the quiet and the play of light are reminiscent of a great cathedral. The caves are in fact chalk quarries. In this area chalk deposits are covered by an extremely hard crust called *nari*. The quarrymen found it most economical to cut only a circular opening 1m in diameter in the *nari*. The chalk was then removed in layers 30–40 cm deep; the tool marks are still visible on the walls. The radius was increased as the pit descended, sometimes breaking through the wall of the pit alongside. The absence of any dumps shows the chalk to have been burnt to create mortar and plaster. There are about 1,000 of these pits within a 3 km radius round Bet Guvrin, and 2,000 more slightly further afield; they were worked between the C4 and C7 AD.

A circular road surrounds Tel Mareshah [3]; the excavations were covered again and nothing is visible on the surface. From the Bible we know that the city fortified by Rehoboam (928–911 BC) as a storehouse and armoury (2 Chr. 11: 8–11) was destroyed by Sennacherib in 701 BC (Mic. 1: 15). After the Exile (586–538 BC) Mareshah became part of Idumaea. The Ptolemies established a colony of Sidonians in the city in the C3 BC and according to Zenon, an Egyptian official who visited Palestine in 259 BC, it was a centre of the slave trade with Egypt. Under Seleucid control (from 193 BC) the city lost its importance, and inscriptions show the colonists merging with the local population. Conquest by John Hyrcanus (134–104 BC) forced the inhabitants to become Jews under threat of exile (*Antiquities* 13: 257). The name of the place to which Herod the Great went

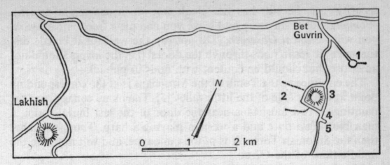

Fig. 47. Bet Guvrin and Lakhish.

on his way to MASADA in 40 BC is textually uncertain; some scholars suggest that we should read Marisa (= Mareshah), which may even have been his birthplace, and this would explain why the Parthians destroyed the city (*War* 1: 263–70).

Thereafter the role of Mareshah passed to the near-by village of Bet Guvrin which grew into a city to which the emperor Septimus Severus gave the *ius italicum* and the name Eleutheropolis in AD 200. He endowed the city with a huge tract of land stretching from EN GEDI almost to the coast. The wealth of the Byzantine city is well illustrated by the elaborate mosaic floor of a C4 villa above which was found the equally beautiful floor of a C6 chapel; both are now in the Israel Museum, Jerusalem. The standing apse on the adjoining hill belongs to the C12 Crusader church of St. Anna (whence the Arabic name for Mareshah, Tel Sandakhanna).

From the north-east corner of a small tarmac parking-lot it is only a few steps to the bush-framed entrance to the Sidonian Tomb [4]. The rock chambers with their 41 gable-shaped loculi are intact, but the paintings of animals which filled the band below the garlands have disappeared. Constructed at the end of the C3 BC as the family tomb of Apollophanes, who headed the Sidonian colony for thirty-three years, it remained in use until the C1 BC. A four-line Greek inscription found in the tomb has given rise to much discussion; the most interesting version is that of Macalister who reads it as messages scrawled by lovers separated when the woman was forced into an arranged marriage. *Woman*: 'I can neither suffer aught for you, nor give you pleasure. I lie with another loving you dearly.' *Man:* 'But, by Aphrodite, I rejoice greatly at one thing; your cloak lies as security' (i.e. he still has her cloak for which she might return). *Woman*: 'But I run away and leave you complete freedom; do what you will.' *Cynical Observer*: 'Do not rap the wall for it breeds disturbance; it lies in nods through the doors' (i.e. the lovers should not advertise, but should be content with nods in public).

The entrance to the Tomb of the Musicians is at the corresponding point at the far side of the little valley [5]. The name comes from the painting of two musicians near the door of the last burial room, a man blowing a flute and a woman playing a harp. Though smaller than the Sidonian Tomb, it is of the same type, and was in use in the middle third of the C2 BC.

The area around Mareshah is honeycombed with underground chambers; the hard *nari* provided a solid roof while the soft chalk below was very easy to work. The most accessible are in the area west of the tel [2]. Clearly defined paths lead from the road, but there are no signs; investigate every hole in the ground which looks interesting. Some of the chambers have elaborate banistered staircases leading down from the surface; others have hundreds of small niches arranged in rows. The purpose of the latter is still unclear. Similar *columbaria* in Rome were burial places, the niches containing urns with ashes, but no evidence supports the hypothesis that this was the case here. Hence the suggestion that they were used for raising small domesticated doves used in the worship of Aphrodite by the Sidonian colony.

BETHLEHEM (J18)

The town is first mentioned in the C14 BC when the king of Jerusalem wrote to his Egyptian overlord asking for archers to help him recover Bit-Lahmi which had seceded from his jurisdiction, but it really enters history with the figure of David. He was born there (1 Sam. 16) to an Ephrathite family who had lived there for many generations (Ruth 1–4). When the jealousy of Saul forced him to become an outlaw, he led an attack on the Philistines (1 Sam. 23: 5) who, in reprisal, put a garrison in Bethlehem (2 Sam. 23: 14). The only piece of information concerning the character of the town at this period is provided by David's nostalgic cry, 'O that someone would give me water to drink from the well of Bethlehem which is by the gate!' (2 Sam. 23: 15); when three of his followers broke through the

Philistines to get it for him, he refused to drink because of the risk they had taken. Even though Bethlehem was a walled city, David decided not to make it his capital, because Saul had greatly diminished his own effectiveness by locating the capital in the territory of the tribe to which he belonged.

David's grandson Rehoboam (928–911 BC) fortified Bethlehem, together with Etam (POOLS OF SOLOMON) and Tekoa, to protect the eastern flank of his kingdom (2 Chr. 11: 6). Two centuries later Bethlehem was an insignificant village, but intimately associated with the Messianic hope, 'You Bethlehem Ephrathah, the least among the clans of Judah, from you shall come forth for me one who is to be ruler in Israel, whose origin is from of old, from ancient days' (Mic. 5: 1). An archaeological survey has shown that the town of this period (C10–C8 BC) was in the area of the Church of the Nativity and that the caves beneath the church were then in use. Presumably the 123 Bethlehemites listed among those who returned from the Exile in the C6 BC (Ezra 2: 21) resettled in their ancient home.

Mary and Joseph were natives of Bethlehem, and only moved to Nazareth because of the atmosphere of insecurity generated by the Herodian dynasty (Matt. 2); their long residence in Galilee gave Luke the impression that they had always lived there and he had to find a reason which would place them in Bethlehem at the moment of the birth of Jesus (Luke 2: 1–7). The Greek underlying the phrase, 'she laid him in a manger because there was no room for them in the inn' (Luke 2: 7) can also be rendered, 'she laid him in a manger because they had no space in the room'. The gospels make no mention of a cave, yet in the C2 AD Justin and the *Protoevangelium of James* speak of the cave in which Jesus was born. Many houses in the area are still built in front of caves, and perhaps we should envisage Joseph (then living with his parents) as taking his wife into such a back area in order to give birth away from the confusion of the living room; the cave part would have been used to shelter animals in bad weather.

In AD 395 Jerome wrote, 'From Hadrian's time [C2 AD] until the reign of Constantine, for about 180 years . . . Bethlehem, now ours, and the earth's, most sacred spot . . . was overshadowed by a grove of Thammuz, which is Adonis, and in the cave where the infant Messiah once cried, the paramour of Venus was bewailed.' (Epistle 58); Cyril of Jerusalem, writing before AD 348, also mentions that the area was wooded. Hadrian had expelled Jews from the Bethlehem area, thus giving free rein to the development of pagan cults; Thammuz was beloved by farmers as the personification of the seed which dies and springs to life again. The commemoration of his mythical death in the cave may have been motivated by a desire to interfere with the veneration of Christians. In this case bitterness would have reinforced the memory of the local tradition attested in the C2 by Justin, and in the C3 by Origen and Eusebius. Pre-Constantinian localizations of sacred sites have much greater validity than identifications which first appear in the C4 when the questions of pilgrims inspired the imaginations of local guides.

Queen Helena dedicated the first church on 31 May 339. The octagonal apse (fig. 48) was sited directly above the cave which was entered by stairs passing under the stone chancel screen [1]. The altar stood on a raised circular dias [2]. The only visible element of this church is the geometric pavement of the nave some 50 cm below the level of the present nave. The cave must have undergone certain alterations but these have been so completely absorbed by later modifications that no details are available. Given the slope of the hill, the natural entrance must have been on the north or east.

In 384 Jerome took up residence in Bethlehem, to be joined two years later by Paula and her daughter Eustochium. Together they made Bethlehem a great monastic centre; within this framework Jerome wrote prolifically, his most notable achievement being a new translation of the Old and New Testaments (the Vulgate) which remained the authoritative version of the Bible for Catholics until the C20. One of the caves (fig. 49) is identified as Jerome's study [1]. This is probably legendary, but the existence of caves adjacent to the main cave [8] is implied by Jerome's assertion that Paula 'was buried beneath the church beside the cave of the Lord'. There he interred Eustochium, and arranged a place for his own burial. A C6 pilgrim noted that his tomb was in a cave.

According to Eutychius of Alexandria (C9), after the Samaritan uprising of AD 529, 'The Emperor Justinian ordered his envoy to pull down the church of Bethlehem, which was a small one, and to build it again of such splendour, size and beauty that none even in the Holy City should surpass it.' He lengthened the church by one bay, added a narthex, and replaced the octagonal apse by a more spacious triapsidal form. This building has remained in use to the present day. The destructive Persians (614) passed it by because they found the Magi in familiar dress represented in the mosaic on the façade (this was quoted at a C9 synod in Jerusalem to show the utility of images).

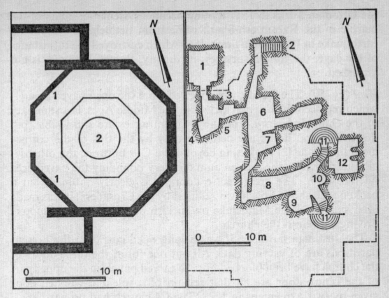

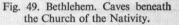

Fig. 48. Bethlehem. Reconstruction of the C4 apse of the Church
of the Nativity (after Bagatti).

Fig. 49. Bethlehem. Caves beneath
the Church of the Nativity.

Muslims prevented the application of Hakim's decree (1009) ordering
the destruction of Christian monuments because, since the time of
Omar (639), they had been permitted to use the south transept for
their devotions.

Tancred's night ride from Latrun on 6 June 1099 secured the
church before the Muslims could react. Crusader kings were crowned
there, and in an extraordinary display of tolerance the Franks and
Byzantines co-operated in the restoration of the church between 1165
and 1169. All the interior decoration was renewed and the roof replaced. After the fall of the Latin Kingdom (1187) Ayyubid respect
for the holy place preserved the church, but this dynasty was supplanted by the Mamelukes in the C13 and they saw it only as a
source of revenue and political leverage. Repairs were permitted only
infrequently; deterioration was assisted by pillage. Felix Fabri, a C15
pilgrim, describes the interior as 'a barn without hay, an apothecary's
without aromatic pots, a library without books'. With the arrival of

the Ottoman Turks in 1517 looting became systematic; much of the marble in the Haram esh-Sharif came from Bethlehem. Despite an earthquake in 1834, and a fire in 1869 which destroyed the furnishings of the cave, the church survives; its dignity, though battered, is not tarnished.

Visit (fig. 50). The façade, when viewed from the open paved area [1] which replaced the original atrium in the Middle Ages, is a summary of the church's history. The three C6 entrances are still visible, but the two lateral doors are betrayed only by the tips of the cornice mouldings, one [2] projecting beyond the C19 buttress, the other [4] all but hidden by the Armenian monastery bounding the paved area on the south. The great centre door [3] is clearly outlined, but a broken arch shows how it was reduced by the Crusaders; it was made even smaller in the Mameluke or Turkish period to prevent looters driving carts into the church.

The Justinian narthex [5] was a long open corridor; the present partitions are of varying date. All but one [6] of the three doors of the church have been blocked up; the carved panels in the upper part of the centre door are all that remain of a splendid wooden door given by two Armenians in 1227. The C4 church had no narthex.

With the exception of the roof and floor, which have been replaced several times, the structure of the body of the church is as it

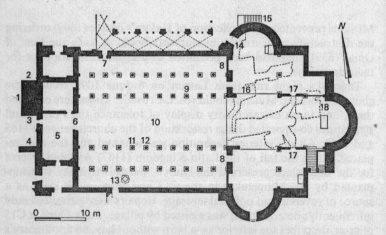

Fig. 50. Bethlehem. Church of the Nativity.

was in the time of Justinian; the closure of the aisles [8] took place in the Middle Ages. The red limestone pillars, quarried near Bethlehem, may have served in the C4 church whose outer walls are still in use. Individual Crusaders decorated the upper part of the pillars with paintings of saints whose names appear in Latin and/or Greek; note particularly Cathal of Ireland [9], Canute of Denmark and England [11], and Olaf of Norway [12]. The heraldic graffiti on the lower part of the pillars are dated to the C14–C15.

The octagonal baptismal font [13] originally stood near the high altar [18] of the C6 church; the inscription reads, 'For remembrance, rest, and remission of sins of those whose names the Lord knows.' Archaeologists found an octagonal bed of exactly the same dimensions over a cistern [12 in fig. 49] which provided the required water. After the Baptistry was moved in the Crusader renovation of the church the cistern became the focus of various legends; it was the well into which the star of the Magi fell, the well where the Magi watered their beasts, and the well to which David's three heroes came!

A small door [7] leads to the restored medieval cloister in front of the Franciscan church of St. Catherine built in 1881. Wooden trapdoors [10] cover the mosaic floor of the C4 church. Similar doors [16] protect another mosaic of the same period showing the Constantinian apse to have been octagonal; these are sometimes opened on request.

The remains of mosaic decoration on the walls of the nave date from the restoration of 1165–9. Each side had three registers; the detailed description made by the Franciscan Qaresmius in 1628 enables us to complete the missing sections. The lowest depicted the ancestors of Jesus according to Luke 3: 23–38 (north wall) and according to Matt. 1: 1–16 (south wall). The middle register of the north wall contained the key decisions of six provincial councils. The text from the Council of Antioch (272), for example, reads, 'The Holy Synod of Antioch in Syria of 33 bishops took place before the Ecumenical Council of Nicaea against Paul of Samosata who held that Christ was a mere man. The Holy Synod expelled him as a heretic'; the other text (to the left) is from the Council of Sardica (347). The corresponding register on the south wall enshrined the decisions of six ecumenical councils; from left to right the preserved fragments recall the Councils of Nicaea (325), Constantinople (381), Ephesus (431), Chalcedon (451), and Constantinople (680). According to Qaresmius, only one council text was in Latin, that of Nicaea (787) which condemned the iconoclast heresy; by deciding in favour of the legitimacy of images it made the flowering of church art possible. The top register on both sides is composed of a series of angels between the windows. The name of the artist appears at the foot of the third angel from the right on the north wall, BASILIUS PICTOR; it is written with the syllables placed one above the other.

The entire west wall was covered with mosaic; prophets, each holding a text considered to refer to Jesus, sat in the branches of the tree of Jesse. The mosaics of the transepts and choir recorded scenes from the life of Jesus; the name of the artist, Ephraim the monk, is given in a Greek and Latin inscription of which part can be seen at the point where the southern end of the C18 iconostasis touches the wall.

A pilgrim in 870 described the present entrances to the cave [17; [11] in fig. 49]; the northern one was used by Arculf in 670 because (subsequent numbers in this paragraph refer to fig. 49) he encountered the birthplace [10] before coming to the site of the manger [9]. The main body of the present cave [8] certainly existed at this period because traces of an earlier entrance have been found at the west end (now blocked by a door). All the furnishings are subsequent to the fire of 1869.

The passage linking the cave of the Nativity with the other caves to the north has not been dated with certitude. Felix Fabri observed it in 1480; then, as now, it was closed to pilgrims. To enter these caves one must leave the church by the small door in the north transept [14] and use a medieval entrance [15 = 2 in fig. 49 to which subsequent numbers refer]. Pottery and pre-Constantinian masonry suggest that these caves were in use in the C1 and C2 AD; they have been significantly modified since and were given their present form in 1964. The various elements are identified as the cell of Jerome [1], the tombs of Jerome [4], Paula and Eustochium [5], and Eusebius of Cremona, the successor of Jerome as head of the monastic community [3], the chapels of the Holy Innocents [6] and of St. Joseph [7]. These identifications have no historical value.

BET SHEAN (M9)

The numerous fishponds in the Harod valley give Bet Shean a unique character. In an arid land it is virtually surrounded by water.

It contains the best-preserved Roman theatre in the country and a unique Byzantine mosaic floor.

The tremendous natural advantages of the site make it easy to understand why it has been continuously occupied for over 5,000 years; the 80 m-high tel contains 18 superimposed cities. The fertile land receives a good rainfall and the Harod is a perennial stream. The valley climbs gently to the west from the Jordan, merging imperceptibly with the Jezreel valley running to the coast. Immeasurably the easiest east–west crossing in the whole country, these valleys have been a trade-route from time immemorial, and they are controlled by Bet Shean.

Stone Age settlements gave way to the first real town about 3000 BC; its name appears in Egyptian texts of the C19 BC. The corresponding levels of the tel provide abundant evidence of Egyptian influence; the city was one of the major strongholds from which the Pharaohs controlled Palestine. After the entrance of the Israelites in the C13 BC, Bet Shean formed part of the territory that fell to the lot of the tribe of Manasseh, but the iron chariots of the Canaanites forbade any attack (Judg. 1: 27). The city fell to another chariot people, the Philistines, in the C11 BC because, after the defeat of the Israelites on Mount Gilboa in 1004 BC, they hung the body of King Saul on the walls of Bet Shean (1 Sam. 31: 10), thus occasioning the famous lament of David (2 Sam. 1: 17–27).

The history of the city from the point where it is mentioned (1 Kgs. 4: 12) as a city of Solomon's empire (965–928 BC) remains obscure until we reach the C3 BC when it reappears as Scythopolis. This name, commonly related to a legendary Scythian invasion in the C7 BC, probably derives from the settlement by Ptolemy II (285–246 BC) of 'Scythian' horse-archers on his estates there. Under Antiochus IV (175–164 BC) the city received the rights of a *polis* and a new name, Nysa. When John Hyrcanus brought it under Jewish control in 107 BC he gave its pagan inhabitants the option of accepting circumcision or exile. The vast majority left and were restored to their possessions only in 63 BC when the Roman general Pompey made the city part of the Decapolis, a league of ten cities designed as a source of Graeco-Roman influence in the area.

In the C3 AD Jewish religious leaders tried to slow the movement of Jewish peasants into the city but, as usual, economics prevailed; Scythopolis was on its way to becoming one of the textile centres of the Roman empire. The Edict of Maximum Prices promulgated by the emperor Diocletian (AD 284–305) consistently ranks the linen produce of Scythopolis as first class. Inevitably Christians were also drawn to the city, and their position improved immeasurably when the empire became Christian in the early C4. The greatest figure the community produced was the C6 historian Cyril of Scythopolis whose biographies of seven Palestinian religious leaders are a mine of accurate detail.

Linen workers began to drift away from Scythopolis in the C6 because state contol of the economy had effectively reduced master-craftsmen to the status of slaves; the weakness of Byzantine authority made it impossible to enforce the law of AD 374 which imposed a heavy fine on 'those who attempt to harbour Scythopolitan linen workers who are bound to the regular public corvée'. The Arab conquest restored the old Semitic name but could not halt the city's decline. From the small Jewish community which survived the presence of the Crusaders came the first Hebrew book on the geography of the Holy Land (1322).

Visit. The town contains two distinct sites: (1) the tel and the Roman theatre; (2) the Monastery of the Lady Mary.

(1) *Tel and Roman Theatre.* Open: 8 a.m.–4 p.m.; Fridays to 3 p.m. The entrance from the main street, Shaul Hamelech, is clearly sign-posted.

Even though the upper part of the seating has disappeared, the theatre, built about AD 200, is a striking monument. Designed for dramatic presentations, it had seating for 5,000.

There is a steep path to the top of the tel, but the only significant remains are the ruins of a gate of the Byzantine or Arab period. Only the view makes the climb worthwhile.

(2) *Monastery of the Lady Mary.* The building is kept locked but the key may be obtained (against deposit of one's passport or identity card) at the museum (open: 8.30 a.m.–3 p.m.; closed Saturdays). The turn south from the bypass linking the Bet Shean–Afula and Bet Shean–Tiberias roads is not marked; there is a café on the corner, and the debris-strewn road runs beside a row of factories; the asbestos-roofed ruin is at the end on the left.

An inscription in the south-east corner of the chapel identifies the builder as 'the Lady Mary'; the title was used by the wives of high Byzantine officials. A tombstone in the chapel shows the monastery to have been erected not long before AD 567. It survived the Persian invasion in 614 only to be abandoned not long after; through some miracle the mosaics escaped the attention of vandals. Many of the floors have simple geometric designs; three are of exceptional interest.

The centrepiece of the mosaic in the main hall is a calendar in which the twelve months form a circle around the Sun and Moon. Each month is represented by a man equipped for an occupation typical of the season; at his feet is the Latin name of the month in Greek script with the number of days (fig. 51): January [1] – effaced; February [2] – man with hoe and sapling; March [3] – soldier; April [4] – man carrying goat and basket; May [5] – man bearing flowers in cloak; June [6] – man holding basket of fruit; July [7] – man holding sheaf of corn; August [8] – effaced; September [9] –

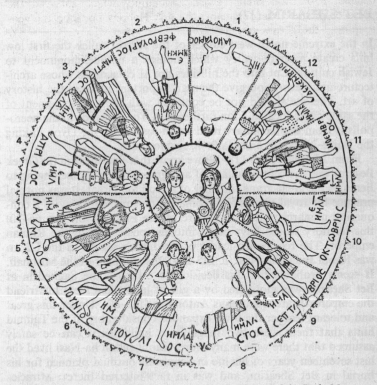

Fig. 51. Bet Shean. Calendar mosaic in the Monastery of the Lady Mary.

man with knife and basket for grape harvest; October [10] and
November [11] – uncertain; December [12] – man scattering seed.

In the room at the far end of the hall from the entrance a vine
trellis is used to create twelve medallions containing (reading left to
right top to bottom) spear-bearer attacking lioness with two cubs;
two damaged; negro leading a giraffe; vintager with load of grapes;
vintager cutting grapes; dog howling accompaniment to pipe player;
treading grapes; man leading pannier-laden donkey; vintager cutting grapes over basket; man thinking about the vintage; damaged.
The circular medallions making up the floor of the chapel contain
eighty small birds in addition to two large peacocks.

BET SHEARIM (J7)

In the extreme north-west corner of the Jezreel valley the first low
hills create a small valley which houses a unique monument to
Jewish culture. Cut into the hillsides are 31 catacombs whose architecture and decoration give them an important place in the history
of art. The site should not be confused with the new settlement of
the same name located 5 km further east. The entrance to the necropolis is from the secondary road south-east of Qiryat Tivon linking
the Haifa–Nazareth and Haifa–Megiddo roads.

From Josephus (*Life* 118–19) we know that Bet Shearim (in Greek
Besara) was the central village of an agricultural estate belonging to
Berenice the great-granddaughter of Herod the Great. It was normal
practice for royal estates to become the personal property of a conquering monarch; after the failure of the First Revolt (AD 66–70)
this territory would have come into the possession of the Roman
emperor. The recognized leader of the Jewish people in the C2 AD
was Rabbi Judah ha-Nasi (*c.* 135–217), the compiler of the Mishnah.
It seems probable that his decision to establish the Sanhedrin at
Bet Shearim was motivated by a gift of land there from his friend
the emperor Marcus Aurelius Antoninus (161–80). Under this great
and tolerant teacher the town expanded considerably; if the Talmud
hints that there were two magnificent buildings it can be safely
assumed that there were many more. Rabbi Judah ha-Nasi lived the
last seventeen years of his life in Sepphoris but had planned for his
burial in Bet Shearim, and was in fact interred there: 'Miracles
were wrought on that day. It was evening and all the towns gathered

to mourn him, and eighteen synagogues praised him and bore him to Bet Shearim, and the daylight remained until everyone reached his home' (Ketubot 12, 35a).

Jews had always desired to be buried on the Mount of Olives where the Messiah was expected to appear, but this became impossible when Hadrian closed the area round Jerusalem to Jews. Bet Shearim became the ideal alternative because of the reverence in which Rabbi Judah ha-Nasi was held, and for a hundred years Jews from throughout Palestine and the Diaspora brought their dead to be interred there. Services to the dead became the main industry of the town, and quarrymen, stonecutters, and sculptors were in continuous employ.

Towards the beginning of the C4 AD the tombs become less ornate, though as numerous as ever. This decline ended in the middle of the century when the town was burnt, presumably when Gallus Caesar in 352 suppressed a Jewish revolt against Byzantine rule. Occupation was sparse in the Byzantine period, and in the Arab period only tomb-robbers frequented the ruins. Memory of the great necropolis vanished so completely that in the Middle Ages Jews venerated the tomb of Rabbi Judah ha-Nasi in Sepphoris; it was rediscovered in 1936 by archaeologists from the Hebrew University.

Visit. Open: 8 a.m.–4 p.m.; Fridays to 3 p.m. An explanatory leaflet is available, and a small museum is located in an ancient rock-cut reservoir near the parking-lot. The site is composed of two parts, the town on the crest of the hill and the necropolis below.

(1) *The Town*. Three buildings have been excavated, all situated on the left of the entrance road. Two are public buildings, one a synagogue and the other a basilica. The third is an olive press.

The synagogue is oriented towards Jerusalem by three doors which give on to a paved street. At the far end a raised platform (*bema*) fills the space between the two rows of pillars; this is an unusual feature, because at KHIRBET SHEMA it is the *bema* which orients the building towards Jerusalem. The foundation of the synagogue is not precisely dated, but it is certainly prior to the middle of the C4 AD. A hoard of 1,200 coins (all C4 but none later than 351), found in the two-storey building between the synagogue and the present road, provides a date for the destruction level covering the whole area.

About 100 m further on is an olive press. Baskets of olives were stacked between two uprights on the circular grooved stone; a heavy horizontal beam let into a notch in the wall acted as a lever to press

out the oil which flowed round the circular groove into a plastered
basin in the rock floor. At a later stage a monumental gate was inserted between the two-room olive press and a building to the west;
note how the doorways on either side had to be modified. The whole
complex is dated to the C4 AD.

The basilica is a simple rectangle divided by two rows of columns,
with a raised platform at the end opposite the doors which opened
on to a wide court. Probably built at the end of the C2 AD, it served
as a meeting place for business transactions.

(2) *The Necropolis*. There are 31 catacombs which vary considerably
in design. To explain the differences the excavators suggest the following development.

Catacomb 20 was cut during the lifetime of Rabbi Judah ha-Nasi
as a public cemetery. The plan is highly irregular with much wasted
space. Two types of burial were envisaged. Some rooms were intended for sarcophagi placed against the walls or in special recesses.
In other rooms single-grave arcosolia (arch recessed into wall) were
cut, some with niches for bone deposits. In addition to 200 such
graves, the catacomb contains 125 sarcophagi whose placement (as
space became a problem) was dictated by expediency.

The plan of the unfinished triple entrance of catacomb 14 was
borrowed from catacomb 20, but the function of this catacomb was
quite different. A vast amount of space is devoted to very few burials;
it can only have been a family tomb. The only inscriptions mention
three rabbis, Shimon, Gamaliel, and Hanina. The first two were sons
of Rabbi Judah ha-Nasi, and the third was a close collaborator. It
seems likely, therefore, that this was the tomb that the Patriarch had
prepared for himself and his family. The simplicity of the graves
here is in vivid contrast to the ornate sarcophagi in catacomb 20;
in a family unit all were honoured by the monumental façade.

Both catacombs (14 and 20) are surmounted by open-air structures
comprising rows of benches and a wall with an apse. These were
assembly places where the dead were remembered in prayer and
study. Above catacomb 23 (between 14 and 20) a plain square mosaic
floor without benches probably served the same function.

The great development of the cemetery that followed on the burial
there of Rabbi ha-Nasi brought with it commercial rationalization,
and all the catacombs cut subsequently conform to a common plan.
A certain flexibility was necessary, however, because some clients
could afford more than others. Catacomb 12 was designed for the

wealthy; it is spacious and well-organized; the one-grave arcosolia in one hall are carefully segregated from the less expensive multi-grave arcosolia in the other hall. Just alongside is catacomb 13 where the intention was obviously to get the maximum number of graves into the minimum space. The area is roughly the same, but whereas catacomb 12 has 56 burial places in two halls on the same level, catacomb 13 has 192 burial places in twelve halls on four levels. No provision was made for sarcophagi in any of the later catacombs; their size and weight (four tons) would have raised costs to an unacceptable level.

In view of the biblical prohibition of images many of the motifs carved in the sarcophagi of catacomb 20 are surprising: Eros, Aphrodite, Nike, and Amazons are the most explicit borrowings from pagan mythology. Their presence in a centre of religious orthodoxy demonstrates that rabbis of the C3 AD made a distinction between images intended for worship and images intended as simply decorative. They mitigated the absolute character of the Second Commandment by emphasizing the second sentence, 'You shall not bow down before them' (Exod. 20: 4–5; Deut. 5: 8–9).

BET YERAH (N7)

The present exit of the River Jordan from the Sea of Galilee is the southern boundary of the 50-acre tel of Bet Yerah. From the bridge over the Jordan the modern road runs through the middle of the tel whose northern extremity is marked by a cemetery. This point was the exit of the Jordan from the lake up to the medieval period. The ruins are located between the road and the lake 400 m north of the second road junction north of the bridge, or 200 m south of the cemetery.

The site was first occupied in the 4th millennium BC, but after these people, who produced the famous Khirbet Kerak ware, moved away about 2000 BC the site remained unsettled until the Persian period (586–332 BC). The city developed greatly in the Hellenistic period; it has been suggested that it be identified with Philoteria built by Ptolemy II Philadelphus (285–246 BC). Occupation continued through the Roman and Byzantine periods but the city does not appear to have been involved in any notable historical events. From Talmudic sources we know only that Jews and Gentiles lived side by side.

Visit. The ruins are in a bad state of preservation, and offer nothing of exceptional interest.

About 100 m south of the cemetery is a Byzantine church. The original building is dated to the first half of the C5 AD, but various reconstructions (the last in the early C6) modified the plan considerably.

South of the church is a C3 AD Roman fort; it is 60 m square with a tower at each corner; the main gate in the south wall was flanked with similar towers. The fort was abandoned late in the C4, and in the next century one of the largest Byzantine synagogues in the country was erected within its walls. An apse in the south wall orients it towards Jerusalem; only part of the mosaic floor is preserved.

In the same period a bath-house was built against the south-east corner of the fort; the heated rooms are arranged on two sides of the square frigidarium with its central pool. This building rests on the corner of a large rectangular structure dated around 2500 BC. It is a broad pavement holding a series of very shallow circular pits 8 m in diameter; each circle is divided into four by stone partitions. These are the foundations for a series of grain silos, showing that the area must have been intensively cultivated.

CAESAREA (G9)

Capital of Palestine for almost 600 years, later a Crusader port, Caesarea was renowned for the splendour of its buildings. Three of its columns are now in Venice, and its most beautiful stones adorn the C18 AD structures of Jezzar Pasha in AKKO. None the less, recent excavations and careful restorations enable the visitor to recapture the highpoints of its colourful history.

The city was founded by Herod the Great (37–4 BC) on the site of an ancient anchorage known as Strato's Tower from its identifying landmark. Strato is the Greek form of a name borne by three kings of Sidon in the C4 BC, and a century earlier, in gratitude for the assistance of the Sidonian fleet in the invasion of Greece, the Persians had granted the coast between Dor and Yafo (Jaffa) to Sidon. The anchorage served traders plying between Phoenicia and Egypt; it is first mentioned by Zenon, an Egyptian official, who landed there for supplies in 259 BC. A fortified town gradually developed which changed hands many times before being given to Herod by the emperor Augustus in 30 BC.

Josephus waxes even more lyrical than usual about the marvels of Herod's constructions (*War* 1: 408–15; *Antiquities* 15: 331–41), being particularly impressed by the size of the port and the ingenuity of the sewer system. He also mentions the grid street pattern, a temple dedicated to Caesar, a palace, a theatre, and an amphitheatre. The extent of the Herodian city is uncertain because no wall has so far been discovered. After the Romans assumed direct control of Palestine in AD 6 Caesarea became the capital. Presumably the official representative of Rome had his residence there from this time, but the first we are certain of is Pontius Pilate (AD 26–36); an inscription bearing his name was found in the ruins of the theatre. Cornelius, a centurion of the Roman garrison, was the first Gentile converted to Christianity by Peter (Acts 10). Paul passed through the port several times on his missionary journeys, and was imprisoned for two years (AD 58–60) in Herod's praetorium until he forced a decision by demanding to be judged by the emperor (Acts 23–6).

Tensions between Jews and Gentiles always ran high in Caesarea; the desecration of the synagogue was one of the contributory causes of the First Revolt (AD 66–70). When Vespasian arrived to put it down he established his headquarters in the city, and directed operations from there until the legions acclaimed him emperor in 69. Thereafter, the city became a Roman colony, though with limited rights. As the principal channel for both exports and imports its prosperity continuously increased, creating an environment which made other developments possible, notably scholarship.

At the beginning of the C3 AD, after the city had been declared levitically clean, Bar Qappara founded a rabbinical school which soon rivalled that of his master, Rabbi Judah ha-Nasi, at Sepphoris (see BET SHEARIM). A graduate of this school, Yohanan bar Nappaha, founded the great academy at TIBERIAS, but the chief glory of rabbinical Caesarea is Abbahu, who was active around the beginning of the C4 AD. The anti-Christian polemic which characterized the rabbis of Caesarea was nullified by the ironic brilliance of Origen (185–254). The tradition of scholarship which he inaugurated during his twenty-year residence here (231–50) was continued by Pamphilius (d. 309); by adding to the manuscript collection of Origen he created a library second only to that of Alexandria; in 630 it had 30,000 volumes. His pupil Eusebius (260–340), who became bishop of Caesarea in 314, is both the first church historian and the first biblical geographer; without his Onomasticon many biblical sites would never have been identified.

The intellectual vitality of Caesarea had virtually disappeared long before the city fell to the Arabs in 640. They permitted the port to silt up, but the fertility of the hinterland continued to make it one of the richest cities in the area. A terrible massacre followed the victorious Crusader siege in May 1101; a hexagonal green glass thought to be the Holy Grail formed part of the booty of the Genoese. Since they relied principally on Akko and Yafo, the Crusaders rehabilitated only part of the Herodian port.

The city was destroyed many times after its capture by Saladin in 1187. The visible fortifications were erected within a year (1251–2) by Louis IX of France, but offered no effective resistance to the Makeluke sultan Baybars in 1265. The inhabitants, who had taken refuge in the citadel on the southern breakwater, escaped by night to Akko in the midst of peace negotiations; in reprisal Baybars levelled the city. It lay abandoned until 1878 when the Turks installed Muslim refugees from Bosnia on the site. Their little mosque beside the port is all that remains of the village obliterated in 1948.

Visit. (fig. 52). The exits from the Tel Aviv–Haifa highway are clearly indicated, as is the access road skirting Sedot Yam.

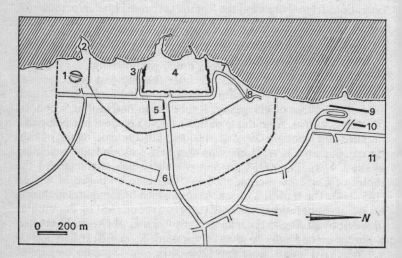

Fig. 52. Caesarea.

The Crusader city [4] is the centrepiece of the site (open: 8 a.m.–5 p.m.; Fridays to 4 p.m.) and a detailed guide is unnecessary because signs identify and date all the excavated architectural remains. The one exception is the Crusader citadel on the breakwater. A restaurant has been built on top of the ruins. On the other side of the road one can see the sea moat dividing the citadel from the town; the marble and granite columes integrated into the base of the tower made it impossible to sap.

The Crusader city represents only a fraction of the area occupied by earlier cities; the Hellenistic city [. . . . . .] was over three times greater, and the Byzantine city [– – – –] nearly eight times larger. Within and without these now-invisible walls are many interesting remains which should not be missed; all are easily accessible by car.

The theatre [1] is the first monument encountered coming from the highway (open: 7.30 a.m.–4 p.m.; Fridays to 3 p.m.). Just inside the ticket office is a replica of the Pontius Pilate inscription; a suggested restoration reads:

> [Dis Augusti]s Tiberieum
> [Po]ntius Pilatus
> [Praef]ectus Juda[ea]e
> [fecit d]e[dicavit]

'Pontius Pilate, Prefect of Judea, made and dedicated the Tiberieum to the Divine Augustus'. The reconstructed theatre is used for concerts. In subsequent centuries some elements of the original Herodian structure were modified and others added; the semicircular platform behind the stage was added in the C3 AD. The great wall with two towers is part of a C6 Byzantine fortress built over the ruins of the theatre.

From the fence around the theatre area one can look down on to a rocky promontory [2] which was the site of a fish farm (perhaps Herodian). Towards the far end (west) of the rectangular (35 × 18 m) rock-cut pool, channels with smaller pools link it to the sea on both sides. A further channel with a stone sluice-gate leads to three parallel pools further west. A mosaic floor was discovered on the terracing at the east end of the big pool. The date and function of the walls is uncertain. The siting of this complex shows that the sea-level has not changed in the last 2,000 years.

Excavations are still in progress just south of the Crusader city [3]. It has been suggested that the series of small rooms with mosaic floors formed part of the famous library founded by Pamphilius. The circular and semicircular structures further west (towards the sea) belonged to a Byzantine bath. From the beach one can see the ends of a series of vaults originally built as port warehouses; one was transformed into a Mithraeum in the C4 AD.

In the eastern section of the main parking-lot a Byzantine street has been brought to light [5]. An inscription at the foot of the steps attributes it to Flavius Strategius, a mayor of the C6 AD. Two columns create a triple entrance to the square paved with marble slabs. The two statues are much older (C2–C3 AD) and originally belonged to temples. The white marble statue is unidentified, but the dark porphyry one is considered to represent the emperor Hadrian (AD 117–38) holding a sceptre and orb. The statue was probably commissioned from the one porphyry quarry in the ancient world, in Egypt, during his first visit to Caesarea (130) and dedicated during his second (133–4). The present chair is not the original; the side had to be broken to take the statue.

A modern arch [6] just beside the road is the easiest way to identify the hippodrome which is now just a great rectangular ploughed field 460 m long. It may have been constructed by Herod; the races at Caesarea were world-famous in the C4 AD. The remains are monumental but uncared for. The square base of the obelisk lies against the east fence; the obelisk itself lies where it fell from the *spina* in the middle of the racecourse. Piled beside it are the bases of the conical turning-points; their upper portions were found in the harbour. The tip of the obelisk is near the fence on a line between the obelisk and the modern pumping-station. Slight irregularities in the terrain, seen in aerial photographs, establish the line of the Byzantine city wall outside the hippodrome.

Immediately north of the Crusader wall is the synagogue area [7]. The remains left by the archaeologists do not offer any coherent pattern. A series of superimposed synagogues were built here from the C3 to the C5 AD. Foundations of houses of the Hellenistic period (C4–C2 BC) were found at the lowest level; the large wall visible in the sea below may have been part of the harbour of Strato's Tower.

A little further to the north the road crosses a massive city wall with two towers [8]. The round tower is evocative of those discovered at SAMARIA; note that the lowest course is all headers. This suggests a date in the Hellenistic period; the wall is certainly earlier than the high-level aqueduct which crosses it. It is uncertain whether the wall served a function in the Herodian city. Inside are two large buildings;

outside, at a higher level, is a paved Byzantine street with a sewer cutting through the wall then out of use; the section outside the wall connects with another sewer running east–west. The oval depression in the fields to the east is thought to be the amphitheatre mentioned by Josephus. From this point on, the road becomes very rough and, in order to reach the aqueducts further north, it is preferable to go back past the hippodrome [6] and take Aqueduct Road, the first turning on the left.

The high-level aqueduct [9] contains two channels with independent foundations. The eastern side (facing the parking-lot) was built by Herod; note the cornice on both sides. The western side (facing the sea) was added by Hadrian; the parallel earthenware pipes are probably Byzantine; the Crusaders blocked this channel completely in order to create a higher and smaller channel. The arched structure is 5 km long; once it reaches the hills north of Binyamina it continues in a series of channels and tunnels which extend it another 10 km.

The roofed low-level aqueduct [10] is dated to the C4 AD by the dams in the Kabbara marches 5 km to the north. These monumental structures (one 197 m long, the other 900 m) created a vast reservoir and raised the water level to the requisite height. Arab troops used the tunnel to infiltrate Caesarea in 640.

A dirt road just east of the low-level aqueduct leads to a curious little building [11] whose construction clearly shows that its function involved the use of water. One immediately thinks of a bath; the excavators note the traces of crosses adorned with precious stones and of Greek letters associated with Christian symbolism. It appears unlikely that it was a baptistry.

CAESAREA PHILIPPI: *see* BANYAS

CAPERNAUM (N5)

Frequently mentioned in the gospels, Capernaum was apparently the closest to a permanent base that Jesus had during the Galilean ministry; it is referred to simply as 'his own city' (Matt. 9: 1; Mark 2: 1). Much of the town that he knew has been brought to light again, together with a primitive house-church later transformed into an octagonal building. The most famous synagogue of Galilee has been partially restored.

Though traces of occupation in the C13 BC have been discovered, the history of the town begins in the C2 BC. When Herod's kingdom was divided after his death, it fell to the lot of Herod Antipas. As the first town encountered by travellers coming from his brother Philip's territory on the other side of the Jordan, it was equipped with a customs office (Matt. 9: 9) and a small garrison under a centurion. The poverty of the inhabitants can be inferred from the fact that the latter, a Gentile, had to build them a synagogue (Luke 7: 1–10). At this period the place had little depth and stretched along the lake front for some 500 m. No unique advantages induced Jesus to settle there; it offered nothing that could not be found in the other lakeside towns. He probably chose it because his first converts, the fishermen Peter and Andrew, lived there (Mark 1: 21, 29). This initial success was not maintained; Jesus' preaching had no more impact there (Luke 10: 15) than it had at Nazareth.

Rabbinic texts attest a rather aggressive Christian presence in Capernaum early in the C2, and two centuries later classify the inhabitants as archetypal sinners (from the Jewish point of view). This hint of continuous occupation is confirmed by archaeology; it was too insignificant to merit destruction. The buildings became steadily more substantial, and by the C4 the town had grown towards the hills. Some doubt regarding the continuity of Christian presence is raised by Epiphanius. Writing in 374 with reference to the time of Constantine, he says that it was one of the Galilean towns in which Jews forbade Gentiles, Samaritans, or Christians to live. This suggestion of extreme orthodoxy is contradicted by the contemporary rabbinic texts mentioned above; the truth probably lies between the two extremes. In any case when the energetic nun Egeria visited the place between 381 and 384 she found evidence of peaceful co-existence: 'At Capernaum the house of [the prince of the apostles] has been made into a church, with its original walls still standing. . . . There also is the synagogue . . . the way in is up many stairs, and it is made of dressed stone.' The anonymous pilgrim of Piacenza, writing in 570, does not mention the synagogue but records 'the house of St. Peter, which is now a basilica'. Archaeology confirms this architectural evolution, and proclaims a complete break in occupation of the site after the Arab conquest (c.700). It was never again inhabited.

Visit. Open: 8.30 a.m.–4.15 p.m.; toilets. On entering one finds oneself in an open-air museum displaying the carved stones of the ruined synagogue. These are worth looking at closely, not only in order to gain an idea of the splendour of the edifice, but because many of the details are of great interest. Enough elements exist to permit precise drawings of how the building might have looked, but no real consensus has emerged.

House of St. Peter (fig. 53). From the C1 BC to the C4 AD the site was occupied by small houses grouped around irregular courtyards [1]. A very good idea of how they looked is provided by Insula II, the only difference being that the buildings here were much poorer. The drystone basalt walls could have supported only a light roof; one automatically thinks of the cure of the paralytic in Mark 2: 1–12. One room in this complex is distinguished from the rest by a succession of floors of crushed limestone; in all the other rooms the floors are of beaten black earth or of basalt pebbles. The walls of this room were covered with plaster decorated by coloured geometric and floral designs. Graffiti were scratched in the plaster but the fragments are not well enough preserved to permit a convincing interpretation.

In the first half of the C4 AD this room was the centrepiece of a complex cut off from other sectors of the town by a wall with entrances on the north and south [2]. The room was given a more solid roof which necessitated the construction of a central arch, and was extended by the addition of other rooms on two sides. There can be little doubt that this was the house-church seen by Egeria. It may have been the work of Count Joseph of Tiberias who, according to Epiphanius, obtained from the emperor Constantine the authority to erect churches in Capernaum and other towns of Galilee.

In the middle of the C5 AD all the buildings within the enclosure were levelled in preparation for the erection of an octagonal church [3]. The central octagon enshrined the venerated room which was now given a mosaic floor. The peacock centrepiece was surrounded by a geometric design with a lotus-flower border identical with that of the Church of the Multiplication of the Loaves and Fishes (HEPTA-PEGON). The proportional relationship between the inner octagon and the two outer ones is identical with that of other churches of the same type in Italy and Syria; the closest parallel in this area is the DOME OF THE ROCK in Jerusalem. Shortly after the church's construction an apse containing a baptistry (?) was added on the east side. It seems that this edifice did not survive the Arab invasion in 638.

Certitude as to the original ownership of this room is, of course,

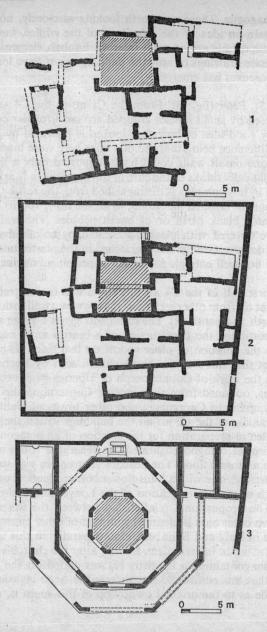

Fig. 53. The three stages in the development of the House of St. Peter (after Corbo).

impossible, but the evidence of persistent veneration in the pre-Constantinian period demands an explanation. There is nothing to contradict the assumption that it was the house of Peter in which Jesus may have lodged (Matt. 8: 20).

Insula II. This group of basalt buildings (plan on site) is bordered on all four sides by streets. Only five doors provided access from the street, suggesting that the houses grouped around small courtyards were perhaps occupied by related families; the complex could accommodate 15 families, i.e. about 100 persons in all. Note the crude windows and the stairways to the flat roofs. Occupation levels run from the C1 to the C6 AD. Insula III near the lake is of the same period, but the two other insulae (IV and V) were developed later, presumably to accommodate those whose houses were destroyed in order to make room for the synagogue.

Synagogue. The date of this building is still a matter of debate. Some assume that such a magnificent building with its doors oriented towards Jerusalem could not have been built when Christians controlled Palestine; they date it to the late C2 or early C3 AD. This prejudice is countered by archaeological evidence; coins and pottery show that the building was erected on buildings from the first part of the C4 AD. A date in the late C4, therefore, seems most appropriate. But this creates a host of other problems, notably, the proximity of a synagogue to a venerated Christian edifice, and the sharp contrast between the style of this synagogue and that of its contemporary at HAMMAT TIBERIAS. No satisfactory answers are yet available, but there may have been greater differences between Jewish groups in the Byzantine period than has been recognized, and perhaps there were places where Jews and Christians lived in harmony. The controversy over the date of the Capernaum synagogue will certainly ensure that others are dug with greater care, and if the late date is proved correct, the dates of a number of other synagogues will have to be reconsidered.

CARMEL CAVES (MEAROT KARMEL) (G7)

These are the most accessible prehistoric caves in Israel, with occupation levels going back 150,000 years. They are located just to the east of the interior road running parallel to the Tel Aviv–Haifa highway, about half-way between En Hod and Kerem Mararal. A tarmac road leads to the parking-lot facing the caves.

There are four caves. The archaeologists' dump is outside the Cave of the Oven. Moving to the left, we have first the Cave of the Camel, then the Cave of the Valley, and round the corner the Cave of the Kid. Excavations provided such an extraordinary amount of data that its interpretation is still being disputed. Nearly 100 human skeletons were brought to light, ranging from a clear Neanderthal through an intermediate type to not quite *homo sapiens*. This unusual combination can be explained in various ways – and is! Tools ranged from the crude flints of the Lower Palaeolithic Age (*c*.150,000 BC) to the sophisticated combination tools of the Natufian period (10,000–7,500 BC), e.g. small flints set in a semicircular bone haft to make a sickle. The Natufian is the first prehistoric culture to produce works of art. The Cave of the Valley (71 m deep) yielded a human head carved in limestone and animals carved in bone; outside it, several cup-marks and a 41 cm-deep pit were cut in the terrace, part of which was paved with flat stones.

CHOROZAIN (KORAZIM) (N5)

A ruined town in the hills above Capernaum, notable for its fine synagogue; entered through a new gate on the right of the side-road to Almagor.

A town existed in the C1 AD; together with Capernaum and Bethsaida it was condemned by Jesus for lack of faith (Matt. 11: 20–4). Presumably it benefited by the concentration of Jews in Galilee after the failure of the Second Revolt (AD 132–5), but at the beginning of the C4 Eusebius saw only ruins. Built in black basalt, the synagogue is similar to the limestone one at CAPERNAUM. In both, the doors face Jerusalem, and rows of pillars run parallel to the other three walls. Both exhibit the same profusion of decorative carving, even though basalt is much more difficult to work. Here the resemblance to highly formalized and rigid Byzantine carving is very marked.

The synagogue is the showpiece of the highest of the three quarters into which terraces divided the 12-acre city; the main residential quarter lay to the west. Very little has been excavated. Occupation ceased in the C8 AD.

Chorozain lies on the edge of an area containing some 300 dolmens, a Breton term meaning 'stone-table'. Large blocks of flat stone are set parallel on their sides, while another is laid over them like a tabletop. It is not unusual for each stone to weigh over a ton. The whole was covered by a mound of earth or stones; often this has eroded, revealing the original nucleus. They were used as burial chambers, and are dated to between 6000 and 4000 BC. The closest are immediately to the east and south-east of the synagogue.

CHURCH OF THE MULTIPLICATION OF THE LOAVES AND FISHES: *see* HEPTAPEGON

CHURCH OF THE PRIMACY: *see* HEPTAPEGON

CRUSADES

The Crusades were a series of military expeditions which established and maintained a European Christian presence in the Holy Land from 1099 to 1291. Groups in fact came annually, but the largest are numbered in a conventional order.

The First Crusade took Jerusalem on 15 July 1099, having breached the north wall near Herod's Gate about noon. Godfrey of Bouillon was elected leader, but Tancred, a Norman from Sicily, made the first territorial gain by conquering Galilee later that year. The foundations of the Latin Kingdom were established by Baldwin I (1100–18) who passed most of the nights of his reign in his battle-tent. He first secured the coast (1101–5), then expanded the northern border to link up with the Principality of Tripoli (1106–10), and finally cut communications between Damascus and Cairo by setting up a line of fortresses on the east side of the Araba, the valley linking the Dead Sea with the Gulf of Aqaba (1115–16).

Reinforcements brought by the Second Crusade in 1147 provided the manpower to hold this territory, but more and more reliance was placed on the permanent standing army constituted by the two great military orders, the Hospitallers (1109) and the Templars (1128). Starting as small groups of dedicated knights, these orders soon became immensely wealthy and powerful organizations furnishing highly trained and disciplined cavalry units.

Castles guarded the major lines of communication, but two groups of fortresses had a special function: one in the north blockaded Tyre (captured 1224), and another in the south blockaded ASHQELON (captured 1153).

Saladin came to power in Egypt in 1170 but he became a serious threat only when he changed his battle tactics. At the beginning he relied on Egyptians whose cavalry, backed up by archers, fought at close quarters; these elements had no answer to the disciplined weight of the Frankish charge. Later Saladin switched to Kurdish mounted archers who never provided a target for the charge, the one tactical weapon of the Crusaders. In reply the Crusaders developed the armoured column which could move through the Kurds guaranteeing a stalemate but never victory. On 3 July 1187, by slowing the advance of a column comprising the whole army of the Latin Kingdom of Jerusalem, Saladin ensured success next day at the HORNS OF HATTIN; the knights had exhausted their water supplies and could not fight effectively.

A new military order, the Teutonic Knights, came into being during the Third Crusade (1189–92) when a combination of military threat and adroit diplomacy led to a new Latin Kingdom with territory in Galilee and around Jerusalem. A series of treaties in the first half of the C13 gave the Crusaders more land, but then the tide turned as the Mamelukes of Egypt began to make forays into Palestine. The Crusaders were first pushed back towards the sea. Then Baybars (1260–77) began his advance up the coast taking city after city in a series of campaigns. Acre (AKKO), the last strong-point, fell in 1291.

There are extensive Crusader remains throughout the country, but only some are really worth a visit:

Churches: in Jerusalem – HOLY SEPULCHRE, ST. ANNE'S, VIRGIN'S TOMB; outside Jerusalem – ABU GHOSH, HEBRON, NABI SAMWIL, SAMARIA, QUBEIBA, LATRUN.

Castles: BELVOIR, MONTFORT, NIMRUD.

Towns: AKKO, CAESAREA.

An excellent map, 'The Crusader Kingdom of Jerusalem (1099–1291)', is published by the Survey of Israel.

DAN: *see* TEL DAN

DEAD SEA (M18–25)

The level of the sea fluctuates so its measurements are not constant: at present it is 80 km long and 18 km at its widest point; at 399 m below sea-level it is the lowest point on the earth. The bottom of a great sink-hole near the north end is 400 m beneath the surface. The sea has no exit and water is lost only through evaporation, in summer as much as 25 mm in 24 hours. This produces a concentrated accumulation of salts near the surface (275 g per litre), notably magnesium chloride, sodium chloride, calcium chloride, and potassium chloride. Being nearly seven times as dense as ordinary sea-water, one can sit in it and read a newspaper comfortably; drowning is impossible but water in the lungs is fatal.

At the turn of the century the Dead Sea was 7 m higher than it is today, but in the first decades of the C19 it was 3 m below its present level. This variation is directly related to the rainfall; in recent times the volume of water coming into the sea has been even further reduced by pumping from the Sea of Galilee and the Yarmuk river. The ford linking the Lisan (HaLashon) with the west bank, passable in 1820, is again emerging. If the earthquake responsible for the southern part of the sea occurred in historical times, it might also have destroyed Sodom and Gomorrah (Gen. 19: 24), traditionally located in that area.

The commercial exploitation of the Dead Sea (today centred on Sodom) was anticipated by the NABATAEANS. As early as the C4 BC they collected bitumen which they sold to the Egyptians for embalming. This remained an important industry well into the Roman period (*War* 4: 480); special boats were developed to sweep it from the surface. The physical properties of the sea excited the curiosity of eminent minds from the time of Aristotle (384–322 BC). He mentions it, as do Strabo, Pliny, Tacitus, Pausanius, and Galen; the last two first used the present name in the C2 AD. The sea carried heavy marine traffic in the Byzantine and Crusader periods, but thereafter became the 'Sea of the Devil' and a magnet for all sorts of legends (e.g. no birds could fly over it) until the successful exploration by the US Navy in 1848.

A magnificent scenic road runs along the west side of the Dead Sea, providing easy access to a number of important sites. Just south of QUMRAN a green area is created by a number of brackish springs collectively called Ein Fashkha or Enot Zuqim. The ruins of an

ESSENE farm are visible on the right of the entrance to the bathing area; the salt of the Dead Sea can be washed off in fresh-water swimming pools. After skirting the headland, Rosh Zuqim, the road emerges on to the alluvial fan of the Wadi ed-Nar (Nahal Qidron); this wadi is easily identified because the detergent from the sewers of Jerusalem is still intact as the evil-smelling stream passes under the road. A small ruin between the road and the sea on the north edge of the delta is called Khirbet Mazin; though dated to the Roman period, it is unclear whether it had any connection with the Essenes.

Other ruins occur further south in the area of dense vegetation between Enot Qane and Enot Samar (Ein el-Ghuweir and Ein at-Turaba). Those between the cliffs and the modern road are from the C8 BC, whereas those just east of the road were occupied from the reign of Herod the Great (37–4 BC) until the middle of the C1 AD. The pottery from this latter building (a large room with a kitchen in the corner) is identical with that of the post-earthquake period at Qumran, and the cemetery 800 m to the north exhibits precisely the same form of burial as at Qumran. The Essenes may have retreated here when they were forced to abandon Qumran during the reign of Herod the Great.

The road to the top of the cliffs at Mizpe Shalem is being extended to connect with the HERODION; from the parking-lot to the left just before the settlement there is an unparalleled view over the Dead Sea. About 1·5 km west of the settlement a small white sign near the road marks the beginning of the trail down to the caves in the Wadi Murabbaat which yielded manuscripts of the Second Revolt (AD 132–5), including an autograph letter of Simon Ben-Kosba (= Bar Kokhba). The dangerous path should be attempted only in the company of someone who knows the desert.

In addition to its archaeological remains the oasis of EN GEDI offers bathing in the Dead Sea and the magnificent nature reserve in Nahal Arugot. During the Second Revolt the Roman camps above the Nahal Hever were supplied through this valley, and from the circular Roman fort on the little plateau to the right (north) of the path near the hidden waterfall one can see the marvellous cliff road (Maale Isiyyim) built by the legion on the far side of the wadi. In order to climb it an experienced guide is essential.

Nahal Hever drains into the Dead Sea about 7 km south of En Gedi. Its vertical cliffs are honeycombed by caves in which followers of Bar Kokhba took refuge; under the eyes of the Romans above they died of thirst and starvation, leaving behind many documents of the C1 and C2 AD. These caves are now totally inaccessible.

The first group of hotels 14 km south of the entrance to MASADA marks the site of En Boqeq. Its present development as a health spa continues an ancient tradition because in the Herodian period pharmaceutical plants were cultivated here. A well-preserved fortress is clearly visible from the main road just north of the hotels. Built in the second half of the C4 AD, it was staffed by agricultural frontier militia who farmed the area where the hotels are now sited. It served until the Arab conquest in the C7.

At Newe Zohar the road divides; one continues south past Mount Sodom to Elat, the other turns west to ARAD. On this latter road two viewpoints permit one to look down into Nahal Zohar where there is another fort of the same period as that at En Boqeq. The valley (entered through the settlement) also contains an Israelite fort because this was the ancient Way of Edom; it is the only route from the Dead Sea to the west which does not involve a cliff climb.

DEAD SEA SCROLLS: *see* QUMRAN *and* ESSENES

DOR: *see* TEL DOR

DRUZE

The eighteen Druze villages in Galilee represent only a small proportion of a religious movement which has almost 200,000 adherents, most of whom live in the Shut and Matan districts of southern Lebanon, on the slopes of Mount Hermon, and in the Jebel Druze in southern Syria.

The movement originated in Egypt when the Fatimid caliph al-Hakim (AD 996–1021) permitted some of his entourage to consider him a divine being. This doctrine was first formulated by al-Darasi who presented al-Hakim as the incarnation of the cosmic intelligence in 1017. His teaching that the faithful were obliged by no moral precepts forced al-Hakim to disown him, and the use of his name to describe the movement was originally intended as abusive. In 1019 the mantle passed to Hamza ben Ali who gave the cult of al-Hakim its definitive form. He took over the classic Ismailite doctrine that all proceeds from the One and returns to the One through knowledge, but modified it by insisting on the immediate presence of the cosmic One incarnated in al-Hakim. The Druze, therefore, call themselves *Muwahhadun*, 'Unitarians'. Knowledge of the One was the only way of salvation; the symbolism and practices of the revealed religions no longer had any meaning.

After the unexplained disappearance of al-Hakim during a nocturnal excursion in Cairo in 1021, Hamza also withdrew after delegating his powers to al-Muktana. The latter encouraged the missionary expansion of the movement by numerous letters written between 1021 and 1042 which gave it a criterion of orthodoxy. Although he himself objected to the importance given to his work, later Druze tradition considers him responsible for the collection of 111 letters (mostly his own but some from al-Hakim and Hamza) which became their canonical scripture, 'The Letters of Wisdom'.

After the withdrawal of al-Muktana all missionary activity ceased, and the Druze became a closed community permitting neither conversion nor defection. Those who believed in the time of Hamza are continually reincarnated as Druze; this long-drawn-out process of purification will make them capable of ruling the human race when al-Hakim and Hamza return to establish justice.

At least since the C15 Druze have been divided into 'the wise' and 'the ignorant'; the latter are not initiated into the secret doctrines of the community. Any adult Druze, male or female, can ask to be initiated. Those who pass the severe test become 'wise'; those who fail have another chance in their next reincarnation. The 'wise' wear a distinguishing garment and a white turban. Their privileged position is also one of greater responsibility, for they are obliged to participate in the cult ceremonies on Thursday evenings, to say the daily prayers, to abstain from drink, lying, theft and vengeance. The 'ignorant' enjoy greater freedom. The more pious or learned among the 'wise' are accorded the authority of sheikhs. They receive instruction in a special school and are expected to spend some time in contemplation in retreat-houses located in remote areas. In addition to copying their sacred scriptures, the sheikhs offer spiritual direction to the 'ignorant' and preside at marriages and funerals. In each Druze district one sheikh, normally from a particular family, is recognized as the supreme religious authority.

The political history of the Druze is one of internal and external struggle. While different dynasties vied for internal power, the community had to fight for its identity against Christians and Muslims; there were two Druze uprisings in the 1920s. They are in consequence a hardy, vigorous people who do not ask for friendship but who demand respect.

The Druze hold Jethro, Moses' father-in-law and adviser, in special reverence. They call him Nebi Shueib, and his tomb below the HORNS OF HATTIN is one of their holiest sites. On 25 April each year thousands gather there for a great festival.

EMMAUS: *see* **ABU GHOSH, LATRUN,** *and* **QUBEIBA**

EN AVDAT (E28)

The plain between Kibbutz Sede Boker and the ancient city of AVDAT is slashed by a deep canyon which is the nature reserve of En Avdat. There are two entrance roads, one leading into the bottom of the canyon from Midreshet Sede Boker, the other, further south, leading to the observation point on the rim of the canyon.

The canyon with its long deep pool is beautiful, but the area on the top of the cliffs is more interesting because prehistoric tribes camped there for over 100,000 years. They dwelt, not in caves, but in huts made of branches. The sections of the plain in which they lived can be detected by observing the concentrations of flint tools: their darker colour makes them stand out from the brown soil. The easiest section to find is on the north rim of the canyon where there is a big Middle Palaeolithic site (80,000–35,000 BC) in the vicinity of a section of the C1 AD Nabataean trade route linking Avdat with the port of Gaza. The road is recognized by the line of untrimmed kerb stones. The density of prehistoric occupation is shown by the fact that flint tools here cover an area of 1 sq. km, and in addition are found up to 1 m beneath the present surface. Other sites appear on the crest of the line of low hills to the north; these yield small tools of the Upper Palaeolithic and Mesolithic periods (35,000–15,000 BC).

EN GEDI (L21)

Date-palms, vineyards, aromatic and medicinal plants made En Gedi in biblical times a symbol of beauty (Sir. 24: 14; S. of S. 1: 14). It is still a vivid slash of green on the barren coast of the Dead Sea;

one can even swim beneath the waterfall in Nahal David (fig. 54). Tribes just emerging from the Stone Age came to the plateau above the waterfall to worship in a little temple from which there is a spectacular view over the oasis and the southern part of the Dead Sea.

Chalcolithic Temple (A). Access is by either of two paths, each 15 minutes' walk. One branches to the left before the waterfall in Nahal

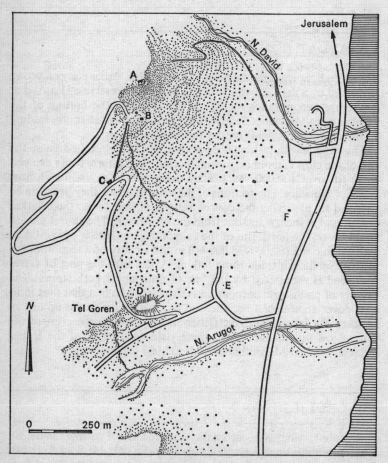

Fig. 54. En Gedi.

David, the other is easier and starts at the parking-lot at the foot of Tel Goren (D); a long detour can be avoided by taking the short cut from the Byzantine building (C).

The temple was in use about 3000 BC and, since no trace of habitation was found in the surrounding area, it must have served as a central sanctuary for the region. Why it was abandoned no one really knows, but some sort of threat is suspected, because it seems likely that the hoard of 416 copper objects, found in the Cave of the Treasure in Nahal Mishmar (6 km south), belonged to the temple. The copper crowns and the wands tipped with figures of birds and animals suggest cult objects. Carbon dating of the straw mats in which they were wrapped show that the dates coincide.

The mud-brick walls have eroded to nothing but their stone foundations remain to reveal the complete plan (fig. 55). Each of the two entrances faces a spring further down the hill. The elaborate main entrance [1] lacks part of the bench; the door was designed to open

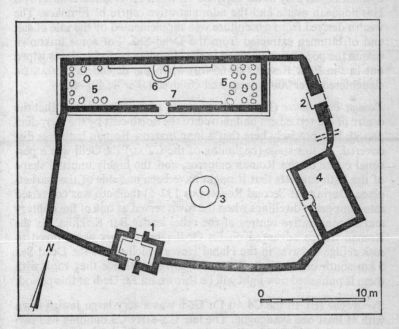

Fig. 55. En Gedi. Chalcolithic Temple (after Ussishkin).

flush with the wall. Beside the other entrance [2] a small opening in the bottom of the wall was the exit for the drain of the once plastered basin [3]. One of the two buildings [4] may have been a storeroom, or even the home of a resident priest. The other was certainly used for cultic purposes. At either end [5] offerings were buried in small pits. Sacrifice was offered in the centre [6] where a thick ash layer contained animal bones, beads, and broken figurines. A neat recess [7] received the opened door.

Tel Goren (D). The amusingly vulgar encounter between David and Saul (1 Sam. 24) suggests that there was no permanent occupation here in the C10 BC. The tel is not worth a visit, but it shows that the first Israelite town was established at the end of the C7 BC when a square tower (B) guarded the precious water supply. From the spring there is a path of this period to the top of the cliff (Ascent of Ziz) and thence the ancient road leads to Tekoa.

Occupation continued after the exile, but intensive economic development began only in the early C2 BC when En Gedi became a royal Hasmonaean estate and the administrative centre of Idumaea. The wealth derived from agriculture was supplemented by the sale of salt and of bitumen extracted from the Dead Sea. For some unknown reason the population declined in the Herodian period and was wiped out in the First Revolt (AD 66–70) when the defenders of MASADA slaughtered over 700 women and children (*War* 4: 401–4).

Roman Bath-house (F). The later strata of Tel Goren show that the centre of the settlement had moved to the north-east by the Herodian period. It is precisely here that a long, narrow Roman bath was discovered. At this stage (beginning of the C2 AD) En Gedi was a personal estate of the Roman emperor, and the highly unusual shape of the bath suggests that it might have been one side of the marketplace. During the Second Revolt (AD 132–5) the bath was converted into temporary dwellings when the town served as one of the military and administrative centres of the rebel leader Bar Kokhba. As the Roman troops advanced on En Gedi rebel officers were forced to seek refuge in caves in the Nahal Hever which enters the Dead Sea 5 km south of En Gedi. When the correspondence they took with them is published new light will be thrown on En Gedi at this period.

Synagogue (E). In the C4 AD En Gedi was a very large Jewish town with at least one synagogue. The late C2–early C3 building had two entrances in the north wall. In the second half of the C5 the orientation was changed. A semicircular niche in the north wall (housing the Scrolls of the Law) was flanked by a stepped seat for the head of the community. The only living things represented in the mosaic floor were birds; the western aisle was composed of five inscriptions in Hebrew and Aramaic. The second from the niche lists the twelve signs of the Zodiac in significant contrast to the figured representations at Naaran and BET ALPHA. Such isolation probably induced the Jews to leave En Gedi after the Arab conquest in the C7. Until this century it was frequented only by bedouin.

ESHTEMOA (SAMMU) (H22)

After his campaign against the Amalekites David (1004–965 BC) divided the spoils among the towns and villages south of HEBRON which had given him and his men hospitality when he badly needed it. Eshtemoa was one of these (1 Sam. 30: 28). In the C4 Eusebius classified it as 'a very large Jewish village'; this assessment is borne out by the monumental synagogue dated to that century.

The access road (signposted) from the main Hebron–Beer Sheva road ends in a T-junction; take the right-hand branch and then turn left in the open space in the centre of the village. The synagogue is just beside the mosque; if the guard is not present, ask anyone to find him.

The disposition of the synagogue, which remained in use until the C7 AD, is identical with that at nearby KHIRBET SUSEYA. The *bema* (raised platform), orienting the building towards Jerusalem, stands in the middle of the north wall; the unusual depression in the centre may have been for the chair of Moses. In the wall above are three niches; the centre one contained the Scrolls of the Law while those on either side housed ritual objects, such as menorah. The niche built above the benches in the opposite wall is the *mihrab* added (by Saladin, according to legend) when the synagogue was converted into a mosque in the Middle Ages.

The walls rise to a considerable height (in one place 8 m) but it is clear that the façade has been badly restored. Vertical moulding betrays that there were originally two lateral doors, now blocked up. The centre door has been narrowed, which means that the lintel cannot be the original one; many such lintels can be seen in the older buildings of the village, particularly those near the T-junction.

ESSENES

The discovery of the Dead Sea Scrolls in early 1947, and the subsequent excavation of QUMRAN, threw new light on the Essenes, already known from detailed accounts in the C1 AD writings of Philo (*Quod Omnis* n. 75–91) and Josephus (*War* 2: 119–61; *Antiquities* 18: 18–22).

The sect originated in Babylon as a reaction against the religious laxity which had provoked the divine punishment of the exile (586–538 BC). The members of this New Covenant dedicated themselves to perfect observance of the Law. Some returned to Judaea about 164 BC, and immediately found themselves at odds with the religious establishment. To their highly conservative eyes the Judaism of the Temple had irremediably compromised itself by assimilating foreign elements. A naïve attempt to convince Jews that the Essenes alone had the truth failed, and the morale of the returned exiles began to crumble. To get away from the hostile pressures of Jerusalem they settled in rural areas. This attempt to salvage their identity was not entirely successful, but only a small number accepted the leadership of the Teacher of Righteousness and moved to Qumran about 150 BC. The tension between the Teacher and the Man of Lies described in some of the scrolls reflects this split in the Essene movement.

The Teacher of Righteousness was the one significant convert made by the Essenes in Judaea. A member of the Sadok family, traditional holders of the High Priesthood until dispossessed in favour of others more amenable to the hellenizing policy of the Seleucids, he was predisposed to radical religious reform. A power vacuum in the religious establishment (159–152 BC) gave him the chance to act as High Priest. His summary dismissal by Jonathan, whom the scrolls call the Wicked Priest, brought him into the Essene camp. A powerful spiritual personality (some of his hymns are preserved), he gave his followers an even more radical orientation,

The rigorous austerity of life at Qumran attracted few adherents until persecution of the Pharisees towards the end of the reign of John Hyrcanus (134–103 BC) forced a number of them to seek refuge in this remote desert settlement. The grudging external obedience they offered in return for security provoked a period of spiritual difficulty attested in the scrolls. The community recovered its equilibrium in time to survive the dislocation caused by the earthquake of 31 BC. When it was broken up by the Romans in AD 68 at least one member escaped to MASADA with a scroll, 'The Songs of the Sabbath Sacrifices'. What happened to the others no one knows.

At Qumran the food supply came from flocks of sheep and from the farm run by the Essenes in the Buqei'a (the flat plain above the cliffs behind the settlement). It is still possible to trace the cliff-path they used. Subsidiary settlements around the brackish springs of Ein Feshkha and Ein el-Ghuweir, further south on the shore of the DEAD SEA, also contributed their share. Some members devoted a considerable portion of each day to such work. Others laboured as potters or scribes, and the kitchen staff must have been large. Saturday was a day of absolute rest; they did not even relieve themselves because their regulations demanded that they dig a hole.

The Law was the *raison d'être* of the Essenes and it was studied twenty-four hours each day. During the day one in each group of ten took it in turns, and the whole community was divided into three to cover the three night watches. The need for copies of the books of the Old Testament is obvious, and the caves yielded copies of all the books of the Hebrew canon with the exception of Esther. Their study was also productive. The caves contained a series of commentaries (*pesherim*) on the prophets in which the Essenes read their own history into the inspired word. Books which now do not figure in the canon had a place in their library (e.g. Henoch, Jubilees), and the needs of liturgy and discipline forced them to generate their own literature. These sectarian documents are easily available in a good English translation by G. Vermes, *The Dead Sea Scrolls* (Penguin Books). The 'Rule of the Community', in particular, furnishes details on the testing of candidates, the procedure in public meetings, and the more common faults of members. Such legislation reveals the very human side of life at Qumran, and balances the rather idealistic, but highly readable, description of their way of life given by Josephus in his *Jewish War* (pp. 125–9 in the Penguin Classics edition).

GAMLA (O5)

Looking due east from the long straight stretch of road at the north end of the SEA OF GALILEE (fig. 98) one can see far into a wild valley (Nahal Daliyyot) split by a steep-sided hill in the centre. The thought of a perfect natural fortress comes at once to mind. From the Golan the site (Khirbet es-Salam) is even more impressive; a narrow ridge links a ruin-encrusted rock island to the plateau. Under planing eagles the Sea of Galilee shimmers in the distance; waterfalls smoke in the valleys on either side.

The place grips the imagination; the temptation to identify it with Gamla is easily understood. According to Josephus (*War* 4: 1–83), Vespasian with three legions began the siege of Gamla (or Gamala) on 12 October AD 67. The Romans quickly broke through the wall, but suffered a defeat in the narrow confines of the town; 'the houses were built against the steep mountain flank and astonishingly huddled together, one on top of the other, and this perpendicular site gave the city the appearance of being suspended in air and falling headlong on itself' (*War* 4: 7). When the Romans had regrouped, the carelessness of the Jewish sentries permitted three legionaries to undermine a tower. This threw the population into panic but the Romans deferred their entry until the following day (10 November), permitting many to take refuge in the citadel. In the fierce battle next day, 4,000 fell before the legions; 5,000 committed suicide by flinging themselves over the cliff. The parallel with MASADA is obvious (in both cases two women escaped to tell the story), but to call Gamla 'the Masada of the North' is a poor compliment to its valiant defenders.

Khirbet es-Salam appears to fit Josephus's description of Gamla until one looks closely at the details, when difficulties begin to emerge: for example, at Gamla the citadel is south of the city on the hump (*War* 4: 8), while here the citadel is west of the hump. Josephus's description applies much more accurately to Tel ed-Dra near the village of Jamle on the Syrian side of the armistice line.

Khirbet es-Salam was certainly a Jewish fortress-town taken by the Romans during the First Revolt (AD 66–70); the slopes are strewn with the round stones fired from legion catapults. Excavations recently begun have so far brought to light a large public building on the southern slope.

GEZER (G16)

As seen from the Jerusalem–Tel Aviv highway, the low, undistinguished silhouette of Tel Gezer yields no hint of its importance. One has to stand on the top to appreciate its commanding position; there is an unimpeded view in all directions. The whole coastal plain from

Ashqelon to north of Tel Aviv is spread out like a map; no force could move there without being seen from Gezer. In antiquity it was sited at the junction of two trade routes. The Way of the Sea, the main commercial link between Egypt and Mesopotamia, passed through the plain to the west; to the north was the road between Jerusalem and the coast. No general or merchant could ignore Gezer, for its ruler had the power to disrupt all communications; the name Gezer is in fact derived from the Semitic root 'to cut', 'to divide'.

The camp-sites of the 4th millennium BC had developed into a fortified city by about 1650 BC. It was destroyed by Thutmose III *c*. 1468 BC and the record of his victory inscribed on the wall of the temple at Karnak is the first mention of the name Gezer. Thereafter, it remained under Egyptian domination, and the relationship during the C14 BC is well documented by letters in the archives of the Foreign Office at el-Amarna in Egypt. There are ten letters from various kings of Gezer and many references in letters from other city-states such as MEGIDDO and Shechem (TEL BALATA).

Egyptian control, lost some time early in the C13 BC, had to be reimposed by Merneptah in 1230 BC; the strategic importance of the city is underlined by the title he gave himself, 'The Binder of Gezer'. Egypt did not hold it long. At the beginning of the C12 BC the Philistines had to extend their authority to Gezer in order to secure their bridgehead on the coast. David skirmished in the region but never took the city (2 Sam. 5: 25; 1 Chr. 14: 16; 20: 4), perhaps because it might have drawn the wrath of Egypt upon the nascent Israelite kingdom.

At the death of David in 965 BC the Israelites had become a force to reckon with in the politics of the region. The succession was not without problems (1 Kgs. 1–2), and the pharaoh Siamun attempted to capitalize on Solomon's difficulties. He gravely underestimated the capacity of the new king and to extricate himself had to give his daughter in marriage to Solomon; her dowry was the city of Gezer (1 Kgs. 9: 16). No other foreigner ever married a pharaoh's daughter; when his request for one was denied, a Babylonian king cunningly suggested that any beautiful woman could be sent from Egypt since none of his subjects would know the difference!

The civil war, which followed Solomon's death in 928 BC, gave Egypt another chance; Gezer was abandoned for a while after its destruction during the pharaoh Shishak's murderous raid into Palestine (*c*. 924 BC). This state could not have lasted for long; its strategic position, fertile fields, and abundant water were too attractive. Gezer must have been one of the first cities taken when the Assyrians under Tiglath-Pileser III undertook two campaigns against the Philistines in 734 and 733 BC. It definitely became part of the Assyrian empire after the fall of the Northern Kingdom, Israel (to which it belonged), in 721 BC. Two business contracts of the mid-C7 BC suggest that Assyrian colonists maintained themselves there until the Babylonian invasion early the following century.

Though inhabited, Gezer seems to have lost all its importance during the C6 – C3 BC. It comes to prominence again only during the Maccabean wars of the C2 BC. First fortified by the Syrians in 160 BC (1 Macc. 9: 52), it fell to Simon Maccabaeus in 142 BC. He strengthened the fortifications and built himself a residence (1 Macc. 13: 43–8). A Greek graffito signed by one of the citizens reveals the resentment caused by the change of regime; in frustration he wrote, 'To blazes with Simon's palace!' In 141 BC Simon gave his son John Hyrcanus command of the army with headquareters at Gezer (1 Macc. 13: 53). Once the Hasmonaean dynasty had been securely established in power, Gezer apparently became a private estate. Seven boundary stones have been found, six with identical Hebrew and Greek inscriptions; the Hebrew reads, 'the boundary of Gezer', and the Greek, 'belonging to Alkios'.

Visit (fig. 56). Gezer is accessible only by means of two good-quality field roads. The shorter and less confusing begins from Kefar Bin Nun; at the right-angled bend of the tarmac road leading from the signposted junction with the old Jerusalem–Tel Aviv road continue straight ahead on the dirt road between the crops and vines which

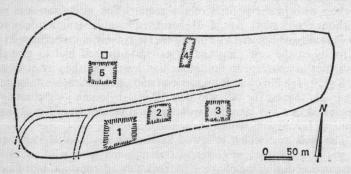

Fig. 56. Excavation areas on Tel Gezer.

goes only to the top of the tel. The alternative route starts from Kibbutz Gezer; it is wise to ask directions.

Despite extensive excavations, erosion and undergrowth limit the areas worth visiting to four, three on the south side of the tel and one on the north.

South Gate and Water System [1]. The dominant feature of this area is a great stone tower over 15 m in width. Built in the C17 BC, it is linked by a 4 m-wide wall to a gate a little further east; orthostats line the entrance and the mudbrick superstructure is beautifully defined. This wall was burnt by Thutmose III in 1468 BC, necessitating the erection of a new wall just outside at the end of the C15 BC; the gate of this period was probably outside the Solomonic gate further east.

A square pit inside the walls and between the tower and the gate is the entrance to the underground water system. Less elaborate than similar installations at MEGIDDO and HAZOR, it cannot be dated with certainty but must have been dug between the C15 and C10 BC.

Iron Age Houses [2]. The oldest houses, one with two square stone pillars, were built under Solomon. Reorganized at the beginning of the C8 BC, the quarter was destroyed by the Babylonians in 586 BC.

Solomonic Gate [3]. This magnificently preserved three-chambered gate dates from Solomon's reconstruction of Gezer in the C10 BC. Each of the chambers has a bench running around three sides; a plastered gutter at the western inner corner carried rain from the roof to the main drain running beneath the street. The large stone basin may have contained water to refresh the guards or the elders who sat at the gate. Traces of a casemate wall are visible on both sides of the gate.

High Place [4]. This row of 10 monoliths was set up about 1800 BC and functioned as a cultic centre, perhaps related to the renewal of a covenant between Gezer and other tribes or city-states. The stone block with a hollow cut in the centre may have been a basin or a socket for another monolith.

Near the edge of the mound are sections of two city walls. The inner one with a tower is contemporary with the High Place and with the South Gate [1]; the outer wall is dated to the C15 BC.

The large excavated area near the ruin of a Muslim tomb at the highest part of the mound [5] yielded private dwellings of all periods of the city's history; nothing is now visible.

GOLAN (O1–6)

The Golan is a high, basalt plateau to the east of the SEA OF GALILEE bounded on the north by Mount Hermon and on the south by the Yarmuk river. The fertile volcanic soil of the southern part gives way to wild pastureland in the north. The whole area is characterized by the small cones of extinct volcanoes.

Very little is known about the Golan; surveys have brought to light a great number of highly interesting sites but as yet there have been no systematic excavations.

The known history of the Golan begins in the C3 BC, even though human occupation has been traced back to the Lower Palaeolithic Age (500,000–120,000 BC). The most significant monuments of the early period are the dolmens built by the nomadic peoples who moved through the area *c*.1500 BC; these served as burial places.

In the C3 BC the Golan was an independent administrative unit (Gaulanitis) of the Ptolemaic empire. True development began when it was granted to Herod the Great by the emperor Augustus in 20 BC. After Herod's death in 4 BC this part of the divided kingdom fell to his son Philip who built his capital, Caesarea Philippi, at BANYAS. The strength of the Jewish population is attested by the part they played in the First Revolt against Rome (AD 66–70). The climax of the struggle for the Golan took place at GAMLA, a fortified town on a narrow rock promontory.

When Hadrian crushed the Second Revolt in 135 and forbade Jews to settle near Jerusalem, the Golan benefited by the movement of Jewish population to the north. Numerous settlements dating from the C2 and C3 AD reveal prosperous and well-organized Jewish communities everywhere throughout the area. The most accessible of these towns is QASRIN.

The victory of Omar's bedouin over the Byzantine army at the battle of the Yarmuk on 20 August AD 636 was followed by massive depopulation of the Golan; 13 Arab settlements replaced the 90 known Byzantine sites. The subsequent history of the region is shrouded in obscurity. The Crusaders were able to build and maintain only one castle, NIMRUD, at the foot of Hermon. Another castle designed to control the rich land of the south was torn down by the Atabeg of Damascus within a year and never rebuilt.

HAMMAT GADER (O7)

The hot springs in the Yarmuk valley are first mentioned by the geographer Strabo (63 BC–AD 21), and their medicinal qualities have continued to attract visitors ever since. From the top of the tel there is a fine view of the fast-flowing Yarmuk river crossed by the bridge which once carried the railway from Haifa to Damascus. The Jordanian frontier is at the far side of the river, and the road which climbs the hill leads to the ancient city of Gadara (today Umm Qeis) on the summit.

The site has never been systematically excavated, but soundings show that it was occupied in the Early Bronze Age (3150–2350 BC) and again in the Roman and subsequent periods. The nature of the area attracted pagan cults of the more uninhibited kind, but some of the most notable Jewish scholars of the C2 and C3 AD gathered there to discuss the problem of the Sabbath boundary between Gadara and the springs.

Visit. Open: 8.30 a.m.–4 p.m.; Fridays to 3 p.m. An explanatory leaflet is available on request.

A synagogue was excavated on the top of the tel, but at present only some of the walls are visible. The mosaic floor was covered for its protection, but it is proposed to expose it again. Except for one panel with two lions the design is entirely geometrical; there are four inscriptions mentioning contributors. One lists 'Moniqah of Susita the Sepphorite, and Kyris Patriqios of Kefar Aqabyah, and Yoseh the son of Dositheus of Capernaum', showing the wide area from which the baths drew clients. The apse orients the building towards Jerusalem, but in synagogues of this type it is unusual to find (as we do here) rows of pillars parallel to the other three walls. The synagogue is dated to the C5 or C6 AD.

There is also a Roman theatre whose 15 rows of basalt seats provided 2,000 places, and a Roman bath built on top of the hottest spring. Both of these, unfortunately, are inaccessible at present.

HAMMAT TIBERIAS (N6)

At least as early as the C1 AD medicinal hot springs attracted visitors to a spot just south of Tiberias (fig. 57). It is still a health spa, and the

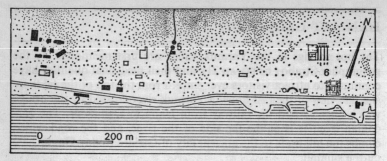

Fig. 57. Hammat Tiberias.

60°C (140°F) waters may be taken either in a picturesque Turkish bath [3] or across the road in a much more modern establishment capable of handling 2,500 bathers per day [2].

The priestly order of Maziah settled here after the destruction of the Temple in AD 70, Tiberias being forbidden to them because it was built over a cemetery. Hammat was later joined to Tiberias for halakhic purposes, and shared its fame when, in the C3, Tiberius became a great centre of Jewish learning. A faint reflection of these days of glory can be caught in the shrine of Rabbi Meir (= the Illuminator) Baal Haness (= the Miracle Worker). A famous teacher of the C2 AD, he died abroad but asked to be buried in the Holy Land. His tomb lies between the two white domes of the C19 Sephardi and Ashkenazi synagogues.

Synagogue [1] (open: 8 a.m. – 4 p.m.; Fridays to 3 p.m.). A plan is available at the ticket office, and the site is well signposted. The most notable feature is a marvellous zodiac mosaic floor, the earliest found in Palestine.

This mosaic belongs to a synagogue of the C4 AD which was an almost square room divided into four by three rows of pillars; the aisle nearest the lake may have been for women. Destroyed in the C5, the synagogue was rebuilt in a different style in the following century. An apse oriented the building towards Jerusalem; a gallery ran round the three other sides. The wall across the mosaic was the foundation for a row of pillars. This edifice survived for only a century; its replacement was destroyed in the middle of the C8. Squatters dwelt in the ruins until the C15. One of the hot springs for which the area is famous is located near the road.

The zodiac mosaic is very different from that at BET ALPHA, clearly betraying its classical origins despite the Hebrew script. In the corners are the four seasons (anticlockwise from the top left-hand corner): *Nisan*, Spring; *Tammuz*, Summer; *Tishri*, Autumn; *Tebeth*, Winter; note that of the four only Winter has her shoulders covered! The zodiac signs differ from those at Bet Alpha in several respects. Not only are the representations here more realistic (fig. 58) but they face outwards, and are correctly placed with regard to the seasons (Bet Alpha is 90 degrees out). The twelve signs start at 12 o'clock and run anticlockwise; for the list see BET ALPHA.

The verve of the upper panel at Bet Alpha is lacking here where the symbolic objects are depicted with greater realism. The rather ridiculous knotted curtain distracts from the meaning of the ark of the Law which, moreover, is overwhelmed by two great flaming menorah. Each menorah is flanked by a lulab (bundle of branches), ethrog (citrus fruit), shofar (ram's-horn trumpet), and incense shovel; their disposition is the same on both sides of the ark.

In the bottom panel two lions flank a series of Greek inscriptions in a nine-box square, but so arranged that four are read facing the zodiac, and four in the opposite direction. They give the names of the principal donors. The most important, Severus, is also mentioned in another inscription just to the left of the zodiac: 'Severus, pupil of

Fig. 58. The figure of Virgo in the zodiac mosaics at Hammat Tiberias (left) and Bet Alpha (right).

the most illustrious patriarchs, completed [the construction]. Praise
be to him and to Iullus the supervisor.' Above it is an Aramaic inscription: 'May peace rest on each one who has given an offering to
this holy place, or will give an offering. May he be blessed. Amen,
amen *sela*, and to me, amen.' Another Greek inscription in the middle
of the aisle nearest the lake reads: 'May he be remembered for good
and for blessing, Profuturus the official who provided this gallery of
the holy place. On him be a blessing. Amen. Shalom.' The inscriptions
show the importance of Greek in the Jewish community at this period.

City Gate [5]. Just beyond the tennis courts of the Ganei Hamat
Hotel [4], in the direction of Tiberias, are the uncared-for 'Tiberias
Archaeological Excavations'. As yet the site is not too badly over-
grown, and the city gate hidden in a shallow wadi is worth a visit.

Two round towers of finely dressed basalt blocks project to the
south. Inside, two small guardrooms flank the street paved with heavy
basalt slabs. Dated to the foundation of TIBERIAS by Herod Antipas
about AD 20, this complex originally stood alone, forming a ceremonial beginning to the street leading to the city. In the C6–C7 AD a
wall 2·7 m wide was built up to the towers, greatly increasing the
urban area. The other structures now visible around the gate area are
dated to the C8–C10 AD. Particularly noteworthy is a perfectly
preserved paved court around a small garden. Some 50 m south of
the gate another excavated area contains houses of the C8 AD; shops
flank the street leading to the gate. The late date of these constructions
shows that the area between Tiberias and Hammat-Tiberias was
uninhabited in the Roman and Byzantine periods.

Baths and Basilica [6]. Earlier excavations brought to light a huge
Byzantine bath-house, a colonnaded street, and a late Roman basilica.
These can still be discerned between the weeds and bushes, but are
not worth a visit. The entrance is from a very rudimentary parking-
lot some 100 m south of the modern cemetery.

HAZOR (N4)

Commanding a well-watered pass at the point where trade-routes
from the north, east, and west joined to enter northern Canaan
(fig. 59), the strategic and commercial importance of Hazor is un-

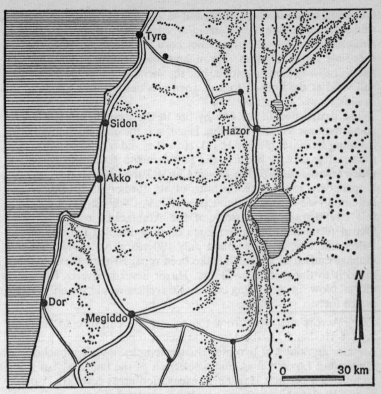

Fig. 59. Ancient trade routes in northern Canaan.

derlined by its sheer size. In its heyday, between the C18 and C13 BC, the city covered 190 acres.

A settlement had existed on the mound for over 1,000 years when in the C18 BC a new people moved in from the north. The mound (Upper City) could not contain them, and they spread on to the plateau to the north (Lower City). Its temples, public buildings, and private dwellings were protected on the north and west by a ditch and rampart and on the east by a steep glacis. Texts of the C18 BC from Mari on the river Euphrates show that Hazor had close political and economic ties with Mesopotamia; one refers to the export of tin and another to Hammurabi's ambassadors resident in Hazor. Egyptian dominion began in the C15 BC, but in the following century Hazor was unique among the Canaanite city-states; according to the Amarna letters (MEGIDDO) its ruler bore the title 'king' and was responsible for other cities. Throughout these centuries the city was periodically washed in blood, but the memory of its grandeur was still vivid at the time of Joshua when it is described as 'the head of . . . kingdoms' (Josh.: 11: 10).

The destruction of the city by fire in the second half of the C13 BC harmonizes with the note that Hazor was the only city burnt by the invading Israelites (Josh. 11: 13). How they did it remains a mystery (contrast MEGIDDO) because the first Israelite settlement reveals a much inferior culture. The Lower City was then abandoned, and the Upper City regained something of its former glory only when Solomon (965–928 BC) rebuilt part of it. A thick ash layer covering this city betrays the passage of the Aramaeans in 885 BC. The Omrid reconstruction in the same century doubled the size of the Solomonic city, but it endured only 100 years. No sooner had the damage caused by an earthquake been repaired than the Assyrians razed it to the ground in 733 BC. Hazor never recovered from this mortal blow. In succeeding centuries travellers would see only lonely police forts.

Visit. Across the road from the tel, at the entrance to Kibbutz Ayelet Hashahar, is the Hazor Museum (open: 8 a.m.–4 p.m.). It contains an exhibit of two pre-Israelite temples, a scale model of the Upper and Lower Cities, and a selection of the finds. A visit is recommended because Hazor's 14 excavation areas revealed 21 occupation levels; only the more accessible are treated here.

(1) *Area G* (fig. 60). With the exception of the C18 BC glacis and its stone-faced ditch [1], all the visible remains are from the C9–C8 BC. The filled double-wall [2] reinforced by towers [3] was built by Omri or Ahab to defend their extension of the Solomonic city. A small postern gate [4], protected by screen walls, gave access to what used to be the Lower City. When news came of the Assyrian advance in 733 BC the defenders filled in the gate with mud-brick, carefully camouflaging the outside with stones to match the wall. Just inside was a large stone-lined grain silo. Another heavy wall [5], providing a second line of defence, ran parallel to the older casemate wall found in Area A.

(2) *Area A* (fig. 61). Elements from all important levels of the city's history appear in this area, so no clearly defined pattern should be

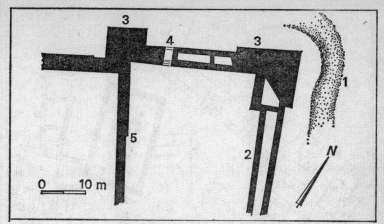

Fig. 60. Hazor. Area G (after Yadin).

expected. The Bronze Age is represented by a temple [1], the corner of a building whose thick walls suggest a palace or a citadel [7], a drain [3], and a flight of steps [4]. A 7·5 m-wide city wall of this period was found further down the slope in the trench [6]; parallel to this wall was a series of fitted clay pipes with drainage holes on top.

The destruction inflicted on this level by Joshua was completed three centuries later when Solomon levelled the area to found his new city. He installed a six-chambered gate protected by two towers [2] and a casemate wall [5]; as at MEGIDDO, only the foundations remain. The line of the casemate wall can be prolonged across the gate to Area M where it turns towards the citadel; at this point the slightly narrower Omrid wall coming from Area G joins it. The columned building [8] is of the C9 BC contemporary with the Omrid wall which, by extending the city, reduced the casemates to the status of store-rooms. The structure of the columned building is identical with that of the so-called 'stables' at Megiddo, but here the contents show indisputably that it served for storage.

When the area was rebuilt in the C8 BC after a great conflagration, the public buildings of previous periods gave way to private dwellings. The house with the pillared corner court [10] is the finest known example of its kind. Its opulence is in vivid contrast to the cramped two-rooms-and-courtyard of Mrs Makhbiram's next door [9]; the

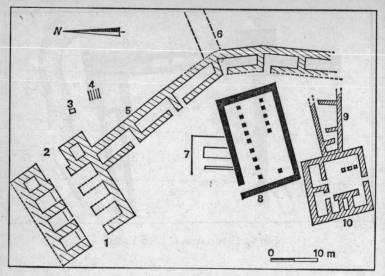

Fig. 61. Hazor. Area A (after Yadin).

name is known from an inscription and the rooms have yielded all the household furniture of an Iron Age home.

(3) *Area L.* Just inside the Solomonic casemate wall the Omrids, with expert geological advice, dug a 19 m-deep rectangular shaft through solid rock and from it a 25 m stepped tunnel to find the water level within the hill. The menace of Assyria made preparations to withstand a siege imperative. The beautifully engineered entrance was controlled from a four-roomed building.

(4) *Area B* (fig. 62). Its position relative to the Solomonic gate (Area A) marks this as the citadel of Hazor. There is no trace of whatever building Solomon placed there, but his casemate walls [1] are evident on both sides of the bottleneck. These were filled in to make solid walls when the Omrids constructed their square fortress [2] which was flanked on both sides by ancillary buildings whose outer walls constituted all the rampart necessary. Two of these buildings remain visible [4 and 5]. The street separating them from the fortress had a monumental entrance [3] with proto-Aeolic capitals, and at the far end a staircase led to the first floor. As in Area G, the threat from

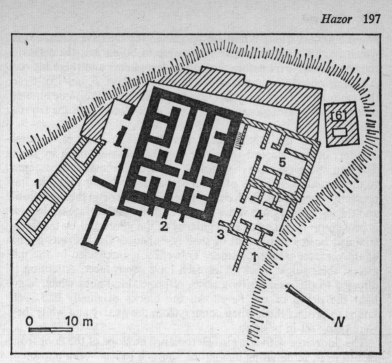

Fig. 62. Hazor. Area B (after Yadin).

Assyria prompted a strengthening of the fortifications in the C8 BC by the building of a tower [6] and a heavy offset-inset wall over the outer part of [4] and [5].

HEBRON (H20)

Sacred to Jews, Christians, and Muslims as the burial-place of Abraham, Isaac, and Jacob, Hebron is notable for the superb wall that Herod the Great (37–4 BC) built around the Cave of Machpelah (Haram el-Khalil). It is perfectly preserved and accessible at all points; the refinement of the construction technique has to be seen to be believed.

The ancient city was on Jebel er-Rumeideh, across the valley from the haram. Excavations (not worth a visit) show occupation from about 2000 BC. There Abraham bargained for the cave (Gen. 23) in which he, his sons, and their wives were to be buried; there David reigned for 7½ years before moving to Jerusalem; and there his son Absalom raised the standard of rebellion (2 Sam. 5 and 15). Even though a city of refuge (Josh. 21: 13), it suffered the same fate as others in wars throughout the centuries until Herod built the haram, today its sole glory.

The size of the stone blocks (the largest 7·5 × 1·4 m) inspires wonder; in Arab legend they were laid by Solomon aided by *jinns*. The largest appear near the corners, imparting tremendous strength to the structure. A series of clever visual deceptions avoids the impression of heaviness. Each course is set back 1·5 cm on the one below, and the upper margin is wider than the others. The surface of the wall is broken up by calculated irregularity of the joints and by the finely trimmed bosses whose hint of shadow enhances the lustrous patina of the *mezzy* ('excellent') stone. This effect is intensified by the pilasters; their single block bases each have seven faces. Attention is directed to this element by a series of projecting knobs which highlight the depth of the bevel. All the blocks originally had such knobs to protect them when coming from the quarry and while they were being set in position.

The floor area within is also Herodian. The slope of the floor from east to west, terminating in a gutter, shows it to have been unroofed. The courtyard probably contained a cenotaph (or several), and was reached by a staircase from an entrance at the base of the wall.

Nothing remains of the Byzantine church (completed after AD 570) save the façade; two buttresses adapted it to the present Crusader building (*c.* 1115) with its lower roof. In the intervening early Arab period the original entrance was blocked by a building housing the cenotaph of Joseph and the existing entrance was then cut in the east wall. Muslim control of the haram has always been marked by a superstitious fear of the burial cavern of the patriarchs. The cenotaphs of Abraham and Sarah were added after the city moved to surround the haram in the C8 AD. By the C10 the disposition of the six cenotaphs was the same as today.

The existing building is manifestly of gothic inspiration; it is a medieval church. The Crusader period is notable for the only serious exploration of the Cave of Machpelah. In 1119 the canons of St. Augustine penetrated beneath the pavement of the church and left a detailed record (fig. 63). Let down by a rope at the point where they later introduced a stairway (A) ,they found themselves in a narrow

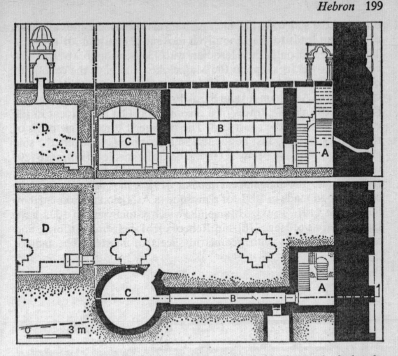

Fig. 63. Hebron. L.-H. Vincent's plan (bottom) and elevation (top) of what the Canons of St. Augustine saw beneath the Herodian floor of the Haram el-Khalil in AD 1119.

corridor of dressed stones (B) leading to a circular chamber with a rock roof (C). Its door opened into a large cavern connecting with a rock-cut chamber (D) which had the present opening in its roof. Bones in quantity came to light. The disposition and the quality of the masonry (compared by the canons to the haram wall) suggests that Herod rearranged the ancient cave before laying his pavement.

The Mamelukes permanently closed the entrance to the crypt at the end of the C14. They also contributed a number of other features to be noted in the course of the visit. Oblivion is too kind a fate for the unknown responsible for the crenellated monstrosity which still disfigures the summit of the Herodian wall.

Visit (fig. 64). Open 7.30–11 a.m.; 12.30–2 p.m.; 3–4 p.m.; closed Fridays. The polychrome entrance-gate betrays the Mameluke origin of the stairway [1] which permits close inspection of all levels of wall and leads to the Djaouliyeh mosque [2] built in AD 1318–20. The passage through the Herodian wall [3] is prior to AD 918. The courtyard owes its shape to the Mamelukes who gave the cenotaphs of Jacob [5] and Leah [4] their present form in the C14. The C9 cenotaphs of Abraham [8] and Sarah [6] are separated by a synagogue [7] installed in 1967; traces of a medieval portico are evident in the corners closest to the courtyard. The tribune [13] reuses elements of the medieval choir. Just beside it a small cupola [14] covers the sole entrance to the cave below (D in fig. 63). The medieval entrance [20] was sealed in 1394. On the right of the *mihrab* [18] stands the glory of the mosque, the magnificent *minbar* [19], a mosaic of exquisitely carved wood made in 1091 for a mosque in Ashqelon and donated by Saladin in 1191. Tankiz, Mameluke viceroy of Syria, in 1332 gave the cenotaphs of Isaac [16] and Rebecca [15] their present form, and adorned the walls with geometric sheets of marble. The marble

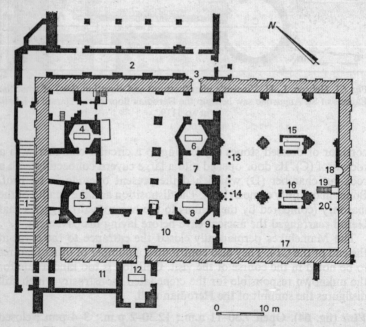

Fig. 64. Hebron. Haram el-Khalil (Tomb of the Patriarchs).

frieze in decorative script is also his; its horizontal line accentuates the slope of the pavement towards the Herodian gutter [17].

The exit is via the mosque of the women [10]. According to Arab legend Adam prayed so frequently in the corner [9] that his foot left a mark in the stone (now part of a small shrine). The mosque [11] and tomb of Joseph [12] with their entrances in the Herodian wall are C14.

HEPTAPEGON (N5)

This Greek word meaning 'seven springs' has been corrupted into the Arabic Tabgha. Egeria, a tirelessly observant nun from somewhere on the Atlantic coast, passed here between AD 381 and 384 coming from Capernaum, and left the following description: 'Not far away from there [Capernaum] are some stone steps where the Lord stood. And in the same place by the sea is a grassy field with plenty of hay and many palm trees. By them are seven springs, each flowing strongly. And this is the field where the Lord fed the people with the five loaves and the two fishes. In fact the stone on which the Lord placed the bread has now been made into an altar. . . . Past the walls of this church goes the public highway on which the Apostle Matthew had his place of custom. Near there on a mountain is the cave to which the Saviour climbed and spoke the Beatitudes.'

Thus, in the C4 Christian tradition located here three episodes in the life of Jesus: the post-Resurrection appearance when he conferred on Peter the responsibility of leadership (John 21), the multiplication of the loaves and fishes (Mark 6: 30–44), and the Sermon on the Mount (Matt. 5–7). Egeria mentions only one church, but three are in fact dated to the C4 (fig. 65).

The Church of the Multiplication of the Loaves and Fishes [1]. Open 7 a.m. – 5 p.m. The present structure is no more than a protective covering erected in 1936; the two wings housing the Benedictine monastery date from 1956. The reconstruction was necessary to preserve the most beautiful mosaic floor in the country. This belonged to a church built in the middle of the C5 AD (plan in narthex), and is the earliest known example of a figured pavement in Palestinian church art. It does not cover the whole floor area but is limited to the two transepts and the intervals between the pillars.

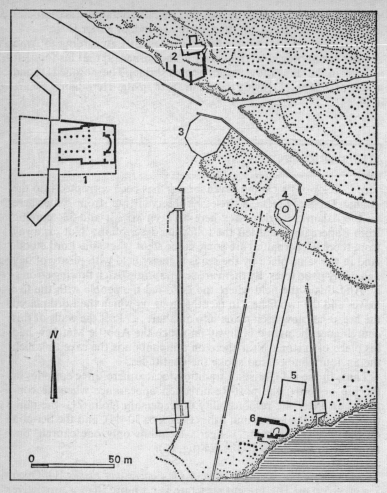

Fig. 65. Heptapegon. Churches of the Multiplication of the Loaves and Fishes (1), of the Sermon on the Mount (2), and of the Primacy of Peter (6).

The artist, indisputably a great master, had enough confidence in his skill to avoid any repetitious pattern and covered the area with a free-flowing design of birds and plants (fig. 66). The prominence of the bell-like lotus flower (not found in this area) betrays the influence of the Nilotic landscapes popular in Hellenistic and Roman art, but the other motifs are drawn from the flora and fauna of the lakeside. Despite the detail which permits the identification of each species, the whole is infused with unique verve and humour. The round tower in the right transept is to measure the water level in the lake; the Greek letters are the numbers 6 to 10.

Immediately in front of the altar is the celebrated mosaic of two

Fig. 66. Heptapegon. Mosaic floor in the Church of the Multiplication of the Loaves and Fishes.

fish flanking a basket of loaves. Below the altar table is a block of undressed limestone ($1 \times 0.6 \times 0.14$ m). It is unlikely that this is the stone altar mentioned by Egeria, though Christians of the C5 undeniably considered it the table of the Lord.

The C4 church lies beneath the present floor. It was much smaller and the two sections left exposed show that the orientation was slightly different. During the restoration of the mosaics in 1936 the complete outline was established (plan in narthex).

Church of the Sermon on the Mount [2]. Above the road the ruins of a small church dated to the end of the C4 are still visible. Beneath it is a cave, probably the one mentioned by Egeria. On the south and south-east are the remains of a little monastery. The remnants of the mosaic floor are on display at Capernaum.

To replace this chapel, put out of commission in the C7, a new church was built in 1938 further up the hill, on what is today called the Mount of Beatitudes. The entrance is not from the lake road but from the main road going up to Rosh Pinna. Although devoid of archaeological interest, it is worth a visit. The octagonal shape of the church commemorates the eight beatitudes (Matt. 5: 3–10) and conveys an impression of immense tranquillity. Its shady gallery is the best place from which to contemplate the spiritual dimension of the lake; one can see all the places in which Jesus lived and worked.

Church of the Primacy of Peter [6] .Open 8.30 a.m.–4 p.m. The modest Franciscan chapel was built in 1933, but at the base of its walls, at the end furthest from the altar, the walls of a late C4 AD building are clearly visible on three sides. The eastern end of this edifice has completely disappeared, but cuts in the rock and the proportions of the comparable C4 Church of the Multiplication suggest that its length was twice its width. It thus enclosed the flat rock projecting in front of the present altar. This is probably the one mentioned by Egeria. In the early Byzantine period it would have been venerated as the table on which Jesus offered breakfast to the disciples: 'As soon as they came ashore they saw that there was some bread there, and a charcoal fire with fish cooking on it' (John 21: 9). This text probably explains why, in the C9, the site was known as the Place of the Coals. The church survived longer than any others in the area, and was finally destroyed only in the C13.

On the lake side of the church are the rock-cut steps of which Egeria speaks. How old they are no one knows. They may have been cut in the C2 or C3 AD when this area was quarried for limestone; the characteristic cuts to liberate the blocks on three sides prior to the insertion of metal wedges (two were found) are visible in the vicinity.

Below the steps, sometimes under water if the lake level is high, are six heart-shaped stones. They are double-column blocks designed for the angle of a colonnade, and never served any practical purpose in their present position. Known as the Twelve Thrones, and first mentioned in a text of AD 808, they were probably taken from disused buildings and placed there to commemorate the Twelve Apostles. It takes little insight to appreciate the mental jump from John 21: 9 (cited above) to 'You will eat and drink at my table in my kingdom, and you will sit on thrones to judge the twelve tribes of Israel' (Luke 22: 30).

Just beside the church is a small Crusader building [5]. The other structures are water towers called Birket Ali ed-Daher [3] and Tannur Ayyub [4]. These date back to the Byzantine period and were designed to raise the water level of the powerful springs so that they flowed into a series of irrigation canals and mill-streams. The existing mills are of recent date.

HERODION (HAR HORDOS) (K19)

The landscape south of Jerusalem is dominated by a peak whose shape suggests a volcano. It is in fact the citadel of a palace complex built by Herod the Great between 24 and 15 BC to commemorate a victorious rearguard action on his flight to MASADA in 40 BC. From the top there is a magnificent view over the Judaean desert, and of the deep WADI KHAREITUN with its prehistoric caves immediately to the south.

The arrangement of the interior of the citadel is reminiscent of Roman imperial tombs. Herod may have built it as his mausoleum; he certainly commanded that he be interred there. Whether he actually was is open to doubt, because Josephus's two accounts do not agree. They can be reconciled if we assume that the solemn cortège walked for only 8 (*Antiquities* 17: 199) of the 200 stadia (*War* 1: 673) between JERICHO and Herodion.

Its insignificant role in the First Revolt parallels that of MASADA; Lucilius Bassus's attack in AD 70 destroyed the towers. In the Second Revolt (132–5) it served as an administrative centre for the rebels, and may even have been the headquarters of Bar Kokhba.

Byzantine monks set up a monastery in the ruins in the C5–C7.

Visit (fig. 67). Open 8 a.m.–5 p.m.; toilets and drinking water. The crude steps of the present entrance are in no way comparable to the original 200 of purest white marble [1]; only traces of the foundations running down the hill remain. The three half-towers [2] highlight the strength of the keep [3]. Here, if anywhere at Herodion, Herod is buried; the combination of a rectangular open court [4] tangent to a circular tomb also appears in the Constantinian Holy Sepulchre (fig. 10). Inevitably there was a Roman bath [5–7]. Since this was the only section with stone roofs, the Byzantine monks installed themselves here, setting up cells and a bakery in the hot-room [7]. The missiles [10] from the Roman catapults would have crashed through the wooden roofs elsewhere. The monks also built a chapel in what was

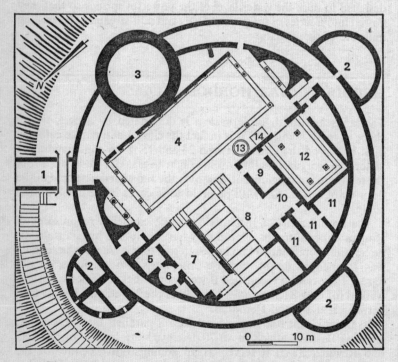

Fig. 67. Herodion. Herod the Great's Palace/Tomb (after Corbo).

originally an open area [8], permitting access from the living (or servant) quarters [11]. A pantry [9] adjoined the dining-room [12], which was turned into a synagogue or meeting hall in the Second Revolt by the addition of benches along the walls. The Zealots also added the furnace [13] and the small bath [14].

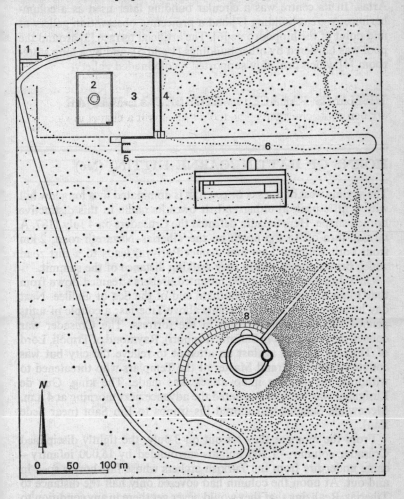

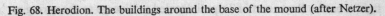

Fig. 68. Herodion. The buildings around the base of the mound (after Netzer).

Herod, according to Josephus, 'around the base erected other palaces for the accommodation of his furniture and his friends' (*War* 1: 421). The outline of some of these can be seen from the top (fig. 68). Openings in the side of the artificial mound [8] lead to cisterns fed by hand from the pool [2] supplied by the aqueduct from Artas. In its centre was a circular building later used as a columbarium. A great building [7] had a projecting observation gallery at mid point of the hippodrome [6]. The artificial terrace [3] around the pool was bordered by other buildings [1 and 5], and by a long storeroom [4] which probably supported a colonnaded gallery.

HISHAM'S PALACE: *see* KHIRBET AL-MAFJAR

HORNS OF HATTIN (QARNE HITTIN) (M6)

The skyline west of the SEA OF GALILEE is dominated by a long low hill with a little peak at either end. It owes its name to this distinctive horned shape. Here Saladin defeated the Crusaders on 4 July 1187. A tarmac turn-off to the north on the Tiberias–Nazareth road, 2 km from both Kibbutz Lavi and Zomet Poriyya, leads to a dirt road which brings one to within easy walking distance of the summit.

On 1 July Saladin's 12,000 mounted archers streamed down from the Golan to camp at the southern end of the Sea of Galilee. Next day he moved them to the heights above Tiberias; a couple of units penned the Crusader garrison in the fortress. The Crusader war council met that night in Safforie (Zippori). Raymond of Tripoli, Lord of Tiberias, argued against an attempt to relieve the city but was countered by the Grand Master of the Templars who threatened to withdraw his support if no attack was made. The king, Guy de Lusignan, was weak and ordered the advance next morning at 4 a.m. Meanwhile Saladin had moved his troops to Ein Sabt (near Sede Ilan).

From the moment they set out on 3 July, the tightly disciplined Crusader column – 1,200 knights surrounded by 16,000 infantry – came under fire from the Turkish archers whose fast horses sped in and out. At noon the column had covered only half the distance to Tiberias. Realizing that they would never get there in any condition to fight a battle, Raymond of Tripoli decided to diverge to the spring at

Hattin (below Nabi Shueib = Jethro's Tomb). At 2 p.m. Balian of Ibelin, commanding the Templars of the rearguard, who had taken the brunt of the attacks, advised the king that they could go no further. The decision was made to camp near Zomet Golani. Saladin's camp was within shouting distance, and that night he sent the regiment of the emir Taqi ed-Din to bar the route to the spring. It formed a line between Nimrin and the Horns of Hattin.

Next morning Saladin attacked only when the brazen summer sun was shining into the Crusaders' eyes as they moved slowly east. He led the first charge himself. It was beaten off by the Templars, but they were not supported; the army thought only of water as they had had nothing to drink for over twenty-four hours. The battle became general. Towards noon the king ordered Raymond of Tripoli to use the vanguard to break a way to the spring. As the huge horses swept down on Taqi ed-Din his troopers wheeled their fast ponies to either side; the charge went through without making contact. As the barrier on the crest closed again, Raymond and his men rode miserably away to the north. This broke the morale of the Crusader foot soldiers who began to swarm to the north peak of Hattin. The remaining knights formed a wall around the red tent of the king on the southern peak. They were overwhelmed by a desperate Muslim charge. The red tent was overturned and the True Cross taken from the dead hands of the Bishop of Acre. Balian of Ibelin, the only knight whose character matched that of Saladin, alone fought his way out of the defeated army.

IZBET SARTAH (G14)

From this barren spur at the very edge of the Judaean foothills Israelites of the period of the Judges (1200–1050 BC) gazed enviously at the well-watered plain below which the Philistines controlled from APHEK (fig. 41). The settlement had a short history and the remains are unexceptional, but nowhere else can one better understand the relationship between the people of the plain and the Israelites who had just returned to the land of their fathers after a long sojourn in Egypt. The Israelites could make sporadic raids into the plain, as Joshua did at Aphek (Josh. 12: 18), but they could not hold it against the chariotry of the Canaanites and Philistines; only in the hill country had they some degree of security, and there they pushed forward as far as they could.

Life at Eben-ezer (the biblical name of the site) must have been rather precarious; the Philistines were only 3 km away and the two nearest Israelite forts were deeper in the hills. Nonetheless, the oval settlement, with houses ranged against the wall, seems to have prospered because it was enlarged *c.*1200 BC. A large four-roomed house (now restored) was built in the open centre previously occupied only by round silos in one of which the oldest known copy of the Proto-Canaanite alphabet was found scratched on a potsherd. From here the word went out (*c.*1050 BC) that the Philistines were massing at Aphek, and it was here that the Israelites assembled to meet them. Things went badly on the first day, and the Ark of the Covenant was brought from SHILOH. The next day brought disaster; the Philistines captured the Ark and routed the Israelite army (1 Sam. 4: 1–11).

After a short interval the Israelites moved back into the deserted settlement, but did not stay there for very long because the military prowess of David opened the plain to them (*c.* 1000 BC). Thereafter no one settled here.

JACOB'S WELL (K12)

A deep well (35 m), located on the eastern edge of NABLUS (D in fig. 92), is venerated as the spot where Jesus encountered the Samaritan woman (John 4). Open: 8 a.m.–12 noon and 2–4 p.m.

The existence of a well in the immediate vicinity of so many springs tends to confirm the traditional attribution to Jacob. When he bought land to settle down (Gen. 33: 18–20) the water rights to the springs would have long been assigned; the only alternative to perpetual disputes was to find his own source of water.

About AD 380 a cruciform church was built, incorporating in a crypt a baptistry constructed at the beginning of the century. After destruction in the SAMARITAN uprising in 529, and again in the early Arab period, a new church was erected by the Crusaders. The abortive reconstruction begun in 1914 retains its main lines, showing that the crypt containing the well was under the sanctuary.

JERICHO (YERIHO) (M16)

The lowest (258 m below sea-level) and the oldest town on earth, strategically located on the border between the desert and the sown, lush green against the surrounding dust-brown, Jericho opens many windows on the past (fig. 69).

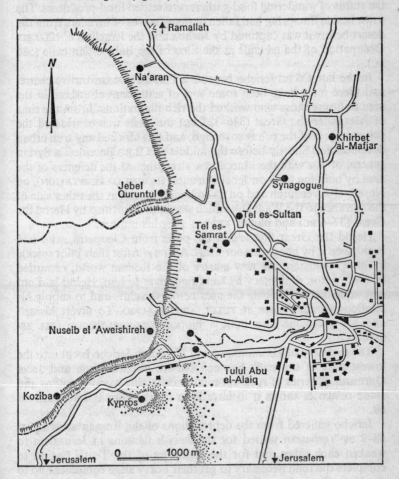

Fig. 69. The Jericho area.

Tropical in summer but beautifully mild in winter, the climate attracted prehistoric nomads to the area. They settled at TEL ES-SULTAN near a powerful perennial spring (Ein es-Sultan; 1,000 gals. per minute) whose water is still distributed throughout the oasis by a complex system of gravity-flow irrigation, producing abundant fruit, flowers, and spices. The first massive defence wall was erected around the settlement *c*.7000 BC, the inhabitants having passed from the status of wandering food-gatherers to settled food-producers. The town beside the spring had fallen to many waves of invaders from the desert before it was captured by Joshua and the Israelites *c*. 1200 BC. Occupation of the tel ends at the time of the Babylonian exile (586 BC).

In the late C6 BC Jericho became a Persian administrative centre, and there must have been some sort of settlement elsewhere in the area to house those who worked the rich plantations. From the time of Alexander the Great (336–323 BC) the oasis was considered the private estate of the ruling sovereign, and this blocked any true urban development. Shortly before the middle of C2 BC Baccides, a Syrian general at war with the Maccabees, strengthened the defences of the area by building forts on Jebel Quruntul (MOUNT OF TEMPTATION), on Nuseib el-Aweishireh and on its companion peak at the other side of the entrance to the Wadi Qilt which was later refortified by Herod the Great (37–4 BC) and named KYPROS after his mother.

Herod the Great first leased the oasis from Cleopatra, who had been given it by her paramour Mark Antony. After their joint suicide in 30 BC Octavian, the new master of the Roman world, rewarded Herod's adroit diplomacy by handing it over to him. Herod laid out new aqueducts to irrigate the area below the cliffs and to supply his fabulous winter palace at TULUL ABU EL-ALAIQ. To divert himself and his guests he also built a hippodrome-cum-theatre (TEL ES-SAMRAT).

The cemetery of Hasmonaean and Herodian Jericho is cut into the lowest part of the cliffs between Nuseib el-Aweishireh and Jebel Quruntul. A series of rock-cut tombs containing wooden coffins and stone ossuaries shows it to have been in use from 100 BC until AD 68.

Jericho suffered from the depredations of the Roman army in AD 68–9 as Vespasian waited for the Jewish factions in Jerusalem to weaken each other and for the engineers of the Tenth Legion to complete the road necessary to get their heavy siege equipment up to the Holy City.

The area was heavily populated in the Byzantine period. In addition to synagogues at Naaran and near Tel es-Sultan there were many monasteries of which the most notable is the MONASTERY OF ST. GEORGE OF KOZIBA clinging to the cliff of the Wadi Qilt. The most remarkable monument of the Arab period is the magnificent hunting palace at KHIRBET AL-MAFJAR which reflects the vast resources of the Umayyad empire in the C8 AD. In the Middle Ages sugar cane was intensively cultivated, and there are very ruined remains of Crusader sugar-mills. At this period churches commemorating the temptations of Christ were erected on Jebel Quruntul (MOUNT OF TEMPTATION).

The departure of the Crusaders from the area after their defeat by Saladin in 1187 left Jericho without protection against bedouin raids from the desert, and a thriving town degenerated into a miserable village. The canals fell into disuse and the desert reclaimed what had been its own. Only with the establishment of effective police control after the First World War did Jericho begin to recover something of its former glory by developing into a great fruit-producing area. The most evident traces of the impact of the C20 on the oldest of towns are the two great Palestinian refugee camps. From 1948 to 1967 these mud huts housed over 70,000 displaced persons, many of whom again fled during the Six-Day War.

JIB (J17)

A picturesque Arab village on a rocky island in the midst of a small intensively cultivated plain (10 km north of Jerusalem), Jib has the most interesting ancient water system in the country.

On reaching the village turn on to the Biddu road and then immediately up the hill with houses on the left and rock threshing floors on the right. From the corner of the parking-lot (courtesy term!) a rough path leads to the two key areas which are all that remain of a much larger excavation. Bring torches.

Jib retains the first syllable of the biblical Gibeon; identification has been confirmed by discovery of inscribed jar-handles on the site. Already a great city (the earliest remains are Ancient Bronze) when the Israelites entered Palestine (*c*. 1200 BC), the old clothes and stale bread of the Gibeonites deceived Joshua into signing a peace treaty (the full story is told in Josh. 9). He nonetheless kept his word and went to their defence when the five kings attacked; in order to prolong the slaughter he prayed, 'Sun, stand still at Gibeon' (Josh. 10: 12). Apart from Solomon's visit (1 Kgs. 3: 4–15), the site is notable only for a series of gory episodes (2 Sam. 2, 20, 21). In the C8–C7 BC the production and exportation of wine made it a prosperous city but this glory never returned after the city's destruction by the Babylonians in 587 BC.

Visit (fig. 70). The round holes cut in the rock [1] are the entrances to C8–C7 BC wine cellars; 63 were discovered, each one capable of storing 42 jars of 35-litre capacity. When sealed by a fitted capstone these cellars maintain a constant temperature of 18°C. The wine was sold in smaller jars with the name of the city and the producer stamped on the handles.

The great rock-cut pool (2 Sam. 2:13) with its spiral staircase [2]

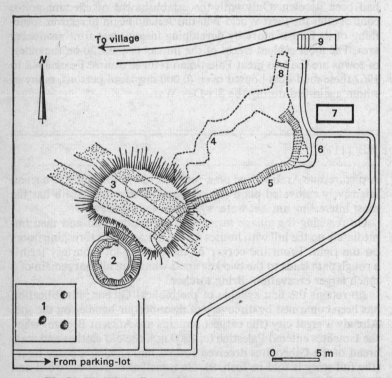

Fig. 70. Jib. Wine cellars and water system (after Pritchard).

is of the C12–C11 BC. The steps continue beneath the rock floor to the water chamber. It could be that the water-table dropped, but it seems more likely that a new administration in the city found a cheaper way of continuing a ridiculously expensive project. At any rate the steps got little use (note the straight edges) because in the C10 BC two new tunnels were cut. One [4] brings water from the spring in the centre of the hill to a pool [8] just inside its edge; piped from here to a series of taps [9], it still serves the village. The other [5] descends from just inside the ancient city wall to the pool. This system denied water to attackers while still making it available to inhabitants under siege. In time of peace they simply walked down the side of the hill and entered the pool from the outside; slots in the walls and floor near the entrance show that it could be sealed quickly in an emergency. The original entrance to the tunnel being blocked by the archaeologists' dump [3], one enters the access tunnel [6] behind a modern house [7]. The worn steps and polished sides bear witness to frequent passage; note the smoke-darkened niches where oil-lamps stood. At the top of the steps one can see how the tunnel was constructed. They first cut a vertical trench 4 m deep outside the city wall and then ran one tunnel under the wall and the other down to the pool. The corbelled roof of this section is still visible; outside it was camouflaged with earth.

KEFAR BARAM (L3)

There are enough architectural elements lying around the sites of CAPERNAUM and CHOROZAIN to give a reasonable idea of what these synagogues looked like. This effort is unnecessary at Kefar Baram because the magnificent façade has been preserved virtually undamaged up to the cornice.

The site (open: 8 a.m.–4 p.m.; Fridays to 3 p.m.) is just over 2 km from the Israel–Lebanon border and 1 km south of the village of Dovev. The rolling hills of Upper Galilee are a perfect setting for the serene dignity of the synagogue which should be on the itinerary of anyone visiting the MERON area.

The plan of the synagogue is identical with that of its sisters at Capernaum and Chorozain. The three entrances face south and there are rows of columns parallel to the other three walls; the floor is paved with stone slabs. The only difference is that here a porch is built along the length of the façade, one column with the architrave connecting it to the building remaining in place. A broken architrave showing the beginning of a curve suggests that the porch was surmounted by a triangular pediment with an arch in its centre. A Hebrew inscription on the sill of the eastern window in the façade reads, 'Built by Elazar, son of Yudan'.

Rabbi Moses Basula, who visited the site in 1522, ascribes the synagogue to Simeon bar Yohai, one of the five disciples of Rabbi Akiva who survived the massacre which followed the failure of the Second Revolt in AD 135. This date is generally accepted, but probably needs to be reconsidered in the light of the excavations at CAPERNAUM.

The buildings in the vicinity of the synagogue belong to a Christian village abandoned in 1948.

KHAN EL-AHMAR (L17)

Surrounded by graceless factories, the forlorn ruin of Khan el-Ahmar bravely continues to bear witness to a spirit which is the antithesis of the crass political materialism behind the establishment of an industrial zone in one of the most beautiful valleys in the Judaean desert. This was the laura (a cluster of solitary cells around a common centre) of St. Euthymius, once the most important monastic centre in the Holy Land (MONASTERIES IN THE JUDAEAN DESERT).

Born in AD 376 in Lesser Armenia, Euthymius came to Palestine and became a disciple of St. Chariton in 405. Six years later he and Theoctistus founded a new laura in a remote part of the desert, Wadi Mukellik. The Arab tribe which pastured its flocks in that region became Christians and Euthymius eventually ordained as bishop the sheikh, Peter Aspebet (a Persian title meaning 'master of horse') who later played a significant role in the Council of Ephesus (431) as Bishop of the Arab Camps.

After moving round the desert in a vain attempt to escape the disciples who flocked to him, Euthymius finally capitulated. In 428 the church of the laura at Khan el-Ahmar was consecrated. Those who desired to participate in the organized hermit life of the laura were first trained in the coenobium (monastery) of Theoctistus in the Wadi Mukellik. This was the major contribution of Euthymius to the development of desert monasticism; in the next century it was made the normal pattern by Sabas, the greatest of Euthymius' disciples (MAR SABA).

Euthymius himself recognized that the site at Khan el-Ahmar was too central to provide the solitude necessary for a laura and left orders that after his death it was to be transformed into a coenobium. He died on 20 January 473, and reconstruction began immediately. The cave of Euthymius became a vaulted cemetery; a new church was erected above the old one which became a refectory. Though ruined by an earthquake in 660, the monastery remained in use until the C12 when it was finally abandoned.

Visit (fig. 71). From the Jerusalem–Jericho road take the turn to Mishor Adummim; go straight through the settlement; the ruin is on the left about 1·5 km from the turn-off.

The entrance [1] to the lower church/refectory is kept locked but one can look through the barred gate. Some of the mosaics on the floor of the upper church [3] (built 478–82) are well preserved; the sacristy [2] projects from the south side. The tomb of Euthymius and his companions [4] is north of the church; to the east is a secondary refectory [5] with a stone table still in place and a storage area [6]. A strong tower [8] provided a place of refuge in case of attack.

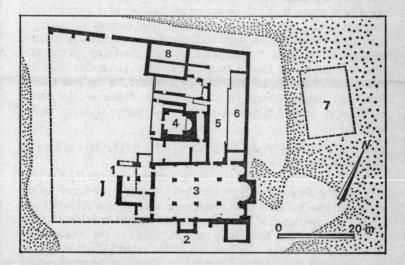

Fig. 71. Khan el-Ahmar. Monastery of St. Euthymius (after Chitty).

Outside the walls of the monastery is a vast underground cistern [7] of the C5; known to the Arabs as the 'Well of Seven Mouths', it collected run-off rainwater from the surrounding area.

KHIRBET AL-MAFJAR (M16)

Located just north of Jericho (fig. 69) and commonly called 'Hisham's Palace', because it was at first thought to have been built by the Umayyad caliph Hisham ibn Abd al-Malik (AD 724–43) who ruled an empire stretching from India to the Pyrenees. Many of the Umayyad dynasty had such hunting lodges which enabled them to recover the freedom and independence of the desert which was their birthright, but the extravagance and unorthodox decoration of Khirbet al-Mafjar is incompatible with the character of the austere, righteous Hisham. It harmonizes best with what we know of his nephew and successor, al Walid ibn Yazid (743–4). 'Banished from the court for wild living and scurrility, passionate aesthete and drinker, habitual companion of singers, himself the best poet and marksman of the Umayyads' (R. W. Hamilton, *Levant* I (1969), 65), Walid first built the bath, which shows signs of having been in use for a number of years. It and the great walled hunting park were his main interests. Walid was assassinated a year after coming to power, so the palace was never completed and, despite an attempted restoration in the C12 (possibly by Saladin's troops), thereafter served as a quarry of cut stones for the people of Jericho. The architecture and the motifs of the stucco decoration (used here for the first time in Palestine) betray strong Persian influence. Much of the ornate plasterwork is well displayed in the Rockefeller Museum in Jerusalem.

Visit (fig. 72). Open: April–Sept. 8 a.m. – 5 p.m. (Fridays to 4 p.m.); Oct.–March 8 a.m.–4 p.m. (Fridays to 3 p.m.).

Toilets are located to the left of the present entrance [1]. On both sides of the forecourt [2] architectural elements scattered by the earthquake of 747 have been arranged in their proper relative positions. The entrance-gate [3] was originally vaulted in brick, showing that master-builders from Iraq were employed in the construction. The monument in the middle of the central court [4] was erected by the excavators. Intended as a window, it illustrates the way in which the Umayyads transformed the motifs (in this case Roman) which

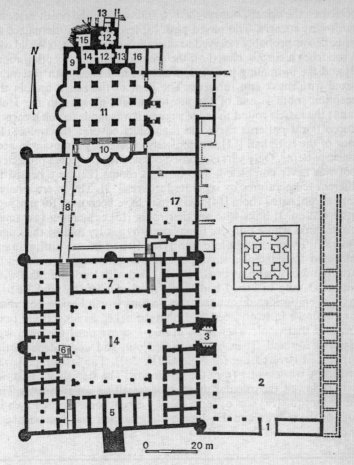

Fig. 72. Khirbet al-Mafjar. Umayyad Palace (after Hamilton).

they found in the lands they conquered. A small mosque abutting on the minaret [5] was probably intended for the personal use of the caliph. A flight of steps [6] leads down to a subterranean bathing hall floored with mosiac. The big hall [7] must have served as a banqueting room. Since few of the rooms round the central court communicate with one another the royal apartments must have been located on the upper floor reached by stairways in the north-east and south-west corners. The paved path [8] leading from the palace to the bath was probably reserved to the caliph because when Walid was in residence a curtain closed off the area between his reception room [9] and the swimming pool [10] which he had filled with rosewater mixed with musk and turmeric. The floor of the raised area in the reception room is one of the most beautiful mosaics in the Holy Land; the tassels round the edge suggest it was modelled on a carpet. Stucco floral patterns carved in high relief covered the walls. The floor of the bath hall [11] is completely covered by a mosaic in geometric patterns. Only part is exposed because the projected protective roof was never completed. The two hot rooms [12] were heated to different temperatures by separate furnaces [13]. They were entered from an unheated room [14] which may have been used for massage or depilation. It links with another room [15] containing two small square tanks whose purpose is explained by a story told by the singer Utarrad: 'I was brought into him [Walid], and he was sitting in his palace on the edge of a small pool, just large enough for a man to turn round in when immersed. It was lined with lead and filled with wine . . . I sang to him. I had barely finished when, by God, he tore apart an embroidered robe that was on him, worth I know not what, flung it down in two pieces, and plunged naked as his mother bore him into that pool; whence he drank, I swear until the level was distinctly lowered. Then he was pulled out, laid down dead to the world, and covered up' (al Aghani III, 303). The latrine [16] was flushed by waste water from the hot rooms. The step shows that the users followed the oriental practice of squatting on foot-rests. The public mosque [17] was open to the sky except for a covered area in front of the mihrab and the door leading to the royal apartments.

KHIRBET MIRD (HYRCANIA) (L18)

The peak stands out from the mass of the Judaean hills, dominating the great plain of the Buqei'a which stretches to the cliffs behind QUMRAN with NABI MUSA at its northern entrance. Here is an opportunity to experience the solitude of the desert.

From the only four-way crossroads on the tarmac road between Abu Dis and Bethlehem it is 6 km on a good dirt road to the parking-lot on the south shoulder of Jebel Muntar, at 524 m the highest point in the area. On the summit, with the panorama of the desert all around, you are among the sparse ruins of the tower built by the empress Eudokia to receive St. Euthymius which later became part of the monastery of St. John Scholarius (early C6 AD). From the parking-lot the walk to Khirbet Mird takes about 90 minutes. Good hiking boots and canteens of water are essential. A good path leads down the side of Jebel Muntar to the cistern (surrounded by drinking troughs) of Bir el-Amarah. From there black trail-markings lead down the bed of the wadi, and eventually along its right side following the line of the ancient aqueduct (fed by run-off rainwater) supplying the fortress. As the wadi deepens, the monastery of Spelaion, founded by St. Sabas in AD 509, becomes visible on the left.

First fortified by John Hyrcanus (134–103 BC), whence its original name Hyrcania, Khirbet Mird served as one of the treasure-houses of the Hasmonaean queen Alexandra (76–67 BC) before being pulled down by the Romans under Gabinius in 57 BC. Herod the Great (37–4 BC) rebuilt the fortress very soon after coming to power, and used it to dispose of those who displeased him (imprisonment or execution). Nonetheless, he brought Marcus Agrippa, son-in-law of the emperor Augustus, to admire its magnificence in 15 BC. Strategically of no importance, it fell into ruins once the security-mad king died; only five days before his death he had sent his last victim, his own son Antipater, to be buried there.

The pain and sorrow which penetrated the stones may account for the atmosphere that St. Sabas encountered there in 492. Having chased away the demons, he constructed the monastery of Castellion. Occupation in the C8 – C10 AD is attested by the discovery of manuscripts in Arabic, Greek, and Christo-Palestinian Aramaic. An attempt to restore the monastery in 1925 by monks of MAR SABA was defeated by the bedouin.

Visit (fig. 73). The drystone surround wall [1] is modern. The masonry of the two parallel vaulted cisterns supporting the sloped floor of the court [4] is Herodian and so, therefore, are the rooms on three sides. One of these [2] was turned into a church in the C6 AD by the addition of an apse, and another [3], with a mosaic floor, was probably the diakonikon (the area in a Byzantine church corresponding to the sacristy or vestry in a Western church). The row of cells [5] may be modern, because the tomb-cave [6] of the original monastery was turned into a chapel in 1925.

The aqueduct bridge and the rock-cut defence trenches on either

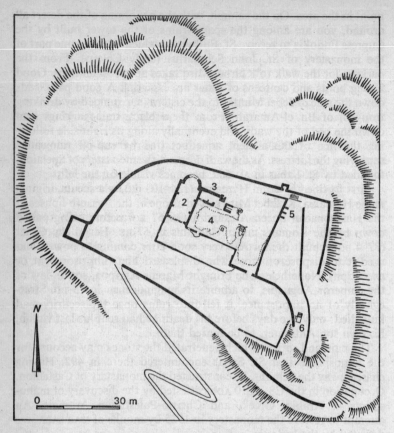

Fig. 73. Khirbet Mird (after Wright).

side are Herodian; the destination of the water is still unclear. The rubble structure crowning a crag 300 m south-west of the fortress was probably a funerary monument, perhaps to be related to the Herodian graves (stone circles in a square enclosure) in the plain below. Are they the resting places of some of Herod's victims, including his son? At the bottom of the narrow section of the Wadi Abu Shale due north of the fortress two stepped tunnels descend into the rock. Their date and function is unknown.

KHIRBET SHEMA (M4)

The impressive assemblage of crude massive blocks, traditionally venerated as the tomb of Shammai the great Jewish teacher (active *c.* 30 BC), has always drawn visitors to one of the eastern spurs of Mount Meron, the highest mountain in Israel (1,208 m). Recent excavations have enhanced the interest of the site by restoring an unusual ancient synagogue.

Separated from the settlement of Meron by a wadi of the same name (fig. 74), the site is reached by a 15-minute walk up the steep slope from the hairpin bend in the main Zefat–AKKO road. Of particular interest (fig. 75) are (1) the synagogue, (2) the mausoleum, (3) the wine-press, and (4) the ritual bath.

The history of the site is a simple one; it was originally only a farming village in an area famous for the quality of its olive oil. In the C2 AD it was a remote extension of MERON, but as the population of Galilee increased owing to the movement of Jews from Judaea, it eventually became an independent village in the second part of the C3. This new identity was marked by the construction of the first

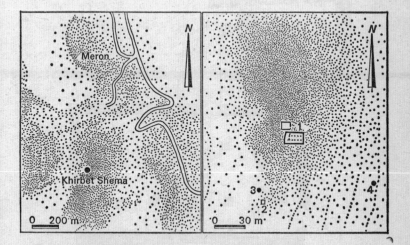

Fig. 74. Relationship between Khirbet Shema and Meron.

Fig. 75. Excavated areas at Khirbet Shema.

synagogue. Destroyed by the earthquake of 306, this edifice was rebuilt only to be again levelled by an earthquake in 419. It was never
reconstructed, even though the site continued to be occupied into the
Arab period.

(1) *Synagogue* (fig. 76). The synagogue complex is made up of two
buildings, a study hall-cum-guesthouse [1] and the synagogue
proper [5]. The former is entered from the paved street [2] to the
east via a short flight of steps; the western side is higher and a rock
bench runs along the walls; when in use the whole room was
plastered.

The unique architectural structure of the synagogue was imposed by
the nature of the terrain. The western end is higher than the body of
the building, part [3] being solid bedrock. A wooden floor laid on
top of the rock extended to the south, covering the room below [4]
and creating a gallery with an entrance at each end; this area may
have been for women. The room beneath [4] was decorated with
frescoes, and probably served for the storage of liturgical objects.
From it there is an entrance to a small cave under the steps from the

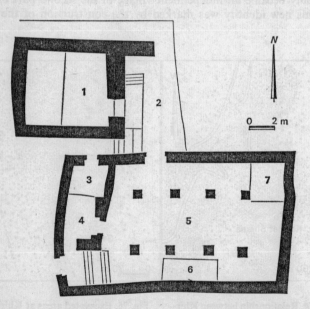

Fig. 76. Khirbet Shema. The C4 AD synagogue (after Meyers).

western entrance; it is suggested that this was the treasury and/or *genizah* (storage place for deteriorating sacred objects).

The broadhouse prayer hall [5] is oriented towards Jerusalem by a *bema* [6], a raised platform from which scripture was read; note that the pedestals of the columns on this side of the building are more elaborate. This *bema* belongs to the second synagogue because it covers a bench of the original building which had a carved stone torah-shrine at this point. In the corner [7] is a ritual bath (*miqveh*) antedating the first synagogue whose construction put it out of commission.

(2) *Mausoleum.* This structure is without parallel and no certain date can be assigned to it. It is assumed to be contemporary with the settlement (C3–C5 AD). The association with Shammai began only in the Middle Ages. The floor of the main level is cut to receive two corpses; a lower level was intended for secondary burial of the bones once the flesh had disappeared. There are many underground tombs in the immediate vicinity, all contemporary with the settlement.

(3) *Wine press.* The installation is cut into bedrock. The grapes were pressed in the area surrounded by a circular groove; the juice flowed automatically into a series of settling basins, becoming progressively purer. No precise dating is possible.

(4) *Ritual bath.* A flight of steps leads down to an antechamber with a small opening on the right leading to a small bath in which the hair was cleansed prior to ritual immersion. An interior chamber contains the steps leading down to the bath proper; it was supplied with rainwater from overhead via a channel coming from a sump which collected rain flowing down the entrance steps. This installation was in use during the C4 AD.

KHIRBET SUSEYA (H21)

Khirbet Suseya is a lonely hilltop in the Judaean hills south of HEBRON. In the springtime it rises above a sea of green when the intense cultivation in the shallow wadis all around begins to produce its fruit. The 4 km access road (signposted) from the main road linking Yatta and ESHTEMOA (SAMMU) is too rough for the average car but at the end lies one of the finest and best-preserved synagogues in the country. The walls stand to a height of several metres and the mosaic floors are intact.

Nothing is known of the history of the Jewish settlement whose ruins cover the adjoining hill. It must have been a thriving agricultural community between the C5 and C9 AD, the period in which the synagogue was in use.

Visit (fig. 77). The roof erected by the Israeli authorities to protect the mosaics is certainly much lower than the original but it gives the monument the air of a functioning building. The two other types of synagogue are oriented to Jerusalem either by their doors or by an apse; Suseya, like its neighbour in Eshtemoa, is oriented by a niche above a *bema* (raised platform) in one of the long walls. Even to the untrained eye it is clear that the principal *bema* [1] is the result of a series of additions. Originally a flight of steps leading up to the niche containing the scrolls cut across the plastered benches which run round three sides of the building. Later a ledge was built in front; the square sockets were for the marble posts of the chancel screen, now lying on the benches opposite. Still later, circular steps were added at each end and the whole was faced with marble, traces of which are still visible low down on the left. The second *bema* [2] is a curious and unique feature; it may have served for the reading of the Scriptures because its importance is underlined by the mosaic in front. Two rams and menorahs flank the gabled Ark of the Law.

The whole centre of the floor is covered by a three-panel mosaic. Nearest the entrance [5] interconnecting octagons are surrounded by

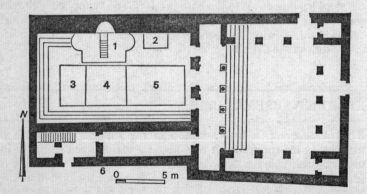

Fig. 77. Khirbet Suseya. The C5 AD synagogue (after Netzer).

birds. In the centre [4] a geometric pattern is laid over an earlier zodiac of which a small part has been revealed. Then comes a three-part panel [3] whose elements are hard to identify.

At some stage the west and south walls were strengthened by the addition of a sloping buttress [6] which, on the west, was subsequently incorporated into a much thicker wall.

KORAZIM: *see* CHOROZAIN

KURNUB: *see* MAMSHIT

KURSI (O6)

The largest Byzantine monastic complex in the country is located 5 km north of En Gev where the road makes a right-angled turn into Nahal Samakh to mount the Golan (fig. 98).

It has been a place of pilgrimage since the C5 AD, presumably because of Jesus' dramatic exorcism where swine cast themselves into the lake. According to the gospels this took place 'in the land of the Gerasenes/Gadarenes/Gergesenes' (Mark 5: 1), 'which is opposite Galilee' (Luke 8: 26). The fact that there are three different names for the same place is suspicious. Jerash and Gadara (= Umm Qeis) are in Transjordan far from the lake. Gergesa has never been identified; it may have been invented to designate this site when local scholars became aware that neither of the two other places fitted the circumstances of the gospel narrative. St. Jerome confused Gergesa with Korazim but his personal knowledge of Palestinian topography was limited. This site thus became known by the name of the town which is in fact located 3·5 km north of Capernaum. Kursi is possibly a dialectical deformation of Korazim.

The monastic area is enclosed by a great rectangular plastered wall (145 × 123 m); decorative paintings can be found on parts of its interior face. The one gate, strongly fortified, faces the lake, and from it a paved way leads to the church located in the middle of the compound. It is most unusual to find a church and the main gate on the same axis.

The church (fig. 78) is a classical mid-C5 AD type. Mosaics cover the entire area of the sanctuary. Most [1, 2, 5, 6] are simple geometric designs, but the medallions of the lateral aisles [4] contain represen-

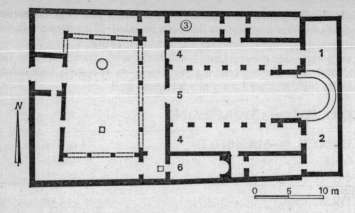

Fig. 78. Kursi. The C5 church (after Urman and Tsaferis).

tations of the flora and fauna of the area; with a few rare exceptions all the living things have been systematically destroyed. One small room [2] was turned into a baptistry in the C6; an inscription at the entrance dates the pavement to 585. The function of the rooms along the north side is not clear; one [3] contained an olive press. A grille at the entrance to an external chapel on the south side [6] is the entrance to a crypt which was the burial place of the monastery.

The living quarters of the monks are located in the area north of the church. Between the enclosure and the lake there are traces of a village of the Roman period with a small port and breakwater 100 m north of the little tel.

KYPROS (M17)

Dominating the entrance of the ancient road from Jerusalem to the rich plain of JERICHO (fig. 69), this strategic peak (Tel el-Aqaba) is a miniature MASADA in terms both of its surprising buildings and of its isolation from the land mass to the west. When the Israeli army is not in occupation two roads lead to a parking-lot just below the summit. It is less nerve-wracking to walk.

A round tower in the south corner of the plateau below the summit is pre-Herodian and shows this to be one of the two fortresses, Thrax and Taurus, built by the Syrian general Baccides during the Maccabean wars and destroyed by Pompey as his legions tramped down the valley to inaugurate Roman dominion in 63 BC. The other (Nuseib el-Aweishireh) is clearly evident on the opposite side of the Wadi Qilt; its history is identical with that of Kypros.

With the exception of a square Byzantine building in the middle of the plateau, all the other ruins are Herodian. His manic fear of revolt suggests that Herod fortified this site, which he named after his mother Kypros, before building his palace at TULUL ABU EL-ALAIQ just below. It was the nearest citadel in which he could take refuge. This might explain the rather elaborate bath (room with two niches) on the very summit. The nearby cisterns were filled by hand (as at Masada) from reservoirs on the north and east slopes fed by an aqueduct coming from Ein Qilt.

In AD 66 the Zealots exterminated the garrison and threw down the fortifications.

LAKHISH (F20)

Lakhish is a very deceptive site. From a distance it is lost among the rolling hills of the Shephelah but its height is impressive as one turns into the rough unpaved access road (fig. 47). It is only when one stands on top that the authority of its situation becomes apparent. From the great palace-fort there is a magnificent view to the west (coastal plain), north (the outline of Mareshah near BET GUVRIN is clear in the middle foreground), and east (the Hebron hills).

Canaanite cities had existed on the mound for almost 2,000 years before it was taken by Joshua. The king of Lakhish had joined the coalition of the five kings defeated by the Israelites at Gibeon (JIB); this prompted a swing to the south-west during which his city fell in two days (Josh. 10: 1–32). Such a speedy end to the siege of a city with the natural advantages of Lakhish would be incredible had the archaeologists not shown that it was not fortified at this period (*c.* 1220 BC). The city was left in ruins until it was fortified by Rehoboam (928–911 BC) as the southernmost of the line of forts protecting the western flank of the kingdom of Judah (2 Chr. 11: 5–12). One of his successors remade the city on a grandiose scale, erecting a great palace-fort on a raised podium and ringing the mound with a double line of walls. At this period Lakhish was probably the most important city in Judah after Jerusalem; King Amaziah (798–769 BC) fled there when a rebellion broke out in Jerusalem, 'but they sent after him to Lakhish and slew him there' (2 Kgs. 14: 19).

An earthquake occurred about 760 BC which necessitated the rebuilding of parts of the city (Amos 1: 1; Zech. 14: 5). In 701 BC Sennacherib invaded Judah and made Lakhish his base (2 Kgs. 18: 13–17; 19: 8). The importance he attached to his successful siege of the city is attested by the carved reliefs of the battle which he installed in the central room of his new palace in Nineveh (fig. 80): archers, supported by infantry, protect mobile battering rams picking at the double wall defended by bowmen and slingers. The passage of the Assyrians is marked by the evidence of fierce fires throughout the city.

The city gate and wall were rebuilt, but not the palace. It is not clear by whom: an inscription of Sennacherib says that he gave the captured towns of Judah to the Philistine kings of Ashdon, Ekron, and Gaza. In the course of the next century, however, the Judaeans regained control because as the Babylonians advanced under Nebuchadnezzar in 587 BC, the commander of an outpost wrote in Hebrew to the ruler of Lakhish, 'And let my lord know that we are watching for the signals of Lakhish, according to all the indications which my lord gave, for we cannot see Azekah'. This note was found in the ruins of the gate; according to the prophet Jeremiah, Lakhish and Azekah were the last cities to fall before Jerusalem (34: 7).

After the Exile (586–538 BC) the area around Lakhish formed part of Idumaea, but the city was resettled by Jews (Neh. 11: 30) A representative of the ruling Persians presumably occupied the palatial residence built on the platform of the Israelite palace-fort (*c*. 450–350 BC). Occupation continued in the succeeding Hellenistic period and then ceased abruptly in the C2 BC.

Visit (fig. 79). The loose stones [1] piled against the side of the mound just north of the crude car park were part of the Assyrian siege ramp. The Israelite access ramp [2] forced attackers to expose their un-protected right side to the defenders on the walls above, the shield being carried on the left arm. From the turn at the head of the ramp one can look down into the Canaanite moat in which successive temples [7] were built between the C15 and C13 BC; nothing visible remains. On the slope of the mound are the outer [4] and inner [5] Israelite walls represented in the Assyrian relief; these walls are best seen in the section between the buttresses [8] and the 44 m-deep Canaanite well [9]. In the C8 BC an attempt was made to develop an

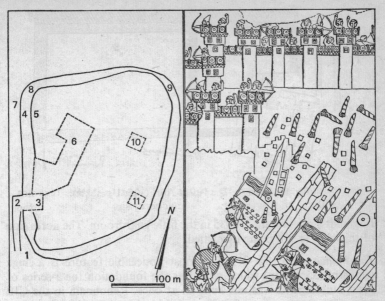

Fig. 79. Fortifications and excavated
areas on Tel Lakhish.

Fig. 80. Relief from Nineveh showing Sennacherib's siege of Lakhish.

alternative water supply by digging a great shaft [11] but the grandiose project was never completed and the pit has been filling since.
There are three excavation areas, the Gate Area [3], the Palace Area
[6], and the Temple Area [10].

The Gate Area. When the gate complex was constructed in the C9–C8
BC it comprised two elements. Having passed through an outer gate
at the top of the access ramp, one had to turn right in an open court
to reach the three-chambered inner gate which is the largest known
in Israel. Similar structures of the same period appear at BEER SHEVA
and MEGIDDO. This gate served until its total destruction by Sennacherib; battering-rams brought down the western wall of the outer
gate. When the defences were rebuilt after the Exile the inner gate
was simply a gap in the stone city wall; a new outer gate was erected
on the ruins of the old one. The south side of this gate is still visible
on the right looking in; the important ostraca (inscribed pottery

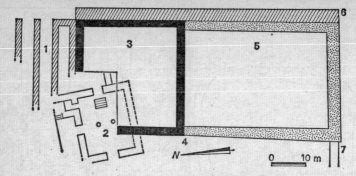

Fig. 81. Lakhish. The Palace Area (after Ussishkin).

fragments) were found in 1935 in the little guardroom. The north side of this area is still being excavated.

The Palace Area (fig. 81). The most noticeable feature is a huge platform (35×75 m) which served as the foundation for a series of great buildings. It was not built all at once. Rehoboam in the C10 BC constructed a square fort [3 – solid black]; one of his successors doubled the area by extending the platform to the south [5], the joint being easily perceived [4]. Some time later (early C8 BC?) additions were made on the north [1] and the width of the east wall was doubled [6]. The intermediate walls in [3] and [5] give some indication of the disposition of rooms in the buildings above. Nothing of the superstructures (probably built of brick) survives; the ruins left by Sennacherib were cleared in order to level the platform for the Persian residence of which only two column bases and a door-sill remain. Prior to 701 BC there were storehouses at the south-east corner [6], and a heavy wall [7] linked the platform to the city wall. Between this wall and the city gate houses of the Israelite period (C10 –C6 BC) are now being brought to light.

Work is still going on in the north-west corner of the platform where a Canaanite temple of the city destroyed by Joshua has been discovered. Entered via a paved antechamber on the west, the main chamber [2] had a brick floor and cedar of Lebanon roof beams, with a flight of stone steps (still in place) leading up to the cella on the east. An earlier three-unit temple appears at TEL BALATA. Such religious edifices were the prototypes of the three-part temple erected by Solomon in Jerusalem.

The Sacred Area (fig. 82). The first Israelite sanctuary was a small room [1] with a low bench and a slightly raised 'altar' in the western corner; it dates from the time of Rehoboam. Subsequently it was covered by a terrace whose retaining wall [2] is visible at the edge of a cobbled street [3]. Traces of a similar street of the same period, which remained in use for several centuries, have been found further down the slope, suggesting that Israelite Lakhish had another gate on the east.

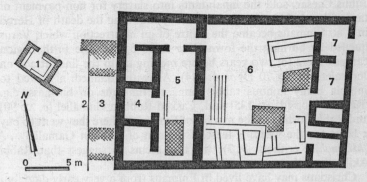

Fig. 82. Lakhish. The Sacred Area (after Aharoni).

Excavations have disturbed the floor levels of the C2 BC temple (solid black) but the plan is still perfectly clear. Its orientation is the reverse of that of the Canaanite temple but the basic plan is the same. Two small chambers with benches inside the door [7] gave access to the courtyard [6] from which a flight of steps led up to the main room [5] paved with stone slabs. Two further steps mark the entrance to the cella [4]. The cult vessels found *in situ* furnish some basis for the belief that the temple was used for Jewish worship.

It has been suggested that the badly overgrown building between the Sacred Area and the great shaft was a temple of the C4–C3 BC; the row of pillars would have divided the main chamber into two.

LATRUN (G17)

Until 1967, when the inhabitants were deported and their homes levelled, the Arab village of Imwas preserved the biblical name

Emmaus; today the site is called Canada Park. Families picnic where the famous scholar Julius Africanus once walked the streets of a Roman city.

Emmaus is first mentioned to locate the Syrian camp taken by Judas Maccabaeus in 161 BC (1 Macc. 3: 38–4: 15); a year later it was again in Syrian possession and Baccides fortified it because it controlled the three routes to Jerusalem from the plain (1 Macc. 9: 50). Josephus records its misfortunes. In 43 BC Cassius, the assassin of Julius Caesar, sold the inhabitants into slavery for non-payment of taxes (*War* 1: 218–22); in the anarchy following the death of Herod in 4 BC Emmaus became the centre of an insurrection which Varus quelled by burning the town (*War* 2: 60–5, 71). The Fifth Legion camped there for two years before moving up to the final attack on Jerusalem in AD 70 (*War* 4: 444). After the Sanhedrin moved to Jamnia many famous rabbis came to Emmaus on business, e.g. 'Rabbi Akiba [d. AD 135] said, I asked Rabban Gamaliel [*c.* AD 90] and Rabbi Joshua in the market of Emmaus, where they went to buy a beast for the wedding-feast of the son of Rabban Gamaliel . . .' (*Mishnah*, Kerithoth 3: 7); the text seems to suggest that Rabbi Akiba lived there.

Christians may have lived in Emmaus from a very early date, but the first we know of is the soldier-diplomat turned scholar, Julius Africanus. In 221, because of his contacts in the imperial court, the city sent him with a delegation to the emperor Elagabalus to request the reconstruction of Emmaus with the rights of a Roman city and a new name, Nicopolis. All requests were granted. The change of name is noted by Jerome (in 386) who adds, 'where the Lord made himself known to Cleophas in the breaking of bread, thus consecrating his house as a church' (Letter 108). The localization here of the gospel event goes back at least as far as Eusebius (330); it was never questioned during the Byzantine period, but seems to have been forgotten after a plague wiped out Emmaus in 639. According to Arab writers (who all revert to the original name, abandoning Nicopolis) the plague started there and spread throughout the Middle East.

The Crusaders built a church where there had been one before, but were attracted to this area for other than religious reasons. A fortress here was imperative to guard the route to Jerusalem and to exercise some control over the raiders from ASHQELON. The Templars built Toron of the Knights on the hill behind the present Cistercian Abbey of Latrun. The ruins are badly overgrown; beneath them may be the acropolis of Nicopolis.

Even though Emmaus-Nicopolis has in its favour the oldest
Palestinian tradition identifying it with the Emmaus of Luke 24, it is
not likely that this is correct. It fits with the distance of 160 stadia
(31 km) from Jerusalem given by some manuscripts of the gospels, but
it is more probable that the alternative reading of 60 stadia (11·5 km)
is the original. This distance suits ABU GHOSH and QUBEIBA but the
identification of both these sites as Emmaus is relatively late. After
crushing the First Revolt (AD 66–70) Vespasian assigned 'to 800
veterans discharged from the army a place for habitation called

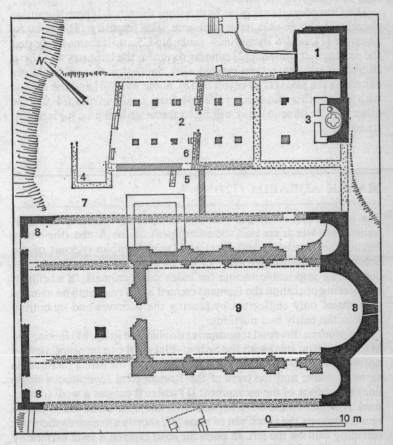

Fig. 83. Latrun. Churches of Emmaus-Nicopolis.

Emmaus, distant 30 stadia from Jerusalem' (*War* 7: 217). Despite the problem of distance, this seems the most likely candidate; the name was quickly supplanted by Colonia (which is why the Byzantines did not know it) and has now become Motza.

Visit. On the highway from Jerusalem take the Ramallah–Ashqelon turn-off. For Latrun Abbey and Toron of the Knights follow the signs to Ashqelon under the bridge. Emmaus-Nicopolis (fig. 83) is just on the right at the end of the ramp. Open: 9 a.m. – 4 p.m.; ring bell and wait for buzzer.

The Crusader church [9] is built within the much bigger Byzantine church [8] and re-uses its central apse. The baptistry [3], fed by its reservoir [1], is also Byzantine – probably C5 AD. It seems likely that the rectangular building [2] running out from the baptistry was also a church; it may have been erected after the destruction of the larger church in the SAMARITAN revolt of 529. Some walls [4] and the mosaic with the panther and birds [7] come from a villa of the C4 AD; the other mosaic floor [5] may belong to the same building. [6] is an entrance to [2].

MAALE AQRABIM (J27)

The prosperity of MAMSHIT was due in great part to the Gaza–Elat trade route which crossed the escarpment of the Araba (the valley linking the Dead Sea and Elat) at Maale Aqrabim (Ascent of the Scorpions). The average slope of the escarpment at this point is 34 degrees, an impossible incline for laden pack animals. In a brilliant engineering operation the Romans created a cliff road with an average gradient of only 16 degrees by making sharp curves and by cutting steps in the really bad portions.

The modern dirt road (continuous double line in fig. 84) linking the Mamshit–Oron road with the Sedom–Elat road can be negotiated by normal cars in dry weather but a jeep increases the safety factor. It is easier to walk: find the trace of the Roman road (continuous single line) at the foot of the escarpment [1] where it crosses a wadi (dotted line). It angles up the ridge between two wadis for some 600 m before one encounters the first flight of steps [2]; shortly afterwards there is a retaining wall on the left. In parts the road is given a level surface by being notched into the slope. There are five flights of steps between

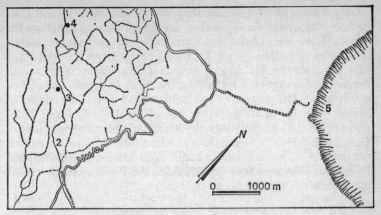

Fig. 84. Roman Road at Maale Aqrabim.

the wadi and Hurvat Zafir [3]; this little ruin may have been a guard-post as was Mezad Zafir [4].

From the modern dirt road a very rough track (broken double line) leads to the top of the rim of ha-Makhtesh ha-Qatan [5]. This roughly circular depression looks as if it had been formed by the impact of a huge meteor but it is in fact the result of severe erosion. The Makhtesh Qatan is the smallest of three such geological phenomena in the Negev. The other two, Makhtesh Ramon and ha-Makhtesh ha-Gadol, can be inspected much more easily because they have been cut by scenic tarmac roads. These depressions began as cracks in the sedimentary surface caused by movements in the Miocene period. After water penetration had worn an outlet to the south-east erosion intensified, eventually exposing the volcanic basalt of the Precambrian period in certain areas.

MAMRE (RAMAT EL-KHALIL) (J20)

Camped beside a great oak, Abraham here received the three mysterious visitors and bargained with the Lord for the salvation of Sodom (Gen. 18). A signpost half-way between Halhul and HEBRON shows the way to the great stone enclosure where 2,000 years later the emperor Hadrian sold the children of Abraham into slavery after crushing the Second Revolt (AD 132–5).

Long a place of popular Jewish devotion because of a great tree, the site became the focal point of local superstitious practices for pagans, Jews, and Christians, culminating in an annual festival. Constantine's mother-in-law, Eutropia, did her best to discourage such practices by building a church (325) whose magnificence merited representation on the Madaba Map (C6; see JERUSALEM: MOUNT ZION). Her gesture was as ineffective as that of the editors of Genesis who, for much the same reasons (Hos. 4:13; Ezek. 6:13), tried to lose the site completely by identifying Mamre with Hebron (Gen. 23: 19; 35: 27). Her architects were forced to cram the church into one end of the enclosure so as not to disturb the pagan altar, and the festival continued into the C7. After the Persian invasion (614) monks built cells in the ruined church.

Visit (fig. 85). The monumental blocks of the enclosure wall [1] make one think of Herod, but the technique (no boss) is quite different. Characteristic Herodian masonry does appear here and there – e.g. pilaster base [11] – suggesting that he may have begun a structure that was never completed. The re-used stone door-sills and lintel [3] were

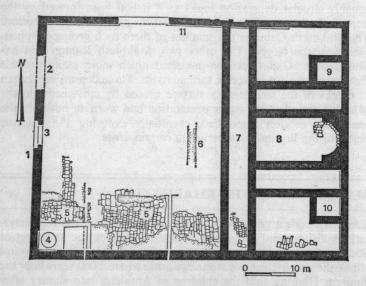

Fig. 85. Mamre.

possibly intended for this edifice. The break in the wall [2] is modern; the original entrance is unknown. According to local tradition, Abraham dug the well [4] with his own hands; the adjoining basin is admittedly modern. No date can be given for the pavement [5] which may be much more extensive. Though unusually cramped because of the position of the pagan altar [6], the church has the classic disposition of a Constantinian basilica: a narthex [7], the central nave [8] with two lateral aisles, having outside them the prothesis [9] and the diakonikon [10].

MAMSHIT (H26)

Brilliant engineering explains the importance of Mamshit. Older trade routes from Gaza to Elat were forced to pass through difficult dry country in order to use natural passages through the high escarpment of the Araba, the valley joining the Dead Sea and the Gulf of Aqaba. Near Mamshit Roman engineers cut a stepped road in the steep cliff (MAALE AQRABIM = Ascent of the Scorpions) which enabled the pack trains to travel the rest of the route on both sides in flat terrain with perennial water supplies every 25–30 km. The trade which used to pass through AVDAT began to flow through Mamshit, and it never needed to develop the agriculture which characterized the other desert cities.

The NABATAEANS founded Mamshit in the C1 AD, and the plan of the city was fixed within a couple of generations. The buildings were of such quality that they were still in use in the C4 AD. The Romans assumed control in the C2 AD; the presence of a garrison to protect the trade route is attested by a military cemetery with tombstones inscribed in Latin. The growing wealth of the city necessitated the construction of a city wall at the beginning of the C4 which encloses an area of 10 acres. Sporadic raids heightened the inhabitants' awareness of nomadic envy, and the Byzantines doubled the width of the wall; but their major contribution to the architecture of Mamshit was the erection of two churches. The absence of any church of the triapsidal C6 type, and the rarity of coins dated after 500, suggest that the life of Mamshit ceased at the end of the C5. Its end was, indeed, violent when riders from the desert tasted the fruits of a victory long denied. The memory of its importance explains its appearance in the early C6 Madaba mosaic map; the name given there is Mampsis (Mamshit is the supposed Semitic original).

Visit (fig. 86). Open: 8 a.m.–5 p.m.; Fridays to 4 p.m.; an explanatory leaflet is available at the ticket office. It is possible to drive to the top of the hill beside the former British police post [1] which now houses toilets. From the roof there is a fine general view of the site. Mamshit has good explanatory signs identifying the purpose of buildings and the function of the rooms within; the periods noted on these signs correspond to the following dates: Middle Nabataean = AD 1–50; Late Nabataean = 70–150; Late Roman = 180–324; Byzantine = 324–640. Everything above the blue line has been restored.

Just north of the old police post is a large complex called the House of Frescoes [2–3]. Off the courtyard with four Nabataean columns

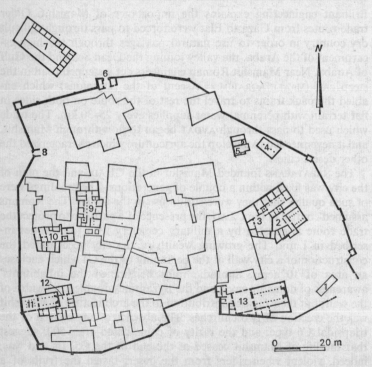

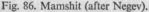

Fig. 86. Mamshit (after Negev).

[2] is a room labelled 'stables'; the troughs do in fact suggest mangers but the animals must have been exceedingly small! Similar structures of a much older period at BEER SHEVA, MEGIDDO, and HAZOR were storehouses. Beside it is a typically Nabataean house [3] built around an open court; note the decantation basin beside the cistern in the courtyard; water from the roofs was collected there and the overflow passed through a channel in the wall to another cistern in an adjoining room.

The great pool [4] was probably roofed over with wooden beams since the space between the arches is too great for stone slabs. The pool cuts through the foundations of an earlier edifice (Building XIX) which projected beyond the line of the Roman city wall. Note the small decantation basin at one end of the pool. It cleansed the run-off rainwater from the slope outside which came through the channel at the base of the city wall.

From the other end of the pool a conduit brought water to the bath-house [5], also built on top of earlier structures. This is a good place to examine the structure of the raised floor of the caldarium; the furnace room is obviously a secondary addition since the much inferior masonry is not integrated into the other walls.

Outside the main gate [6] was a large caravanserai [7] where the Nabataean drivers rested while the caravan masters and merchants were entertained in the city. The only other gate [8] faces the wadi in which a Nabataean dam is still visible; three watch towers ensured the protection of the precious water supply.

A very big house [9] is typically Nabataean in its general plan but much more elaborate than usual; it may have been the residence of the governor. Two features are noteworthy. The staircase tower is preserved to a considerable height and the care expended on the underside of the steps is remarkable. One room has two sets of arches, one running north-south, the other east-west; they could not have been in use together and show that the room was reconstructed. The cistern outside the single entrance collected rainwater from the street.

Beside the governor's house is a tower [10] which may have served as an administrative centre; storerooms were built around the courtyard in which a cistern was sunk. Rainwater from the roofs was carried to the cistern by a gutter running along the outside of the building. The upper part of the tower has been reconstructed as an observation point.

A Greek inscription in the middle of the magnificent mosaic floor of the West Church [11] shows it to have been erected by Nilus; no date is given but it must have been about the middle of the C5. The square rooms on either side of the apse probably contained reliquaries. In addition to storing rainwater from the roofs, the cistern in the courtyard of the church was served by a channel under the city wall which collected run-off from the slope outside.

The West Church was built over part of a fine Nabataean house [12]. The eastern end of the church virtually blocks the doorways of the southern portion of the house, and destroys the proportions of the courtyard. The roof of the cistern is almost intact and is a perfect illustration of the way the Nabataeans overcame the lack of trees for rafters; arches set closely together supported stone slabs which were then covered with plaster. The same roofing technique is found throughout the city.

The East Church [13] is the oldest church in the central Negev. The excavator dates it to the second half of the C4; it was certainly built before 427 because there are two crosses in the mosaic floor and such decoration was forbidden after this date. In the square rooms on either side of the apse one can see the marks of the legs of the stone tables which stood above the reliquaries built into the floors. At a later stage a second reliquary was added in each room; the purpose of the hole in the covering slab was to permit objects to touch the bone and become imbued with its virtue. The baptismal font in a room on the south had steps on three sides; the purpose of the depression in the surface of the font is unknown. The circular plastered basin in the adjoining room may have served for the disposal of water used in baptism. The staircase in the little courtyard beside the bathroom suggests that there was a gallery on top of the colonnade round the atrium; the drainpipes in each corner of the atrium lead to the central cistern.

MAR SABA (L18)

From the last turn in the road only two towers are visible; the buildings pour over the side of the deep Kidron valley almost to the bottom. The stark landscape and the colourful airiness of the structures combine to leave an indelible memory of the greatest of the desert monasteries.

In Bethlehem follow the signs to the HERODION, and at the bottom of the hill branch left on the road going past the Latin Shepherds' Field. The road offers a magnificent panorama of the Kidron valley and Jerusalem. Past the big monastery of Deir Dosi (restored 1893), which housed 400 monks when its founder St. Theodosius died in AD 529, one road descends to the bed of the Kidron, the other continues along the ridge to Mar Saba. Where the tarmac ends the road to the left leads to the monastery.

St. Sabas (439–532) built the first monastery on this site in 482 when the number of his disciples forced him from the cave (grille with cross and letters A and C on far side of wadi) which he had occupied for five years. Despite the number martyred by the savage Persian attack in 614, the monastery enjoyed its golden age in the C8–C9. Of all the celebrated figures who then lived there (historians, poets, musicians) St. John Damascene (d. 749) deserves special mention; without his classic defence of the legitimacy of images the culture of Western Europe would be very different and our heritage immeasurably poorer. Surrounded by hostility which periodically erupted into murderous violence, even as late as the C19, the monastery nonetheless survived. Severe damage in the earthquake of 1834 necessitated almost complete reconstruction.

Visit. Open 8 a.m.–5 p.m. throughout the year; no women admitted. Pull bell cord in door at foot of ramp. The body of St. Sabas, borrowed by the Crusaders and restored by Pope Paul VI in 1965, can be seen in the principal church dedicated to the Annunciation. Most of the icons and frescoes are modern; the two lateral doors in the iconostasis are said to be medieval. The chapel of St. Nicholas is located in the cave where St. Sabas founded the first church. The royal doors in the iconostasis are C15, as are the set of five icons above the painted wooden band on the wall facing it. A series of reliquaries contain skulls of the martyrs; many others are entombed behind a grille. The tomb of St. Sabas in the courtyard between the two churches was built in 1929 in place of a much smaller edicule. A chapel is built out from the cave in which St. John Damascene did much of his writing. It was also his tomb but the Crusaders removed the body and its present whereabouts is uncertain. From the gallery outside the lateral narthex of the Church of the Annunciation the cell of St. Sophie, mother of St. Sabas, can be seen 300 m to the north in the bed of the wadi. Directly below this gallery is the basin of a tiny spring within the cliff reserved for emergencies; normal water needs are met by cisterns which collect the run-off from the occasional winter rains.

The isolated Tower of St. Simeon (built 1612) can be entered by women but is rarely open. From its base a good path descends into the wadi; the view into the monastery from the other side is well worth the effort. From the top of the cliff the sides of the wadi appear strewn with remnants of ancient walls, showing how dense was the occupation in its age of glory. In 1978 there were only eight monks.

See also MONASTERIES IN THE JUDAEAN DESERT.

MASADA (L22)

A great rock curiously like an aircraft-carrier moored to the western cliffs of the Dead Sea, Masada is the most spectacular site in the country and the scene of one of the most dramatic episodes in its history.

Access is easier from the Dead Sea side where there is a choice between the cable car (starts 8 a.m.; last car down 4 p.m.) and a very steep path which, according to Josephus, 'they call the Snake, seeing a resemblance to that reptile in its narrowness and continual windings' (*War* 7: 282); minimum 40 minutes for the very fit. On the west a tarmac road from Arad leads to the base of the Roman ramp which must then be climbed on foot (15 minutes). Open: 6.30 a.m. – 3.30 p.m.

All our information on the history of Masada comes from Josephus's *Jewish War* to which the bracketed numbers refer. First fortified by Alexander Jannaeus (103–76 BC) to protect his south-eastern border (7: 285), it was taken by Herod the Great (1: 237) in the power-struggle which followed the murder of his father Antipater in 43 BC. Forced to flee Jerusalem in 40 BC when the invading Parthians made Antigonus king, he put his womenfolk (mother, sisters, Mariamne his fiancée, and her mother) for security in Masada with a guard of 800 (1: 267) while he escaped across the desert to Rome. In his absence Antigonus besieged Masada. Shortage of water forced the defenders to begin girding themselves for a break-out, but a sudden cloudburst replenished the cisterns (1: 286–7). Shortly afterwards Herod relieved the garrison (1: 293–4).

This experience showed Herod the value of Masada, and he replanned it as a last refuge in case the Jews should turn against him, or Cleopatra should persuade Mark Antony to have him killed (7: 300). This must have taken place between 39 and 31 BC. Under the Procurators the Romans controlled Masada, but in the summer of AD 66 Jewish rebels took it over by a trick (2: 408). Menachem was the first to see that Herod's stores would provide the weapons the rising needed (2: 433–4). This gave him the edge on his rivals, but he was quickly assassinated because of his brutality and arrogance, and some of his supporters, including his relative Eleazar ben Jair, barely escaped to Masada (2: 442–7). Thereafter they took no further part in the war against Rome, occupying themselves with raids on the surrounding villages (4: 400). The worst episode occurred at EN GEDI where, during Passover, they slaughtered over 700 women and children (4: 401–5). When Simon ben Giora tried to persuade them to carve out their own territory in the south they refused, preferring to stay close to their base (4: 503–7).

Masada, therefore, posed no threat to the Romans, and they were in no hurry to move against it. Some time after the fall of Jerusalem in AD 70 Lucilius Bassus was appointed legate in Judaea and saw the capture of HERODION and Machaerus as his first priorities (7: 163–4). Having taken Herodion first, it would have been natural to continue south to Masada, but instead he swung round the north end of the Dead Sea to deal with Machaerus which was a real danger. The site offered the defenders the same advantages as Masada, and an energetic defence prolonged the siege. Bassus followed his victory there with a foray into the forest of Jardes (7: 210), and it was left to his successor, Flavius Silva, to turn his attention to Masada (7: 252), probably in the autumn of 72.

Coming in from the Arad side, he set up his command camp just beside the present parking-lot (7: 277). His first step was to surround Masada with eight fortified camps linked by a wall (7: 276); any visitor will see the futility of this rigid adherence to the military textbook. To reach the defence wall on the summit 150 m above he built a huge ramp which enabled an iron-sheathed tower equipped with quick-firing balliste on top and a battering-ram below to reach the wall (7: 304–10). The Zealots had time to prepare their defences, and when the Romans made a breach they found a new wood-faced wall in front of them. The defenders had a moment of hope as the torches thrown against this wall flamed back against the tower, but the wind changed and the wall began to burn (7: 311–19).

Confident that the next day would see the end, the Romans rested for the night. No hope remained to the Zealots and they decided on communal suicide. Ten were appointed by lot to slay the others, and when the deed was done, 'the nine bared their throats, and the last solitary survivor ... set the palace ablaze, and then collecting his strength drove his sword clean through his body and fell beside his family' (7: 389–97). It was the 2nd of May AD 73.

An awful solitude greeted the Roman vanguard next morning, and Silva departed leaving a small garrison in the corner of his command camp where they remained for some thirty years. His standard textbook operation merited no mention in Roman records.

As with most of the Herodian fortresses which provided a ready-made supply of cut stone, Masada was occupied by Byzantine monks in the C4–C5. This was the only truly peaceful moment in a history which began in fear and culminated in tragic despair.

Visit. It would be superfluous to provide details for a tour of Masada. All the buildings except the church are of the Herodian period, and detailed signs (with plans where necessary) contain all the useful information on each edifice. An excellent guide to the site is available at the ticket-office. At least two hours should be allowed for the visit, not counting the ascent and descent. Shaded rest areas, toilets, and drinking water are provided on the summit.

MEGIDDO (J8)

Megiddo is the royal box in one of the great theatres of history. From time immemorial armies have surged from the surrounding valleys to play their parts on the flat stage of the Jezreel valley. Not surprisingly, Armageddon (= Har Megedon = Mountain of Megiddo) has become the symbol for the battle to end all wars (Rev. 16: 16).

Its position at the head of the most important pass through the Carmel range (Nahal Iron) gave Megiddo control of the Way of the Sea, the ancient trade-route between Egypt and the east (fig. 59). Traders from all over the known world passed its gates, as did invading armies. It was a strongly fortified city before 3000 BC, but its name first appears on the walls of the Temple of Karnak where Thutmose III had carved a detailed record (the earliest known) of the battle he fought at Megiddo in May 1468 BC. From the top of the tel, with the account in hand (*The Ancient Near East: an Anthology of Texts and Pictures*, ed. J. Pritchard, London: OUP, 1958, pp. 179–82), every movement of the swirling chariot squadrons can be plotted; that day Thutmose captured 924 enemy chariots! It remained a vassal city-state of Egypt for over a hundred years; six letters from its king, Biridiya, were found in the archives of the Egyptian foreign ministry at Amarna (*Ancient Near East*, pp. 263–4), one howling for aid against Shechem (TEL BALATA). The quality of the architecture and hoards of ivory, gold, and jewellery bear witness to the great prosperity of the city.

Too strong to be taken by the invading Israelites (Judg. 1: 27), it probably fell to David. Solomon (965–928 BC) surrounded the summit with a casemate wall and filled the surface with public buildings, as befitted one of the most important cities of his realm. Destroyed in pharaoh Shishak's campaign in 923 BC, it was rebuilt even more magnificently by Omri or Ahab in the mid-C9 BC. Megiddo fell in 733 BC to the Assyrians who made it the capital of the province of Galilee. They gave it spacious private dwellings and a new grid street system.

In the C7 BC Megiddo suddenly and inexplicably loses all importance; it became an open settlement with a small fortress. By the C4 BC it was uninhabited, and was never resettled.

Visit. Open 8 a.m.–5 p.m. Megiddo is a complicated site; there are 20 superimposed cities. The reception area has a highly instructive exhibit with a model of the city as it looked in the time of Omri or Ahab. A general plan of the site is available on request.

(1) *The Gate Area* (fig. 87). The ruins visible here did not all exist at the same time; different shading in the plan shows elements that were contemporary. The path from the reception area [1] leads up a ramp which formed part of the entrance to the city from the time of Solomon. Earlier gates employed the same technique [8 & 11], necessitating a right-angled turn to enter the city. Just in front of the forward gate [4] a flight of steps [3] leads to a post-Solomonic water system; the wall just inside [5] is pre-Solomonic. The earliest gate discovered at Megiddo [12] is dated to the C18 BC. Only big enough to accommodate pedestrians, it was built of mud-brick on stone foundations. A new stone gate [9], wide enough to take chariots, was built in the C16 and served the city for some 400 years. Just beside it is the corner of a large building [10] whose rooms surrounded a wide courtyard. The rich collections of carved ivories and jewellery found therein justify calling it a palace. It was balanced, on the far side of the gate, by another building [2] with thinner walls but the same room arrangement.

The excavators left only one side of the Solomonic gate [7]. All

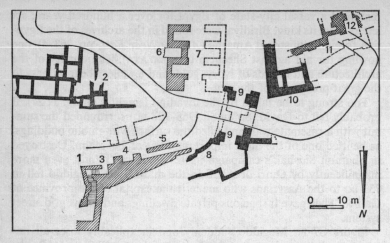

Fig. 87. Megiddo. The Gate Area (after Loud).

that remains visible was below ground; the street level was at the top of the finely bonded piers. At a later stage the space between the piers was filled in to create the foundations for a C7 BC one-bay gate; its inner pier [6] is still in place.

(2) *The Palace Area.* On the higher ground just to the east of building [2] is a palace (28 × 21 m) built by Solomon. The five rooms north of its courtyard formed part of the casemate wall with which he fortified the city. A 10 m-wide street separated the 2 m-thick south wall of this palace from another large Solomonic edifice.

(3) *The Sacred Area* (fig. 88). The viewpoint on the south side of the deepest trench cut by the archaeologists is the best spot from which to appreciate the four temples. The city worshipped here for over a thousand years. The oldest temple [5] was built about 3000 BC. The long room has an altar opposite the door which gives on to an open courtyard similar to its contemporary at EN GEDI. The round stone altar [4] came into being some 500 years later. Originally an independent unit enclosed by a wall, it was shortly afterwards linked to a two-room temple [3]. From the vestibule one entered a chamber with an altar at the far end; two pillars supported the roof. Within the same period (2650–2350 BC) two further temples [1 and 2] were constructed identical in plan with [3]. What happened then is not clear,

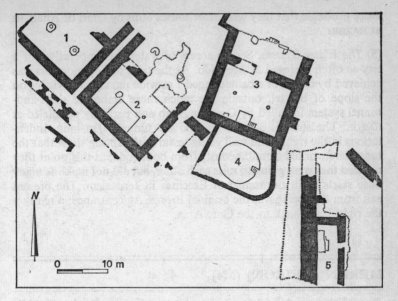

Fig. 88. Megiddo. The Sacred Area (after Loud).

but temples [1] and [2] went out of use first, and temple [3] some time later; by 2000 BC no traces remained.

The ruins surrounding the viewpoint belong to a large building of the time of Omri-Ahab and to its protective offset-inset wall.

(4) *The Stable Area*. Continuing clockwise around the tel, one passes a large grain silo. Just behind it is the entrance to a large square enclosure (now unfortunately overgrown). Dated to the time of Omri-Ahab, it then contained no buildings as the palace built there by Solomon had been destroyed by Shishak in 923 BC. Adjoining it is another large courtyard with a series of long, narrow buildings along one side. Each was divided into three by two rows of pillars; the two outer aisles were cobbled, the centre one plastered. In some cases a stone trough was found between the pillars. Immediately, the excavators visualized two lines of horses face to the centre, and proclaimed the discovery of Solomon's stables, but it is now certain that they are not from the time of Solomon as the south-east corner lies over one of his ruined palaces. And if they were stables they must have housed very small, house-broken ponies. It is

more probable that they were storehouses built by Omri or Ahab, as at HAZOR.

(5) *The Water System*. Secure access to water was imperative for a city as often besieged as Megiddo. At the time of Solomon this was achieved by means of a camouflaged 1 m-wide passage still visible on the slope of the tel, outside the much more elaborate shaft-and-tunnel system installed by Omri or Ahab and perfectly paralleled at HAZOR. The shaft is 30 m deep, and the tunnel 70 m long. Indentations in the right-hand wall going towards the spring show that the tunnellers worked simultaneously from both ends; at this point they realized they were going to miss each other, but did not make as many false starts as in the tunnel of Ezechias in Jerusalem. The present exit from the spring was the original Bronze Age entrance; a path on the right leads back to the Gate Area.

MERON (MEIRON) (M4)

One of the great Jewish pilgrimage centres since the late Middle Ages, Meron is now a settlement of Oriental Jews whose customs reveal a little-known side of Judaism: animal sacrifices are still practised regularly. A magnificent synagogue and fine houses attest its prosperity in the Late Roman period.

Jewish territory since the time of Alexander Jannaeus (103–76 BC), Meron was fortified by Josephus in AD 66 (*War* 2: 573). The migration of Judaeans into Galilee after the failure of the Second Revolt in AD 135 produced a great increase in population and Meron expanded from a village into a true town. One of its attractions was the presence of Rabbi Simeon bar Yochai, one of the five disciples of Rabbi Akiva to escape execution by the Romans in 135. His fame as a teacher was reinforced by his determination to continue the fight, and both Jews and Gentiles felt the lash of his tongue; two of his sayings were, 'Slay the best of the Gentiles' and 'If Israel were to keep two Sabbaths according to the laws they would be immediately redeemed'.

As the centre of a rich agricultural area, Meron grew continuously between 135 and 360. By the C3 its inhabitants had become so numerous that part formed an independent village on an adjoining hill, KHIRBET SHEMA. The end came abruptly in the reign of Constantius II (337–61) when excessive taxes prompted a mass exodus; exile was preferable to payment.

The town came to life again only in the C8; thereafter occupation was more or less continuous. Simeon bar Yochai enjoyed a revival of popularity with the publication of the Zohar in the C14, since the greater part of this cabbalistic work purports to record his sayings as well as those of his close companions. It became the basic text of Jewish mysticism, and his tomb acted as a magnet for the cabbalists of Spain who settled at nearby Zefat (Safed) in the C16. Tens of thousands still congregate there every year on the feast of Lag Be'omer (33 days after Passover).

Visit. After the turn-off (signposted) from the main Zefat–Akko road keep bearing left to the parking-lot beside the tomb of Simeon bar Yochai (a large domed building). From the corner of the parking-lot a stepped path leads up the hill to the ancient synagogue beside the rock outcrop on the summit. The two housing complexes are on either side of the unpaved field road which starts just outside the entrance to the parking-lot.

(1) *Synagogue*. Oriented towards Jerusalem by its doors, the synagogue is the largest in Galilee; the monumental façade stands to the height of the centre lintel but the east door has been restored. The building is dated to the very end of the C3 AD by material found in the annexes along the eastern side.

(2) *Lower City* (fig. 89). Located about 150 m from the parking-lot on the right (east) side of the field road, this is the largest and best-preserved complex of the C2–C4 in the country. Its purpose seems to have been industrial with living quarters in an upper storey.

The beautifully dressed doorposts [1] of the entrance from the street give access to a narrow corridor with benches along one side. It leads to a paved courtyard [2] in which there is a column base and a flight of steps [3]; the dwelling area was above the entrance corridor and the adjoining rooms [4 and 5].

Below the level of the courtyard (which took it out of commission) is a ritual bath or *mikveh* [6] of the C1 AD. The water and the surrounding air of this bath were heated by fires lit in the adjacent pit [7]; the winters of northern Galilee can be very cold.

The semicircular stone platform and the stone bench in a room [8] off the courtyard suggest that it was a cooper's workshop; barrels were needed for Meron's famous olive-oil industry. Josephus's enemy

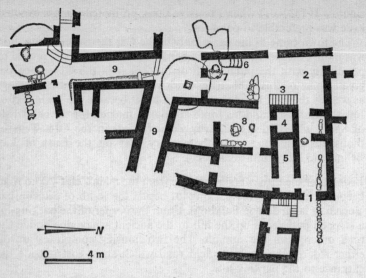

Fig. 89. Meron. The Lower City (after Meyers).

John of Giscala (today Jish, 4 km to the north) made a profit of 800
per cent when he cornered the market in this essential commodity
(*War* 2: 591–3).

Streets [9] separate this block from other home industries of the
same type; one street has a deep plastered drain running along one
side.

(3) *Wealthy Houses* (fig. 90). Directly opposite, on the other (west)
side of the field road, a massive lintel resting on two monolithic doorposts draws attention to a definitely upper-class house [1]. The space
[2] between it and the next house [3] was filled in to create a terrace.
The plan of the 'Patrician House' [3] has one unusual feature, a
room with no doors [4]. This was a storage area entered through a
trap-door in the roof and was used to store first-fruits. Because of the
cool climate the first-fruits of the spring harvest in Upper Galilee
were not ready by Passover and had to be held over for the next year.

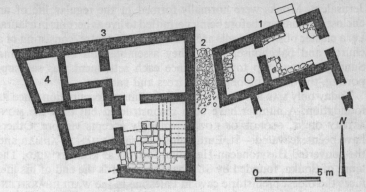

Fig. 90. Meron. Houses of the wealthy (after Meyers).

MONASTERIES IN THE JUDAEAN DESERT

D. J. Chitty called his book on Byzantine monasticism *The Desert a City* (Oxford: Blackwell, 1966), a title which perfectly characterizes an extraordinary phenomenon of life in the C4 to C6 AD. In all the provinces of the now Christian empire hundreds of thousands left the comforts of home to dwell in remote, desolate areas. Why? In sharp contrast to the centuries of persecution, Christianity now offered security and respectability. However, the standard of Christian commitment had been set by the martyrs, and so the fervent, stifled by the mediocrity of an official politicized religion, sought risk-situations elsewhere. If men were no longer offered a challenge to survival they would find it in the wild places. In order to live fully they were drawn to the desert; they did not flee the world. In fact, the desert monks were intensely involved in all the major politico-religious movements of their time. From among them came poets, critical historians, and great theologians whose writings had incalculable influence.

Monasticism in the Judaean desert is indelibly associated with three saints, each of whom formed his successor: Chariton, who founded the first laura *c.* AD 330, Euthymius (376–473), who attracted thousands of recruits, and Sabas (439–532), the great organizer. By the time of Sabas there were 130 settlements in the desert east of

Jerusalem. Monks were normally formed in the regular life of an enclosed monastery before being permitted to live as hermits in a laura, i.e. a cluster of solitary cells around a common centre, consisting of a church and bakehouse, where they assembled on Saturdays and Sundays to worship together. Since each settlement was self-supporting, the desert bloomed with trees and gardens.

Today only MAR SABA can boast of continuous occupation since its foundation. A number have been reconstructed but only the MONASTERY OF ST. GEORGE OF KOZIBA willingly accepts visitors. Others have been excavated – St. Euthymius's laura at KHAN EL-AHMAR and the converted Hasmonaean-Herodian fortress at KHIRBET MIRD. The laura of Souka, founded by St. Chariton towards the end of his life, faces the oldest prehistoric cave in Palestine in the WADI KHAREITUN.

MONASTERY OF ST. GEORGE OF KOZIBA (L17)

Clinging to the steep cliff of the Wadi Qilt above a small garden with olive trees and cypresses, this perfect example of a Greek Orthodox desert monastery has always been famous for its hospitality which, from the C6, has also been extended to women.

The dirt road from Jericho is good (fig. 69); the path down to the monastery begins at a broken vaulted cistern (Manzil Gibr) on the north side of the road where, in the Byzantine period, the monks distributed water to pilgrims passing between Jerusalem and Jericho. Hikers (who do not suffer from vertigo) can reach the monastery by a path which follows an Herodian aqueduct on the north side of the wadi in about 40 minutes from TULUL ABU AL-ALAIQ. Below this path a number of Byzantine hermitages, some still in use, are visible.

A small oratory built by five hermits (AD 420–30) was transformed into a monastery by John of Thebes towards the end of the C5. The numerous cave-dwelling hermits came there for the divine liturgy on Saturdays and Sundays. The direction of St. George of Koziba gave the monastery its period of greatest renown in the second half of the C6. Virtually abandoned after the destructive visit of the Persians (614), it was restored by Manuel I Comnenus in 1179. The legends which still influence its iconography came into being at this time. The prophet Elijah stayed there on his way to Sinai; there St. Joachim wept because of the sterility of his wife Anne and an angel announced to him the conception of the Virgin Mary. In 1483 Felix Fabri saw only ruins. Reconstruction of the monastery began in 1878 and was completed in 1901.

Visit (open: 8 a.m.–5 p.m.). From the balcony of the roofed inner court Herodian aqueducts are clearly visible on the far side of the wadi. The C6 mosaic floor of the church of SS. John and George is the oldest part of the building. A long reliquary contains the skulls of the 14 monks martyred by the Persians. A niche contains the tomb of St. George. Linked with this church by a narthex is the principal church dedicated to the Blessed Virgin. The double-headed Byzantine eagle in black, white, and red mosaic recalls the C12 restoration. The iconostasis is of recent date, but the royal doors in its centre are attributed to Alexios II Comnenus (1167–83). The vast majority of the paintings and icons date only from the last restoration. The cave-church of St. Elijah is reached by stairs from the inner court. According to legend the prophet lived there for three years and six months, being fed by ravens (1 Kings. 17: 3). There, too, St. Joachim hid for 40 days bewailing the barrenness of his wife. From this cave a narrow tunnel runs deep into the mountain; it was used as a place of refuge in times of persecution.

MONTFORT (K3)

When compared with the other Crusader castles of NIMRUD or BEL-VOIR, Montfort is of limited interest. Though finely situated on a high wooded promontory jutting out into Nahal Keziv (which reaches the sea half-way between Nahariyya and Rosh Haniqra), it commands only a limited perspective to the north-west. The 5 km track starts at the village of Miilya, 13 km due east of Nahariyya, and is not in good condition.

In the C12 AD the area was a fief of the Courtenays. The ruins of their small fortress (Castrum Regis) can be seen in the village of Miilya. As times grew more dangerous, this was considered to afford insufficient protection and a new castle (Castellum Novum Regis) was built on a site with greater natural defences. This gave rise to the new name, Montfort, which was changed to Starkenberg when the Franks sold the castle to the Teutonic knights (1228) who had already bought Miilya in 1220. These knights were the German equivalent of the older Frankish military orders, the Templars and the Hospitallers. Originally the branch of the Hospitallers which administered the hospital/hospice of St. Mary in Jerusalem (see p. 54), they had become an independent order in 1190 and were in quest of a site to serve as their central treasury and archives. Though Montfort had no strategic value, it could offer the isolation which enhanced economic security; moreover, it was located in the midst of rich farmlands. On taking possession they immediately enlarged and strengthened the castle which became their headquarters in the Holy Land.

A valiant defence repulsed Baybars who laid siege to the fortress in 1266. When he returned in 1271 his troops, protected by mantlets, worked their way up the steep slope at the western end, and succeeded in undermining the southern wall after a week. For a short while the knights held out in the keep, but eventually surrendered and marched out to Acre (AKKO). On Baybars's orders the fortress was demolished.

Visit (fig. 91). The state of the ruins does not permit a complete plan, and the one offered here is deliberately schematic. On the left of the present entrance [3] a semicircular retaining wall (of a garden?) dominates the outer screen wall further down the hill. To the right is the residence of the governor, always the Treasurer of the Order. The tower straight ahead [2] is preserved to its original height; inside, deep-set balconies and high ceilings provide restful shade. The two vaulted chambers [4] are the basement of a 20 m-square hall in which

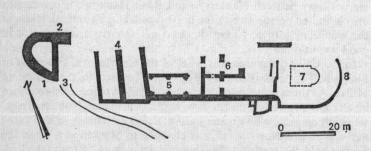

Fig. 91. Montfort. Castle of the Teutonic Knights (after Dean).

the knights met. Adjoining it is the chapel [5] which is entered from the inner ward. Further east are a series of service rooms [6]; one may have been a kitchen, another was certainly the armourer's workshop. The ruins of the keep [7] look out over the moat [8] which cuts across the saddle linking the fortress to the adjoining land mass. The great stones at the base of the keep originally formed part of a building of the Roman or Byzantine period; under the floor there is a large cistern.

Below the castle in the wadi bed is a 50 m-long two-storey building of the C13 AD. It was probably part of the farm, and may have guarded a dam which conserved winter floods.

MOUNT CARMEL (G6–J9)

The majestic promontory of Mount Carmel, which creates the Bay of Haifa, is known in Egyptian texts of the C15 BC as the 'Holy Headland'. This tradition of sanctity, inaugurated by the Phoenicians, is its dominant characteristic. An author of the C4 BC calls it 'the holy mountain of Zeus'. The Roman general Vespasian came there to make a sacrifice at the end of the C1 AD, enabling the historian Tacitus to comment, 'Carmel lies between Judaea and Syria; the same name is given to the mountain and a god. This god has neither statue nor temple; so willed the ancients; there is only an altar and worship' (*Hist.* ii, ch. 78). In the C4 AD Jamblicus, the biographer of Pythagoras, thought it appropriate to have his hero visit Carmel, 'a mountain holy above all and regarded as inaccessible to the vulgar' (*Life*, iii, ch. 14); the fact that he wrote 800 years later makes the accuracy of his information suspect, but it underlines the reputation of Mount Carmel.

The promontory dominating Haifa is in fact the tip of a ridge widening to the south-east for some 25 km until it merges with the mountains of Samaria. There are two passes, Nahal Yoqneam and the more important Nahal Iron, which in antiquity was guarded by MEGIDDO because of the great trade route, the Way of the Sea, which passed through it (fig. 59).

There is much evidence of Stone Age occupation in the little wadis which reach the sea on the west; the most accessible group of caves are those in Nahal Mearot (CARMEL CAVES). At the mouth of the River Qishon the Egyptians had a port (now Tel Abu Hawam) which served as a naval base and the point of entry for imports from Mycenae and Cyprus. This settlement flourished during the C14–C13 BC, but did not survive the onslaughts of the Sea Peoples a century later. The site was occupied sporadically down to the Byzantine period, but from the C10 BC onwards the most important town was at Tel Shiqmona on the other side of the cape. Destroyed time and time again, it was always rebuilt, and the Byzantine town covered an area of some 50 acres, spreading up the side of the hill where hundreds of tombs were cut into the rock; some of these can be seen in Histadrut Park, and there is a good exhibition of finds from the excavations in the Haifa Municipal Museum of Ancient Art in Bialik Street.

The 'majesty of Carmel' (Isa. 35: 2) had a great impact on the Old Testament prophets; they used it as a symbol for strength, beauty, and fertility (Isa. 33: 9; Jer. 46: 18; 50: 19; Amos 1: 2; Nahum 1: 4; S. of S. 7: 5). It was often visited by Elisha, who had inherited the mantle of Elijah (2 Kgs. 2: 25; 4: 25), but the episode that has fired the imagination of all succeeding generations was the epic trial of strength between Elijah and 450 prophets of Baal (1 Kgs. 18). Carmel is still the territory of Elijah.

Just at the traffic lights which mark the turn from the coast road into Allenby Road, a flight of steps leads into a public garden. A winding path brings one to the Cave of el-Hader, known as the School of the Prophets, on the left of a modern building. From remote antiquity Baal-Adonis was worshipped here, but from the C3 AD he began to be replaced by Elijah; graffiti scratched on the walls in the C5–C6 AD attest the veneration of both Christians and Jews. Islam shares the same respect, and the site was a mosque until taken over as a synagogue in 1948. Despite the change, the tradition of a Roman Catholic mass once a year (14 June) has been maintained.

Beneath the church of the Carmelite monastery further up the hill behind the lighthouse (from Allenby Road turn right into Stella Maris Road) is another cave associated with Elijah; every 19–20 July it becomes the focal point of a great assembly of Christians, Muslims, and Druze, who come to beg the intercession of Elijah. The fortress-like monastery (built 1826), which includes a pilgrim hospice, is the latest in a succession of buildings which began with a medieval Crusader castle. It belongs to a Roman Catholic religious order which developed from a C13 group of hermits who came together in the Wadi Siyah (the valley between the western suburbs of Kababir and

Karmeliya) where archaeologists have discovered a small medieval monastery.

From the lighthouse Tchernichovsky Street brings one to the gilt-domed Bahai Shrine. This is the centre of a religious movement which broke away from the Shiah branch of Islam in 1844. The founder, Mizra Ali Mohammad, was a Persian who proclaimed himself the mysterious Twelfth Imam (Mahdi) expected by Shiah Muslims; the basic principle of the movement is that no religion has a monopoly of the truth, and it tries to integrate the wisdom of all great religious teachers. Such tolerance naturally provoked violent opposition, and this area became the centre of the movement only because the Turks exiled Mirza's successor, Baha 'u-ullah, to Akko in 1868.

The scenic road along the top of the ridge passes Haifa University before climbing Rom Hacarmel (528 m), the highest point of the Carmel range, whence it descends to two DRUZE villages, Isfiya and Daliyat el Karmil. The former is identified with Husifah, a Jewish village of the Roman-Byzantine period. A hoard of 4,560 silver coins (the latest dated AD 53) was discovered there; it may have been the annual collection for the Temple. An early C6 AD synagogue was also brought to light; it had a badly damaged zodiac mosaic floor which has been removed.

Traditionally Elijah's contest with the prophets of Baal (1 Kgs. 18) is located at el-Muhraqa (= the sacrifice), a peak (482 m) offering a splendid view of the Jezreel valley. The reliability of the tradition is, of course, open to doubt, but site and text in fact harmonize perfectly. From the platform in front of the little Carmelite monastery (built 1868) one can see the sea (v. 43), and there is a spring, Bir el-Mansoura, just below (v. 33). The brook Qishon runs at the bottom of the hill (v. 40) in the Jezreel valley (v. 45–6). The colourful narrative comes vividly to life when read in this setting.

MOUNT GERIZIM (K13)

From the top of the sacred mountain of the SAMARITANS, dominating NABLUS (B, fig. 92), there is a panoramic view of central Samaria. The ancient trade route from the great highway on the coast, the Way of the Sea, came through the pass (whence the importance of TEL BALATA) and continued down the deep cut of the Wadi Farah (Nahal Tirza) to the Jordan valley. A north-south route, never as important,

passed through the fertile plain to the east. The view to the north is
blocked by the slightly higher Mount Ebal. It is considered accursed
by the Samaritans, and one can see the reason why if one compares
the sterility of its grey rocks with the luxuriant trees surrounding
TEL ER-RAS (C, fig. 92) in the foreground.

A tarmac road from Nablus brings one first to a plateau with a
number of new houses. These belong to the Samaritans who live
there during the 40 days of the feast of Passover; the lambs are sacrificed in what looks like a basketball court south of the road, just
before the dirt track leading to Tel er-Ras. Previously the sacrifice
took place in a fenced area of flat rock on the very summit.

The Muslim tomb of Abu Ghanem is on the north-east tower of
the wall built by Justinian in the C6 AD to protect the octagonal
church of the Theotokos erected by Zeno after the suppression of the
Samaritan uprising in AD 484. The Muslims destroyed the church in
the C8, and the fortress was dismantled in the C9.

MOUNT TABOR (HAR TAVOR) (L7)

The perfect breast shape of Mount Tabor excites awe and wonder; it
has the aura of a sacred mountain. From the dawn of history it was a
place where humanity found contact with the unknown and it is
hardly suprising that Christian tradition eventually located there the
transfiguration of Jesus.

Neanderthal people came there from 80,000 to 15,000 BC to make
flint tools; because of the lack of water, it served only as a factory site.
The mountain is first mentioned in the Bible in connection with the
defeat of the army of the king of Hazor at the hands of Deborah and
Barak in 1125 BC. The 900 Canaanite chariots swept across the plain
of Jezreel from near MEGIDDO, but a sudden downpour bogged them
near the foot of Tabor, holding them for the Israelite charge from the
mountain (Judg. 4–5). Heterodox Jewish worship on Tabor is condemned by Hosea (5:1); for Jeremiah it symbolized the might of
Nebuchadnezzar (46:18). In 218 BC Antiochus III of Syria, by
feigning retreat, enticed the Egyptian garrison from their position on
the summit and slaughtered them in the plain. The same stratagem
enabled the Roman general Placidus to defeat the Jews who, under
Josephus, had built a wall around the summit in 40 days (AD 67).
This latter text (*War* 4:54–61) incidentally suggests that a village

existed on the summit in the C1 AD, possibly inhabited by the descendants of a garrison left behind by Alexander Jannaeus (103–76 BC) when he consolidated Jewish control over the centre and north of the country.

The localization of the Transfiguration fluctuated at the beginning of the Byzantine period. Eusebius (d. 340) hesitates between Tabor and Hermon, while the Pilgrim of Bordeaux (333) places it on the Mount of Olives. In 348 Cyril of Jerusalem decided on Tabor, and the support of Epiphanius and Jerome established the tradition firmly. The date of the first religious constructions is uncertain. The anonymous pilgrim of Piacenza saw three basilicas in 570. Willibaldus (723), on the contrary, mentions only one church dedicated to Jesus, Moses, and Elijah. The contradiction disappears if we assume three chapels architecturally linked, as in the present building.

A Crusader text suggests that the Byzantine edifice was still standing when Tancred installed Benedictine monks on Tabor in 1099. They were massacred and their buildings destroyed by a Turkish attack in 1113. When the Benedictines returned they defended the new church and monastery with a stout wall which successfully resisted Saladin's attack in 1183; the nearby Greek church of St. Elijah was destroyed. The fortress-monastery capitulated after the defeat of the Latin Kingdom at the HORNS OF HATTIN in July 1187.

The threat of the Fourth Crusade (1202–4) inspired Melek el-Adel, ruler of Damascus, to fortify the mountain; this was in fact done by his son Melek el-Mouadzam between 1212 and 1214. The presence of a Muslim fortress on the site of the Transfiguration was made the occasion of the Fifth Crusade. A 17-day Crusader siege in 1217 failed, but a year later Melek el-Adel ordered the fortress to be dismantled because he recognized that it would be a continuous provocation. A series of truces permitted Christians to return to Tabor later in the C13 but they were expelled by Baybars in 1263.

Visit. After leaving the village of Dabburiya (where Byzantine tradition located the cure of the epileptic boy (Luke 9: 37–43), the miracle immediately subsequent to the Transfiguration) the road runs above the ancient Way of the Sea before turning to climb the mountain. The summit is divided equally between Greek Orthodox and Latin Catholics; a wall highlights the character of the relationship.

The first turn-off leads to the Greek sector. Just inside the medieval Arab wall an iron door, flanked by two small windows in a broken wall, is the entrance to the Cave of Melchisedek; according to a bizarre medieval tradition this was the dwelling where he received Abraham (Gen. 14: 17–20). The key is kept in the Church of St. Elijah at the end of the drive which is built on Crusader foundations. All the ruins visible throughout the area are medieval.

The entrance to the Latin sector is through the main gate of Melek el-Adel's fortress; today called the Gate of the Wind, it was restored in 1897. The defence wall of which it formed part can be traced all round the summit; there are 12 towers. About 150 m from the gate on the right (south) is a small chapel built on Byzantine foundations; unmentioned in any ancient document, it today commemorates the conversation between Jesus and the disciples after the Transfiguration (Mark 9: 9–13). It is bracketed by two cemeteries, that on the north is medieval while the southern one contains tombs of the C1 AD.

The drive ends in the piazza in front of the basilica constructed in 1924. The new building to the right (south) is the Franciscan monastery and hospice; to the left are the ruins of the medieval Benedictine monastery. A small oratory, the chapter room, and the refectory are easily discernible. Two rooms between the oratory and the chapter room contain entrances to an Arab bath.

The towers of the basilica cover the Byzantino-medieval chapels of Moses and Elijah; in the crypt traces of the earlier main church are still visible.

The ruins of Mount Tabor are less interesting than the panorama its altitude provides. A flight of steps in the medieval refectory to the north of the basilica brings one to the top of the fortress wall of the monastery. The line of Melek el-Adel's wall with its two towers leads the eye to the north and the mountains of Upper Galilee. Slightly to the east is the great mass of Mount Hermon with the Horns of Hattin in the foreground above the depression (further east) containing the Sea of Galilee. NAZARETH crowns the crest to the west.

There is a similar viewpoint south of the basilica on the medieval walls near the Tower of the King's Daughters, but it is not as good as the balcony of the Franciscan hospice. This offers an uninterrupted panorama of the plain of Jezreel bounded by the south-eastern part of the Carmel range and the northern extremity of the mountains of Samaria. This vast arena resounded to the tramp of the armies of all the great generals who campaigned in the Middle East, from Thutmose III (MEGIDDO) to Allenby, and including Alexander the Great and Napoleon. The BET SHEAN valley is clearly a natural highway connecting the Jordan valley with the route across the plain to the coast at Haifa. It has carried trade since the beginning of commerce, but was less important than the Way of the Sea, the trade route linking Damascus and Egypt, which swung round the Nazareth side of Tabor. From Afula the highway followed the modern road across the plain to the pass of the Nahal Iron guarded by MEGIDDO.

MOUNT OF TEMPTATION (JEBEL QURUNTUL) (M16)

A 30-minute climb on a good path, passing through the monastery (open: winter, 7 a.m.–2 p.m., 3–4 p.m.; summer, 7 a.m.–3 p.m., 4–5 p.m.; no shorts or sleeveless blouses allowed), permits a magnificent panorama of the entire JERICHO area (fig. 69) with the DEAD SEA to the south and the towers of the Mount of Olives on the western skyline. The monastery is open to women. On payment of a small fee permission to go to the summit is granted by the superior.

The legendary association of the mountain with the first and third temptations of Christ (Matt. 4: 1–11) begins only in the C12 when two churches were built, one in a cave half-way up, the other on the summit. Both these edifices were in ruins by the C14. The present monastery (rebuilt 1874–1904) contains the medieval cave-church in which, it was thought, Christ fasted and refused to turn stones into bread; the stone on which he sat during the argument is still shown.

A new church on the summit was begun in 1874 but only the surrounding wall was completed. The area it circumscribes is within the fortress of Doq built by the Syrian general Baccides just before the middle of the C2 BC. There Ptolemy, the governor of Jericho, assassinated his father-in-law Simon Maccabaeus in 134 BC (1 Macc. 16). According to the Copper Scroll from QUMRAN, a treasure of 22 talents is buried under the east angle of the fortress. About 70 m due north of the enclosure wall is an aqueduct coming from the west. It is particularly well preserved at the point where it disappears over the cliff-edge and swings south to terminate at nine big cisterns with a total capacity of 2,000 cubic metres.

The cave of St. Elijah (40 m below the monastery) was rebuilt in 1949–65. It is kept locked and contains no datable remains.

MUHRAQA: *see* MOUNT CARMEL

NABATAEANS

In pre-Christian centuries trade ships from the east could not sail against the strong winds in the north of the Red Sea. They had to land their goods in the Arabian peninsula whence they were carried overland to the Mediterranean coast. The Nabataeans were an Arab tribe who had the wit to see the possibilities of this trade route crossing their territory. At first they offered only 'protection', but soon controlled the whole trade from their centre at Petra.

The first historical reference to the Nabataeans is in 312 BC when they defeated an army sent against them by one of Alexander the Great's successors. At this time they were already involved in the exportation of bitumen from the DEAD SEA to Egypt. The collapse of the Ptolemaic (Egypt) and Seleucid (Syria) empires towards the end of the C2 BC permitted them to develop into an independent state. Immense revenues were generated by taxes levied on the caravans; the cost of incense from Dhofar, pearls from the Persian Gulf, silk from China, spice and cotton from India doubled during transit through Nabataean controls.

The Negev was always a critical area in the Nabataean route system because it gave them access to the coast. At AVDAT the route from Petra divided, one section going to the port of Gaza, the other joining the ancient Way of the Sea at el-Arish for Egypt. The loss of Gaza to the Jews under Alexander Jannaeus c.100 BC cost the Nabataeans dearly; there is a break in their occupation of Avdat, Haluza, and Nizzana. When the Romans marched into Syria-Palestine in 63 BC an arrangement with the Nabataeans was worked out by Antipater, father of Herod the Great; his wife, Kypros, was a Nabataean. The civil wars in Rome, which led to the end of the Republic, made this arrangement irrelevant and the Nabataeans had effective control of Transjordan until the advent of Augustus (27 BC–AD 14). He confirmed their lack of control in the north by giving the area to Herod the Great (BANYAS), and sapped the commercial basis of their power by having ships land their goods on the Egyptian side of the Red Sea.

The effect of this measure was not immediately apparent. Under Aretas IV (9 BC–AD 40), whose daughter married Herod Antipas, the Nabataeans had control of Damascus in the time of St. Paul (2 Cor. 11: 32). The defeat by Aretas of Herod Antipas, who had thrown his daughter aside to marry Herodias (Mark 6: 14–29), was a significant factor in this expansion northwards; according to Josephus the Jews saw this victory as divine vengeance for the murder of John the Baptist (*Antiquities* 18: 116). In this period Nabataean cities in the Negev flourished again. As the century progressed, however, the consequences of the Roman economic squeeze became more manifest; in AD 106 Trajan was able to annex the kingdom of Nabataea without a struggle. Thereafter the Nabataeans assimilated more and more into other elements of the local population. The last remnants of the proud trade-masters appear as camel drivers in southern Sinai in the C2 and C3 AD.

NABI MUSA (M17)

To the south of the Jerusalem–Jericho road, just before the final descent into the Jordan valley, the numerous domes of a great building stand out from the humps of the low barren hills which hide the entrance to the Buqei'a. A new tarmac road leads to the site venerated by the Muṣlims as the tomb of Moses. Entrance to the building depends on the availability and humour of the guardian.

In AD 1269 the Mameluke sultan Baybars built a small shrine at a point on one of the old roads from Jerusalem where Muslims were accustomed to venerate Moses whose tomb on Mount Nebo was visible on the other side of the Jordan valley. This act of piety inspired others to build rooms for travellers adjacent to the shrine. Between 1470 and 1480 the hospice was extended to its present spacious dimensions. In the minds of simple people the place *from which* the tomb of Moses was venerated inevitably became the tomb itself. About 1820 the Turks completely restored the buildings which had fallen into total disrepair, and actively encouraged a seven-day pilgrimage for the Muslims of the area. Their purpose was to provide a counterbalance to the Easter ceremonies, and the date was fixed according to the Christian calendar. Accordingly, on Friday of Holy Week a tumultuous procession of thousands of pilgrims left the el-Aksa Mosque in Jerusalem for the day-long march to Nabi Musa and five full days of prayer, feasting, and games. It became one of the most popular and colourful Palestinian institutions. As tensions in the area grew it acquired political overtones which led to tight controls by the British authorities and ultimately to suppression by the Jordanian Government in 1948.

Muslim legend identifies two of the tombs in the immense cemetery surrounding Nabi Musa as the resting places of Hasan er-Rai, the shepherd of Moses, and of Aisha, the favourite wife of Muhammad.

NABI SAMWIL (J17)

The skyline north of Jerusalem is dominated by a peak with a large mosque whose stark lines are softened by one great tree. This is the traditional tomb of the prophet Samuel; from it there is a magnificent panorama of the territory of the tribe of Benjamin with JIB in the foreground. On a clear day one can see both the Mediterranean and the mountains of Jordan.

It may have been the great high place of Gibeon on which Solomon offered sacrifice for the gift of wisdom (1 Kgs. 3: 3–14). It certainly has nothing to do with the burial of Samuel: he was buried in Rama (1 Sam. 25: 1). No one has yet explained how the tradition shifted, but by the C6 AD it was well established. The Crusaders called the spot Mountjoy; from there the army of 1099 and subsequent pilgrims got a first glimpse of the Holy City. The church built in 1157 was still intact in 1674. A mysterious destruction in the C18 paved the way for the present mosque begun in 1911. Free access to the roof is permitted except during times of prayer.

NABLUS (SHECHEM) (K12)

Whereas a political decision made Jerusalem capital, nature itself gave this status to Shechem, 'the uncrowned queen of Palestine'. In the mouth of the only east–west pass, surrounded by springs, the centre of an ancient road system, it is the natural capital of the mountain region (fig. 92).

The site first settled by Chalcolithic people (*c.* 4500–3100 BC), TEL BALATA (E), was just in the process of becoming an imposing city when Abraham arrived (*c.* 1850 BC). Having crossed the Jordan by a ford, he would have come up the beautiful Wadi Farah (Nahal Tirza) to Shechem where he received the promise of the land (Gen. 12: 6–7).

The political significance of the city decreased in the C9 BC when

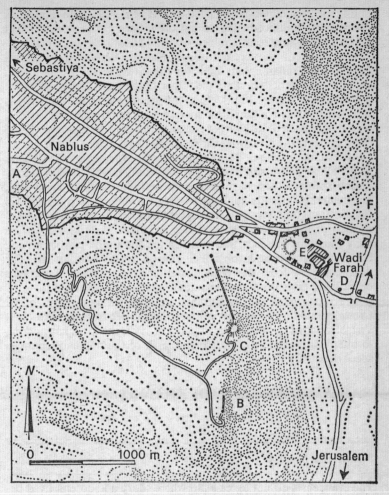

Fig. 92. Antiquity sites in the vicinity of Nablus.

the capital of the dissident northern kingdom was moved to SAMARIA (Shomeron). In succeeding centuries historical forces conspired to give the SAMARITANS their distinctive identity. In opposition to Jerusalem, they built their own temple in the C5–C4 BC on a promontory of Mount Gerizim called TEL ER-RAS (C). John Hyrcanus destroyed this edifice in 128 BC but the memory of it was still vivid (John 4: 20) when Jesus stopped to drink at JACOB'S WELL (D).

The name of the present town, Nablus, derives from Flavia Neapolis, a Roman colony built for the veterans of Titus in AD 72. One of these settlers became the father of the great apologist Justin Martyr, born there *c.*100. Despite intense pressures the Samaritans prospered; witness a grandiose monumental tomb (dated *c.* AD 200; now reconstructed) at Khirbet Askar (F). A visit to their synagogue (A) highlights the disastrous difference in their present condition.

According to John 3: 23, John the Baptist 'was baptizing at Aenon near Salim'. Salim still exists, 5 km east of Nablus. Aenon simply means 'springs'; these have been located at Ein Faria (10 km north), but the term is equally applicable to the ten springs surrounding Tel Balata. Jesus' ministry paved the way (John 4: 38) for the successful mission of Philip, followed by Peter and John (Acts 8: 4–25). This early Christian presence intensified in the Byzantine period, leaving traces in churches at Jacob's Well and on MOUNT GERIZIM (B). The dominant view from this point underlines the strategic importance of the city; the natural trade routes are immediately evident.

The rapacity of the inhabitants removed the cut stones of all Crusader buildings; Queen Melisande lived there from 1152 to 1161. Virtually wiped out by the earthquake of 1927, the town has nothing to offer visitors, and the uncertain temper of the populace counsels speedy transit.

NAHAL TEQOA: *see* **WADI KHAREITUN**

NAZARETH (K7)

The evangelists do not agree as to where Mary and Joseph lived before the birth of Jesus. Matthew implies that it was Bethlehem (Matt. 2), but Luke says that it was Nazareth (Luke 2: 4–5). It is more probable that Matthew is correct. Joseph belonged to a Judaean family, and Mary was related to Zachary, a priest who had to live near the Temple. Were Nazareth their home it would have been more natural to return there when Herod menaced the family than to go to Egypt. Judaeans, on the other hand, automatically thought of Egypt as a place of refuge (1 Kgs. 11: 40; 2 Kgs. 25: 26; Jer. 26: 21). If she lived near Jerusalem it would have been natural for Mary to visit and stay with Zachary's wife Elizabeth (Luke 1: 39–40); no young Jewish girl would have been permitted to make the three-day journey from Nazareth alone.

When Archelaus showed that he had inherited the murderous unpredictability of his father, Herod the Great (37–4 BC), Joseph decided to move his family to a remote village in the north and perhaps other members of his family moved with them. Luke knew that the family had lived in Nazareth for so long that it was Jesus' 'home town' (Matt. 13: 54; Luke 4: 16) and that they had relatives there (Matt. 13: 55–6). He therefore assumed that Joseph and Mary had been born there.

Slender evidence suggests that a Judaeo-Christian community survived in Nazareth during the C2 and C3 AD. Conon, martyred in Asia Minor during the reign of Decius (AD 249–51), affirmed in court, 'I am of Nazareth in Galilee, I am of the family of Christ to whom I offer a cult from the time of my ancestors.'

The early Byzantine pilgrims do not seem to have paid much attention to Nazareth. In 384 Egeria was shown 'a big and very splendid cave' in which Mary had lived. Then silence descends for almost two centuries, a period in which many legends were born. The Piacenza pilgrim (*c.* 570) writes, 'We travelled on to the city of Nazareth, where many miracles take place. In the synagogue there is kept the book in which the Lord wrote his ABC, and in this synagogue is the bench on which he sat with other children. Christians can lift the bench and move it about, but the Jews are completely unable to move it, and cannot drag it outside. The house of Saint Mary is now a basilica, and her clothes are the cause of frequent miracles. The Jewesses of that city are better looking than any other Jewesses in the whole country. They declare that this is Saint Mary's gift to them, for they also say that she was a relation of theirs.' A hundred years later Arculf saw two 'very large churches', one in the centre of the city on the site of the house where Jesus was brought up, the other on the site of the house where Mary received the angel Gabriel.

One of Tancred's first concerns on becoming Prince of Galilee in 1099 was to erect a church above the cave in the centre of the city. Dedicated to the Annunciation, it was visited by the Russian pilgrim Daniel in 1106; every corner of the cave is related to something in the daily life of the Holy Family. He also mentions a second church built above a well and dedicated to the angel Gabriel.

After the collapse of the Latin Kingdom at the HORNS OF HATTIN in 1187, a series of truces permitted pilgrims to get to Nazareth for just over a hundred years. Thereafter it became too dangerous, and only the very brave attempted to visit the city of ruins and murderous Moors (to paraphrase a traveller in 1598). In 1620 the Franciscans were permitted to buy back the ruins of the church of the Annunciation thanks to the benevolence of the DRUZE emir Fakhr ed-Din, and managed to maintain a Christian presence despite incredible difficulties. With the approbation of another Muslim rebel, Daher el-Omar, they built a church in 1730 which was demolished in 1955 to make room for the new basilica.

Visit. Nazareth of today is dominated by the massive basilica of the Annunciation; visible from anywhere in the town, it serves as a perfect orientation point (fig. 93).

Basilica of the Annunciation [A]

Open: 8.30–11.45 a.m. and 2–5 p.m.; 6 p.m. in summer; closed Sunday morning except for those who wish to attend mass. The building has been designed to enclose and protect the discoveries made in the exhaustive archaeological excavations which can be seen in the lower church.

The centre of the underground church is the apse of the Byzantine church of the mid-C5. In front is a 2 m-square basin which the excavators identify as a pre-Constantinian baptistry on the basis of its form and the graffiti scratched on its plaster walls; it was found sealed by a mosaic oriented north-south. More remains of this period are preserved outside the north wall of the Crusader church: granaries, oil presses, storage areas, even traces of the foundations of

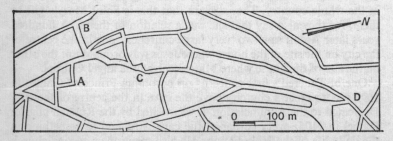

Fig. 93. The centre of Nazareth.

houses; these are visible from outside the modern church but accessible only by special permission.

To the left of the baptismal basin a short flight of steps leads down to a mosaic floor with the inscription, 'Gift of Conon deacon of Jerusalem'; this was the floor of the venerated cave in the Byzantine period.

Behind the Byzantine apse one can see the triple apse of the C12 church with a staircase in the north-east corner. In the south apse are displayed six exquisite capitals intended for the Crusader church. Created by sculptors from northern France, they were never installed; after Saladin's victory at Hattin they were buried for safety. They depict scenes (both biblical and legendary) from the lives of the Twelve Apostles; the detail of the attitudes, gestures, and dress of the 48 figurines defies description.

Convent of the Sisters of Nazareth [B]
May be visited only by previous appointment. Beneath the convent lies a Jewish necropolis containing one of the best examples of a tomb sealed by a rolling stone. The masonry structures are medieval, probably belonging to a Crusader monastery or convent. After the expulsion of the Franks the site was used by the Muslims as a place of worship.

Church of St. Joseph [C]
Open: 8.30–11.45 a.m. and 2–5 p.m.; 6 p.m. in summer. The church, built in 1914, follows the trace of a triapsidal medieval church. In the crypt a 2 m-square basin cut in the rock has a white mosaic floor carefully arranged to fit round a piece of black basalt let into the floor; six rectangles are outlined in black. Seven steps lead down into the basin. The arrangement is immediately evocative of the pre-Constantinian baptistry in the Basilica of the Annunciation; the pieces of pottery in the plaster of the basin could be Late Roman or Early Byzantine. No traces have been found of a Byzantine church.

Beside the basin a flight of rough steps leads down to a narrow passage which, after a 180-degree curve, opens into a 2 m-high underground cave; it has been enlarged and contains a number of bell-shaped silos at a still lower level. At the end furthest from the entrance there were four such silos one above the other; the enlargement of the cave cut into the second from the top. The silos were developed by the pre-Byzantine village. It is not certain whether the extension of the cave had any relationship to the baptismal basin.

From the C17 the cave has been identified as the workshop of

Joseph, a pious tradition that has no foundation. The gospels identify Joseph simply as a 'worker' (Matt. 13: 55), not specifically as a 'worker in wood' or carpenter; he might have been a smith or a stonecutter.

Church of Saint Gabriel [D]

Open: 8.30–11.45 a.m. and 2–5 p.m.; 6 p.m. in summer. This Greek Orthodox church has taken the place of a round medieval church which itself was the adaptation of an earlier Byzantine edifice. Here is located the spring which feeds the present Virgin's Fountain some 150 m to the south-east. A church above a spring was an important place of pilgrimage for both Byzantines and Crusaders, and there can be little doubt that this is the location of the second great church seen by Arculf.

Attention must have been directed to the spring by the version of the Annunciation found in the C2 (?) *Protoevangelium of James*: 'And Mary took the pitcher and went forth to draw water, and behold, a voice said: "Hail, thou that art highly favoured among women." And she looked on the right and on the left to see whence this voice came. And trembling she went to her house and put down the pitcher and took the purple and sat down on her seat and drew out the thread. And behold, an angel of the Lord suddenly stood before her and said, "Do not fear, Mary, for you have found grace before the Lord of all things and shall conceive of his Word." ' (11: 1–2.) It is difficult to say exactly when this text was localized. The church was built very late in the Byzantine period – Arculf (670) is the first to mention it – but Jewish opposition may have forced a delay; the Piacenza pilgrim noted in 570 that 'there is no love lost between Jews and Christians' in Nazareth.

The crypt is not beneath the present church but juts out on the north at a right angle. As one descends the steps one can hear the sound of running water; it bubbles up in the small apse at the far end. The spring is in a cave 17 m inside the hill.

The Synagogue

The synagogue that Jesus attended was shown to the Piacenza pilgrim (570); in 1285 Burchard noted that it had been transformed into a church. Efforts have been made to find it, but no satisfactory evidence has come to light. The location is unknown.

NIMRUD (O1)

The keep towering above a long narrow-waisted enclosure gives the great fortress of Subeibe (now known by its Arabic name Qalaat Nimrud) the air of an alert guard-dog ready to spring. Its raised head faces Damascus; behind and below is BANYAS, its responsibility. From the battlements one can see its sister castles Beaufort (AD 1139) on the cliffs of the Litani river (north-west), and Chateau Neuf (1178) on the heights to the west of Qiryat Shemona (south-west) at the head of the Hula valley.

The site was given to Baldwin II in 1129 by the sect of the Assassins in order to spite the atabek of Damascus who had massacred a number of its members. The Crusader king confided it to Renier Brus who built the castle in three years. He lost it to the Damascenes in December 1132. It was taken from them in 1137 by Zengi, atabek of Mosul and Aleppo, who had set his heart on becoming master of Damascus. He was an equal threat to the Crusaders, and in 1140 a combined Crusader-Arab force retook the fortress after a month-long siege. This alliance lasted until 1154 when Zengi's son, Nur-ed-din, won control of Damascus. He laid siege to Subeibe twice in 1157, each time retreating when a Crusader relieving force appeared on the horizon. He was more successful in 1164; the garrison surrendered before the Crusader army could return from Egypt. The Crusaders tried to retake Subeibe twice, in 1174 and 1253, but failed. With other fortresses it was dismantled during the Fifth Crusade (1217–21), but inscriptions attest various restorations during the later part of the C13. Under the Mamelukes it served as a prison.

Visit (fig. 94). The approach road from the route linking Banyas and Neve Ativ runs underneath the south wall which is an unusual mixture of round and square towers. The square towers [1, 3, 5, 7] belong to the original structure (1129–32). The postern at the base of [7] was the normal entrance, because just inside another door gives access to the forecourt [9] of the keep [11–12]. There are other posterns in [3] and [15]. The round towers [4, 6, 8, 13] were added after 1164 by the Muslims who also doubled the size of the square towers [1 and 16] by adding to their external faces; in the former [1] it is easy to see that five of the eight original firing-slits have been enlarged into doorways leading to a series of small rooms with thirteen firing slits.

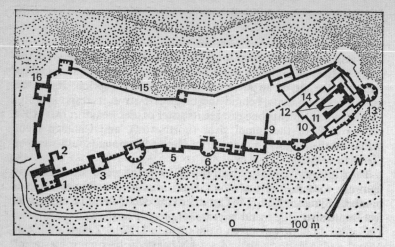

Fig. 94. Nimrud (after Coupel).

A glance at the plan shows that the north wall [15] is not nearly as strongly defended; the steep slope meant that no serious attack could be mounted from this side. The shape of the hill determined the form of the fortress which is very different from that of BELVOIR, but Subeibe is also a concentric castle. The rectangular keep [12] is entirely independent of its six-tower defence wall [11] which was cut off from the outer ward by the inner ward [9]. Attackers who managed to penetrate the inner ward found themselves confronted by a moat [10] which forced them into a narrow rectangle [14] commanded by fire from the towers.

The present entrance is through a breach in the west wall near the corner tower [1]. Just inside is a vast vaulted cistern [2]. The first round tower [4] contains a fine example of Arab fan vaulting; in the second [6] note the projecting stone on one side of the firing slits to protect the hand of the archer. The keep area is very ruined but a rudimentary trail enables one to make a circuit which brings out the main dispositions.

QASRIN (O4)

This deserted village was one of the oldest Jewish settlements in the Golan. The large synagogue, some of whose walls are preserved to a height of 3 m, was built in the first part of the C3 AD. The site is in the process of being developed as a park.

Contemporary texts (Tosephta, Erubin 4: 5) describe how Jewish cities were accessible from main roads but did not lie directly on them, being constructed on naturally elevated positions. It is also noted (Tosephta, Arakhin 5: 12) that, instead of a city wall, the back walls of houses formed a continuous line serving the same purpose (SHIVTA). Qasrin fulfils all the details of this description. Despite re-use by Syrian bedouin, the structures are well preserved and manifest impressive design and high-quality workmanship.

QUBEIBA (J17)

Venerated since 1500 as the site of Emmaus where Jesus, in the breaking of bread, revealed himself to Cleophas and another disciple (Luke 24: 13–35); a wall of the very house of Cleophas is shown within the Franciscan church.

The truth is rather more prosaic. The site lies on a Roman road leading down to the plain. Along its edge Arabs built houses in the C8–C9 AD. Some time between 1114 and 1164 the Canons of the Holy Sepulchre founded a village here which they called Parva Mahomeria, possibly because of a small Muslim shrine (el-Qubeiba = 'a little cupola'). Their purpose was to intensify the agriculture of the vast domain from which they drew their substance. They may also have had the charitable thought of providing a resting-place for pilgrims en route to Jerusalem as the ascent from the plain is steep. The complex included a church and a small castle in addition to the usual buildings of a farming village. At a later period Christians assumed that the foundation commemorated an event in the life of Christ. What could it be? The distance from Jerusalem given by Luke (according to certain manuscripts) suggested Emmaus. And so it was. The Crusaders themselves located Emmaus near the castle of Belmont on the Jaffa road (see ABU GHOSH).

Visit (fig. 95). Open: 6.30–11.30 a.m. and 2–6 p.m. The Crusader castle was to the left of the present entrance [1]. The church [2] was reconstructed in 1902, but the lower part of the three apses is medieval. The wall preserved in the floor [3] is not parallel to those of the church. At one time thought to be part of a Jewish house which the

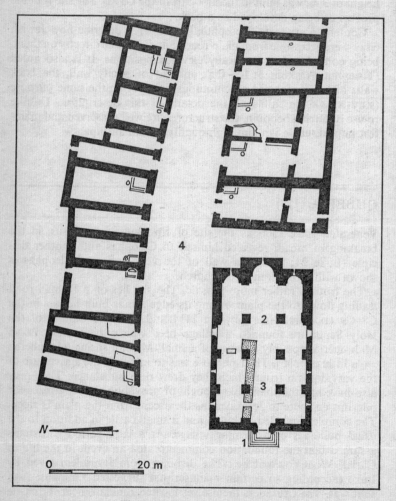

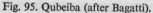

Fig. 95. Qubeiba (after Bagatti).

Crusaders preserved by incorporating it in their church, it is more likely to be a later edifice built in its ruins. The Roman road [4] is bordered by the houses of the medieval village; the basins for the preparation of olive oil or wine and the millstones underline its agricultural character.

QUMRAN (M18)

Community centre of the ESSENES who produced the famous Dead Sea Scrolls. They lived in natural caves in the adjoining cliffs, in tents, and in underground chambers cut in the soft marl. They gathered here for all the religious and economic activities of the sect. The well-preserved ruins, situated on a little plateau on the north-west shore of the DEAD SEA, make it easy to visualize the daily life of these people whose austere dedication excited the admiration of the Roman statesman Pliny the Elder and the Greek orator and philosopher Dio Chrisostom.

The Essenes were not the first to occupy this site. In the C8 BC the Israelites established here a small fort (A in fig. 96); it may have served as the centre of a farming settlement, the 'City of Salt' mentioned in Josh. 15: 61–2. The fort had been long abandoned when the Teacher of Righteousness and some fifty Essenes settled there about 150 BC. They took over the earlier building with its round cistern, and modified the plan only to the extent of adding two rectangular stepped cisterns beside the round one, and two kilns in the south-east corner (B in fig. 96).

At the end of the reign of John Hyrcanus (134–103 BC) an influx of new members brought the number to two hundred and necessitated an extensive rebuilding programme (C in fig. 96). These buildings (which we visit) were damaged by an earthquake in 31 BC, forcing the Essenes to abandon the settlement for some thirty years. Where they went during this period is unknown, but they returned to continue their monastic form of life until the Romans expelled them in AD 68. They were no threat to the Romans, but the fortress-like building would have been visible when Vespasian came to the north end of the Dead Sea to test its reputed properties by throwing in two bound non-swimmers to see if they would float (*War* 4: 477). A small Roman garrison remained on the site to control the traffic on the Dead Sea until the fall of MASADA in AD 73.

Visit (C in fig. 96). Open: 8 a.m.–5 p.m.; to 4 p.m. Fridays. A platform on the tower [4] permits a good general view of the whole complex. In particular one can see the double line of the aqueduct going towards the cliffs. The Essenes had constructed a dam (no longer visible) in the Wadi Qumran; water was directed through a rock-cut tunnel (still extant) into the aqueduct and so into the large decantation pool [3]. Sand sank to the bottom and clear water flowed from the top of the pool into the channel system. This area naturally silted up when the site was abandoned after 31 BC. Rather than dig it out when they returned, the Essenes simply extended the channel to a new smaller decantation pool [1].

As gravity moved the water through the system, each of the cisterns (shaded) filled in turn; some have their own decantation basins. Associated with the water system, but not part of it, are two baths [2 and 10]; the Essenes had to purify themselves by bathing in cold water before entering the 'holy temple' of the refectory.

This refectory [7] was easy to identify. The adjoining room [8] contained over 700 bowls arranged in piles of a dozen, 210 plates, 75 beakers, and assorted other vessels for food and drink. In addition, the floor sloped from a water inlet to the external door at the far end; this ingenious cleansing system shows the room to have been a place where dirt was inevitable and cleanliness essential. The members of the community received bread, wine, and a single bowl of one kind of food; this was sometimes meat (mutton, beef, goat), usually boiled but sometimes roasted. At least some of these meals had a religious significance (at present not fully understood) because the meat bones, carefully covered with broken potsherds, were found buried in most of the open areas.

The community was run on strictly democratic lines, making a council chamber [5] necessary. Just inside the door is a water basin which could be filled from the outside. Perhaps they worked on a conclave system; no exit without a decision! The stairs outside the door led to the scriptorium [6] on the first floor; a 5 m-long plastered table and two inkwells were recovered from the debris in the room below. Here, presumably, many of the scrolls found in the cave were copied.

Near the cistern [9] cracked by the earthquake in 31 BC is a complete pottery workshop. The clay was first washed in a plastered basin [13] with a small cistern fed from the main channel. It was then left to mature in a storage pit, before the final mix was made in a shallow tank beside the circular pit [12] in which the wheel was set.

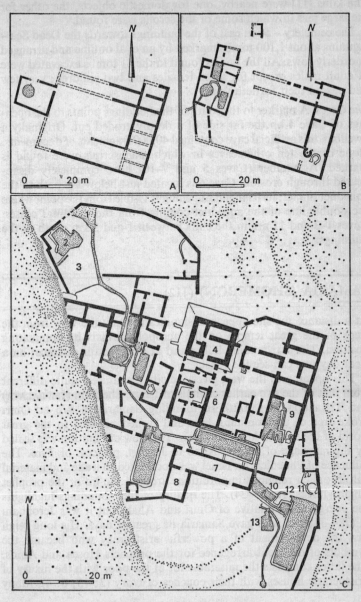

Fig. 96. Qumran (after Couäsnon).

The kilns [11] were nearby, one for domestic objects, the other for the large jars in which some of the scrolls were found.

The cemetery – 50 m east of the buildings towards the Dead Sea – contains about 1,100 tombs marked by an oval outline and arranged in orderly rows. All the bodies found in the 41 tombs excavated were of adult males except for seven females and two children; very few had passed their fortieth year.

The Caves. A marker to the south of the buildings points to the openings of Cave 4 on the far side of a deeply eroded cut. Originally a dwelling, this artificial cave contained 40,000 fragments of documents. None of the ten other caves in which manuscripts were found is marked. A number (Caves 5 and 7–10) have completely disappeared through erosion. Cave 6 is located just below the path to the aqueduct tunnel; its triangular opening is visible from the point where the double line of the aqueduct coming from the buildings ceases. Caves 1–3 and 11 are in the cliffs between 1 and 3 km north of the buildings.

SAMARIA (SHOMERON) (J12)

At a distance the site appears insignificant. Only the view from the steps of the great temple on the acropolis reveals its dominating position. The surrounding hills stand at a respectful distance; on a clear day one can see the coast.

This opening to the west gives the city a character quite different from that of the two earlier capitals of Israel, Shechem (TEL BALATA) and Tirza (TEL EL-FARAH). In founding Samaria in 876 BC Omri broke free of the confining hills and turned his face to the great world of the eastern Mediterranean. This new orientation was sealed by the marriage of his son Ahab to Jezebel, princess of Tyre. The influence of Phoenicia on Israel was not limited to trade and material culture; alien religious importations aroused the ire of the prophet Elijah (1 Kgs. 16: 29–34). The quality of their buildings highlights the energy and initiative of Omri and Ahab, but it was Jeroboam II (784–748 BC) who gave Samaria its greatest days. His long reign saw the development of a powerful aristocracy who became the symbols of decadent arrogance for the prophets Hosea and Amos. The latter contrasts the miserable lot of the poor with the luxury of aristocratic houses with their couches of ivory (3: 15; 6: 4). Many of these plaques of carved ivory (produced in Damascus or Tyre but with Egyptian motifs) that were used to decorate furniture are on display in the Rockefeller Museum, Jerusalem.

After the Assyrian invasion (724–722 BC) 30,000 citizens were deported and their places taken by foreigners (2 Kgs. 17: 24); a significant contribution to the origin of the SAMARITANS. Under the Persians Samaria became the capital of a province, and with the fall of that empire it passed to Alexander the Great. He may have come there in person in 331 BC to punish the rebels who had burnt his representative alive. Some of the leaders escaped, but were betrayed and died, with their documents, in the cave of Abu Sinjeh in the Wadi Daliyeh. Alexander installed his veteran Macedonians in Samaria, forcing the Samaritans to move back to Shechem.

Razed by John Hyrcanus (108 BC), restored by Gabinius (57 BC), it was granted to Herod the Great by Octavian in 30 BC. He did his usual first-class building job and to honour his patron renamed the new city Sebaste (the Greek for Augustus). He further intensified the non-Jewish character of the population by installing foreign mercenaries. At Sebaste he celebrated one of his many marriages and executed two of his sons. In an effort to live up to its new status when Septimus Severus made it a Roman colony with full privileges in AD 200, the Herodian structures (weakened by age and earthquakes) were restored. The vitality thus injected did not last long, and the city steadily lost population to NABLUS. The legend that John the Baptist was buried there attracted Christians in the Byzantine and Crusader periods.

Visit (fig. 97). Open 8 a.m.–5 p.m. A new road entering through the West Gate avoids the twisty narrow streets of the village of Sebastiya, an Arabic corruption of Herod's Sebaste.

The West Gate served the city at least from the time of Alexander the Great. A Hellenistic square tower [2], but not its wall [3], was incorporated into the reconstruction of the gate under Septimus Severus when the three towers [1, 2, 4] were built. At this stage the city wall was over 3 km in circumference.

The colonnaded street ran through the business section below the acropolis. A series of small one-room shops of the Roman period opened on to covered pavements 4 m wide. The width of the street between the columns averaged 12 m, but this spaciousness was lost in the Byzantine period when the covered area was used as a second room and shops were built in the street [5].

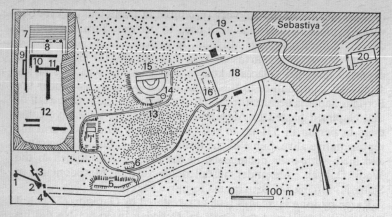

Fig. 97. Excavated areas at Samaria. Enlarged inset: the Temple of Augustus.

The great open area [18] corresponds to the Roman forum. The row of columns nearest the parking level are all that remain of the porticos that once surrounded it. These are at a lower level than the other two rows which were part of the basilica [16] and may have belonged to the original Herodian basilica; but in AD 200 the level of the north end was dropped 1·5 m and a small semicircular tribune added. The curve of a much wider semicircle can be seen just alongside. Beyond the toilets a viewpoint [19] overlooks the rectangular stadium, similar to the one which Herod built in Jericho (TEL ES-SAMRAT).

Just behind the Roman theatre [15], which may rest on an older Herodian one, is a round tower [14] described as the finest monument of the Hellenistic period in Palestine. It sits astride an Israelite wall breached for insertion, and links with a Hellenistic wall [13] forming part of the defences of the acropolis in the time of Alexander the Great. The way the stones in the tower are laid is unique, as is the bevel cut on the outer face.

The summit of the acropolis was crowned by the temple Herod dedicated to Augustus. To prepare the site he had to level and fill in ruins of the Israelite and Hellenistic periods [12]. One beautiful wall [9], with bossed foundations (see [17]) and perfectly smooth header-stretcher upper courses shows the skill of the builders employed by Omri or Ahab. Two walls [10 and 11] supported the columns framing the porch of Herod's temple. In the time of Septimus

Severus the front of the building was moved forward some 5 m; the present steps [7] are from this period as is the wall supporting the column bases [8].

Christian tradition very quickly (before 361) identified Samaria as the site of the infamous birthday party at which Herod Antipas had John the Baptist executed (Mark 6: 17–29). Josephus locates the murder at Machaerus in Jordan (*Antiquities* 18: 119), but this information was not available to all Christians and Samaria was both associated with the name of Herod and much more accessible. Two churches were built in John's honour, one near Herod's temple and the other in the modern village.

A small church [6] commemorates the finding of the Baptist's head. A C6 three-aisled monastic chapel was radically transformed at the end of the C11. The original apse was retained but the other three walls and narthex were rebuilt; four granite columns were introduced into the nave to support a central dome. In the seond half of the C12 Greeks reconstructed the west door, and encased the four columns in masonry in order to support a heavier dome. In the northeast corner they built a chapel of St. John and beneath it a crypt in which, according to John Phocas (1185), the head of the Baptist had been found. The bases of the four pillars of the C11 narthex are still visible on the inside of the crude wall outside the main door.

Just to the south of the basilica three courses of an Israelite wall of the C9 BC are still visible [17]. They are laid on a foundation bed of headers; in the courses stretchers alternate with pairs of headers. The bosses are not decorative since there are margins on only three sides. In contrast to the much more refined Herodian technique (HEBRON), the masons received rough stones from the quarry. They cut a margin on the bottom in order to align the stone precisely. The stone in position, they cut a vertical margin on the side towards which they were working. A vertical line ruled on this margin enabled them to cut the edge back square to receive the next stone. When the whole course had been laid, they cut a margin on the upper edge in order to permit them to dress the top down to a horizontal bed for the next level. Different shifts with idiosyncratic foremen may explain why the working direction changes twice in the middle course and three times in the top and bottom!

The great cathedral [20], enshrining the reputed tomb of John the Baptist, is built in the Burgundian style of the mid-C12. The lower courses visible on the outside of the north wall are all that remain of a C5 church which was already in ruins at the beginning of the C9.

Saladin transformed the Crusader building into a mosque whose subsequent history is unclear. The present mosque, and the other buildings inside, were erected in the latter part of the C19 when the triple apse was pulled down to make a straight wall. The tomb-chamber is entered via a staircase from a small domed building in the north side of the nave. The stone door and the six burial niches reveal it to be a Roman tomb of the C2 or C3 AD. Another tomb of the same period can be seen at the bottom of a deep hole some 50 m south of the cathedral among the houses; the rise in ground level (due to the accumulation of rubbish) round the cathedral explains why this tomb is now buried. One hopes it will be made accessible because it contains possibly the earliest instance of the use of pendentives (triangular segments of a sphere) to impose a dome on a square chamber.

SAMARITANS

A tiny dissident Jewish sect (300–400 members) with one community in NABLUS and a smaller one in Holon. In opposition to other Jews, they recognize only the five books of Moses as inspired scripture. Their origin goes back to the split between the northern (Israel) and southern (Judah) kingdoms which followed the death of Solomon (1 Kgs. 12–13).

In the north religious differences, introduced to make the political separation effective, were intensified when the Assyrians settled great numbers of foreigners there in 721 BC. Thereafter, for Jerusalem, the Judaism of Samaria was suspect. However, when the Jews of the south returned from sixty years' exile in Babylon, they found the Samaritans claiming to be the guardians of the pure faith of Moses. They refused the Samaritans' offer of help in rebuilding the Temple. In return the Samaritans made things as difficult as possible, resorting to every dirty trick in a large repertory. In the C5 BC Nehemiah persuaded the Persians to withdraw Judah from the political control of Samaria. The resentment this provoked was exacerbated by the religious reforms of Esdras, and the Samaritans built their own temple on Mount Gerizim (TEL ER-RAS). This serious breach in the unity of Judaism became definitive only in the late C2 BC when John Hyrcanus, anticipating the tactics of the Spanish Inquisition, destroyed the temple and brutally imposed the Jerusalem version of

Judaism on the Samaritans. When Pompey freed them from the political control of the south in 64 BC they would have nothing more to do with Jews.

The Samaritans prospered under direct Roman rule, and enjoyed sufficient credit to procure the dismissal of Pontius Pilate in AD 36. With the ineptitude that characterized his tenure as Procurator of Judaea he had massacred a crowd assembled because a visionary had promised to find the sacred vessels hidden by Moses on Mount Gerizim. The golden age of the Samaritans came in the C4 AD when Baba Rabba secured a high degree of political autonomy for Samaria and inspired a great revival in worship, literature, and language, to which Markah and Amram Darah made major contributions. Influential in trade and learning, their communities were established in the most important cities of the empire.

The greatly increased Christian presence in the Byzantine period inevitably provoked incidents which led to repressive measures. The response was a revolt in NABLUS in 484. In order to make it clear who was master the emperor Zeno removed Mount Gerizim from their jurisdiction and built a church on the summit. The resentment thus engendered simmered for a generation before bursting out with even greater force in 529. The Samaritans swept across the country venting their frustration on churches and monasteries. Justinian's response was savage. The Samaritans were well-nigh exterminated, and new legislation made the existence of the survivors as a religious body virtually impossible.

The advent of the Arabs did not relieve the pressure and they lost many converts to Islam. They retained some sort of identity at the price of keeping an extremely low profile. Denial of access to Mount Gerizim forced them to elaborate a secondary liturgy celebrated in their city quarters. Apart from this there has been no development in the last 1,500 years. In the C18 they were able to purchase a piece of land on MOUNT GERIZIM for their sacred rites. This was soon annulled, but they reacquired the right to celebrate there in the C19. Each year the whole community moves to houses below the summit for the six weeks of Passover; one lamb is sacrificed for each family according to the ancient tradition. Unfortunately crowds of tourists tend to turn a dignified ceremony into a rather vulgar circus.

SAMMU: *see* **ESHTEMOA**

SEA OF GALILEE (N5–7)

In the Old Testament the Sea of Galilee (fig. 98) is known as the Sea of Kinnereth (Num. 34: 11; Josh. 12:3 ; 13: 27), a name that is imaginatively associated with the Hebrew word *kinnor* meaning a harp; for some the lake is shaped like a harp, for others the music of its waters resembles the sound of a harp. Matthew and Mark call it the Sea of Galilee (Matt. 4: 18; 15: 29; Mark 1: 16; 7: 31) or simply the Sea (Mark 2: 13 etc.) to which John adds the Sea of Tiberias (6: 1; 21: 1). Luke pedantically calls it the Lake (8: 22) or the Lake of Gennesaret (5: 1), a name which reflects the usage of Josephus who calls it the Lake of Gennesar because of the remarkable qualities of the region north of Tiberias: 'There is not a plant which its fertile soil refused to produce, and its cultivators in fact grow every species. The air is so well tempered that it suits the most opposite varieties. The walnut, a tree which delights in the most wintry climate, here grows luxuriantly, beside palm-trees, which thrive on heat, and figs and olives, which require a milder atmosphere. One might say that nature had taken pride in thus assembling, by a *tour de force*, the most discordant species in a single spot, and that, by a happy rivalry, each of the seasons wished to claim this region for her own.' (*War* 3: 516–18.)

The lake is 21 km from north to south and 12 km wide at its broadest point. The water level fluctuates considerably, depending on the rainfall each year and on the quantity pumped from the lake which serves as the reservoir for the National Water Carrier; the mean level is 210 m below sea-level. The water is sweet, and in summer (when the temperature averages 33°C) too warm for a really refreshing swim. Twenty-two species of fish are found in the lake; fishing is again the important industry it was in the time of Jesus, and the small boats have still to watch for the sudden gusts from the surrounding wadis which can whip the normally tranquil surface to turmoil in a matter of minutes (Matt. 8: 23–7; 14: 24–33).

The physical charm of the lake is enhanced by its historical associations. Prehistoric tribes lived in the AMUD CAVES, and BET YERAH was an important Canaanite city in the third millennium BC. Some thirty years after the Roman general Pompey made SUSITA part of the Decapolis, one of the most brutal espisodes in Herod the Great's rise to power took place in the ARBEL CAVES. His son, Herod Antipas, founded TIBERIAS in AD 20, but a little later CAPERNAUM

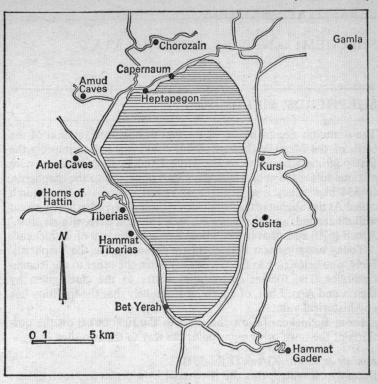

Fig. 98. Antiquity sites around the Sea of Galilee.

became the most important site on the lake when Jesus made the fishing village the centre of his ministry in Galilee. In the First Revolt (66–70) GAMLA was the scene of a famous battle between Jews and Romans. After the fall of Jerusalem Galilee became the centre of Jewish life in Palestine. Great schools of learning developed, and magnificent synagogues were built at CHOROZAIN, CAPERNAUM, HAMMAT TIBERIAS, and HAMMAT GADER. Christians flocked to the area in the Byzantine period, and the glory of the synagogues was rivalled by splendid churches at HEPTAPEGON, CAPERNAUM, KURSI, SUSITA, and BET YERAH. The next attempt to establish a Christian kingdom in Palestine occurred in the Middle Ages, and 88 years of effort came to nothing when Saladin defeated the Crusaders at the HORNS OF HATTIN on 4 July 1187.

SEBASTIYA: *see* SAMARIA

SHECHEM: *see* NABLUS *and* TEL BALATA

SHEPHERDS' FIELDS (K18)

The dramatic circumstances of the first public proclamation of the birth of the Messiah (Luke 2: 8–14) could not fail to impress the first pilgrims who came to the Holy Land in the C4. They were anxious to see the spot where the angels appeared to the shepherds. In 384 in a valley near BETHLEHEM Egeria was shown 'the church called At the Shepherds; a big garden is there now, protected by a neat wall all around, and also there is a very splendid cave with an altar.' Arculf (670) adds that it was 'about a mile to the east of Bethlehem'.

Today two sites near Bethlehem are pointed out as the Shepherds' Field, one belonging to the Greek Orthodox, the other to the Roman Catholics. The former corresponds better to the clues given by Egeria and Arculf but, of course, it is unlikely that the tradition has any historical value.

From Bethlehem follow the signs to the HERODION; on the outskirts of the town other signs point the way to the two sites.

Kenisat er Ruwat (Greek Orthodox)
Recently excavated, this site is covered by a protective roof. Open: 8–11.30 a.m. and 2–5 p.m.; 6 p.m. in summer.

In the second half of the C4 AD a natural cave was given a mosaic floor. Soon afterwards the rock was cut away to permit the erection of a church within the cave; the barrel-vault ceiling is still intact, and this church served the Greek Orthodox community of Beit Sahour from the beginning of the C14 until 1955. It is the only C5 church outside Jerusalem to have survived intact. A chapel was built on the roof of this Cave Church; its mosaic floor (set on an axis different from that of the later buildings) is perfectly preserved together with the two holes which permitted visitors to look through to the cave below.

By the C6 these facilities had proved inadequate to cope with the number of pilgrims; Bethlehem was a major site and the cave lay on the main road to the MONASTERIES IN THE JUDAEAN DESERT. The Roof Chapel was removed to make way for a much larger church which was destroyed by the Persians in 614; the collapse of the burning roof ruined the colourful mosaic pavement. The church was rebuilt in the C7 as the centre of a monastic community which survived until the C10.

Khirbet Siyar el Ghanem (Roman Catholic)
The Franciscans consecrated this site by the erection of a tent-like chapel in 1954. Open: 8–11 a.m. and 2–5 p.m.; 6 p.m. in summer.

The ruins on the other side of the parking-lot from the chapel are from the Byzantine period. The first monastery was founded at the end of the C4 AD on a site occupied during the C1 AD by nomadic shepherds. The monastery was enlarged during the C6, the apse of the church being reconstructed with stones from the original polygonal apse of the Church of the Nativity at BETHLEHEM.

Since the excavations did not reveal the existence of a venerated cave it is impossible to reconcile this site with the description given by Egeria. It was simply one of the many monasteries scattered throughout the area during centuries when Byzantine monasticism was at its zenith. Its lack of special significance is shown by the fact that it was not reoccupied after having been destroyed by the Persians in 614.

SHILOH (K14)

Loose stones without plan or structure on a small mound at the end of a long quiet valley are all that remain of the first temple of the God of Israel. At some time in the period of the Judges (C13–C12 BC) it became the permanent resting place of the Ark of the Covenant. 1 Sam. 1–3 gives a vivid picture of life in this remote sanctuary whose importance is difficult to estimate. It was not a central sanctuary creating a tenuous religious bond among twelve anarchically independent tribes, but seems rather to have served as a focus for private devotion culminating in an annual pilgrimage (Judg. 21: 19).

The site (fig. 99) had been occupied for a thousand years when it was destroyed by the Philistines (*c.* 1050 BC) after their capture of the Ark of the Covenant (1 Sam. 4). The non-specialist will find nothing intelligible on the mound [1] because of erosion and the small scale of the excavations, but enough evidence came to light to show intense occupation in the Roman and Byzantine periods. Persistence of a religious tradition is a plausible explanation, even though Shiloh

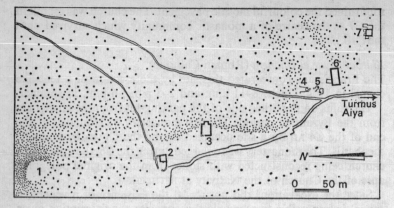

Fig. 99. Shiloh.

drops out of Israelite history once the Ark was removed; the lack of a spring was compensated for by the fertility of the land and abundant winter rains. Two churches, called the Basilica [3] and the Pilgrim's Church [6], show Shiloh to have been a religious centre in the C5 AD. Their concrete walls are an eyesore, but the intention was to preserve the mosaics. Two disused Arab sanctuaries, Weli Yetin [2] and Weli Sittin [7], attest Muslim veneration. Both re-use elements from the ruined churches, and Weli Sittin may originally have been a synagogue; the niche faces Jerusalem.

Just north of the Pilgrims' Church are two tomb complexes of the Roman period. In the first [4] graves were cut and then adapted to a reservoir, whereas in the second [5] a cistern was turned into a burial cave.

SHIVTA (D27)

Although much deeper in the Negev (40 km south-west of Beer Sheva) than either AVDAT or MAMSHIT, Shivta offers something unique. In order to survive in an area where the rainfall averages only 86 mm per year, the city was planned to catch and store every drop that fell.

The NABATAEANS first settled here in the C1 AD; their town occupied the southern third of the present city, and the double reservoir on its northern edge collected run-off from the slope to the east. Little is known of Shivta in the C2 and C3, but in the C4 it began a period of expansion which continued into the next century. Christianity made its presence felt in the construction of two churches. One was squeezed in next to the double reservoir, the other was erected some distance outside the city to the north so that it would not interfere with the catchment area. As more and more land around the city was brought under cultivation in the C5 the population increased, necessitating the construction of new quarters. Buildings now filled the area between the double reservoir and the North Church, but the streets were laid out to respect the Nabataean catchment channels. The paved areas of the unusually wide streets and frequent open spaces acted as highly efficient water collectors. The upkeep of the water system was a public duty; citizens who participated presumably got a tax rebate because receipts for service were provided.

The city was not walled, but the exterior buildings formed a continuous line save for nine openings which were simply the ends of major streets and these were secured by gates. The Arab take-over in the C7 was extraordinarily peaceful; in building their mosque the Muslims took great care not to damage the adjoining South Church. The city survived for a further two centuries, gradually dying as the quality of water management decreased.

Visit (fig. 100). From BEER SHEVA take the Nizzana road; the turn south to Shivta is 15 km west of the turn-off to Sede Boqer; the tarmac road ends at the parking-lot on the west of the city.

The gate [1] left of the excavators' house leads into a typical street lined with houses. The average house [2] is built around a courtyard which provided light and air; very few have windows on the street side. Each house has its own cistern to which clay pipes in the walls led water from the roof. In a land without trees for beams, roofs were made of stone slabs laid on arches set closely together; rubble walling levelled up the spandrels.

The public water system is well illustrated in the road on the north edge of the double reservoir [3]. Parallel channels collected the run-off from the street. One filled a cistern [4] whose overflow was carried to another cistern under the narthex of the South Church [5]; its overflow went into the other channel which brought street water

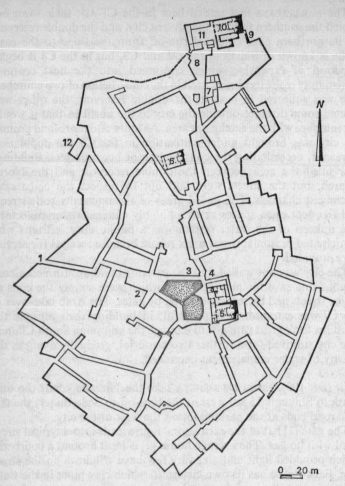

Fig. 100. Shivta (after Woolley).

directly to the south reservoir. The total capacity of the double reservoir is 1,550 cubic metres.

The awkward entrance to the South Church [5] shows the builders to have been limited by existing structures; there is no atrium, and the narthex is entered from the street. Originally there were two square rooms on either side of the central apse; at a later stage these were transformed into smaller apses each containing a built-in receptacle for the bones of martyrs. According to one inscription, the floor of the southern aisle was laid in 640. Another, engraved on a lintel, commemorates the building of an addition to the church in 415/430; this may refer to the rooms around the little court to the north. The cruciform baptismal font is cut from a single block. The *mihrab* of the mosque is cut in the outside of the north wall of the baptistry.

The Central Church [6] has three apses, a feature paralleled (in the Negev) only in the early C7 South Church at Nizzana. It is the latest of the three churches in Shivta; the adjacent buildings may have been a monastery.

The monastic(?) complex adjoining the North Church [10] contains a fine wine press [7]. The grapes were trodden in a square stone-lined pit from which an underground pipe carried the liquid to a square basin where most of the skins could be trapped; thence it flowed into a round settling tank. There is a similar wine press near the parking-lot [12]; there the only difference is the provision of separate chambers around the treading floor where farmers could store their grapes while waiting their turn.

The North Church [10] is the most elaborate, showing that space was not a factor in its construction. The whole complex is girdled by a retaining wall suggesting that the structure had been weakened by an earthquake in the C5. A single entrance led from the square [8] to the atrium [11] with its large cistern and stylite column. The church [10] was originally monoapsidal; the two lateral apses with their reliquary niches are secondary, as are the chapel and baptistry to the south. The beautiful mosaic floor of the chapel can be seen by anyone prepared to take the trouble of scraping away the protective covering of sand which, of course, should then be immediately replaced. Above the monolithic baptismal font a pipe comes through the wall; to fill the font, water was poured by hand from a cistern outside. Water from the catchment area on the slope flowed through the wall [9] into a division box; thence part went to the baptistry cistern and part out into the square [8] where it was integrated into the public system. Members of the clergy were interred in the baptistry; the dates on the tombstones run from 614 to 679. Graves in the church and atrium date from 506 to 646.

Byzantine Farm. Just 1 km from the parking-lot the exit road crosses a shallow wadi; 200 m up the wadi bed to the right (east) is a Byzantine farm which Israeli botanists have brought back into use. Here one can see all features mentioned in the section on Desert Agriculture appended to the description of AVDAT. Fine crops of carobs, figs, grapes, pomegranates, olives, almonds, peaches, and apricots have been produced here using ancient techniques. The reconstruction of the farm and its catchment area gave the researchers an idea of how long it would take to set up a complex of this size; a family with three or four children could have done it in two years.

From the top of Mizpe Shivta (422 m) there is a magnificent view of the way stones were cleared from the water catchment areas. The climb takes about 40 minutes from a point just before the junction with the main road.

SOLOMON'S POOLS (BEREKHOT SHELOMO) (J18)

Even if it is only a legend that Solomon frequently came here to disport himself among the waters and gardens (*Antiquities* 8: 186), one can easily see why he might have. The leafy shade around the three great reservoirs (until very recently crucial to Jerusalem's water supply) with their attendant Turkish fort, makes it a perfect picnic spot. Just to the south the well-preserved remains of the ancient aqueduct system are definitely worth a visit.

This area contains the closest large springs to Jerusalem at a higher altitude than the city. As the city's need for water grew (possibly during the Israelite monarchy, certainly under Herod), an aqueduct was built terminating in the Temple; traces can still be seen on both sides of Birket es-Sultan, the great pool outside Jaffa Gate. A second was built later, possibly by Pontius Pilate who, according to Josephus, in AD 26 appropriated Temple funds to build an aqueduct. Constructed at a higher level, it fed the Upper City where the Procurator had his residence. Part of the great stone pipe, which acted as a syphon, is still in place 400 m south of Rachel's tomb below a row of cottages; one block is displayed in the courtyard of the American Colony Hotel in Jerusalem.

The supply to the pools was augmented by two aqueducts from the south. The lower aqueduct comes 45 km from the great pool at 'Arrub, dropping only one metre per kilometre. Built by Herod the Great (37–4 BC), it was extensively repaired by the Mamelukes. The upper aqueduct begins at Bir el-Daraj, 5 km south of the pools; the construction technique shows it to be Roman.

Visit (fig. 101). Strong rubber-soled shoes are essential; the complete circuit takes two hours. A crude channel of uncertain date [1] leads to the upper aqueduct. Follow it to your left (south), around the head of a small wadi, until it disappears into a tunnel [2]; impress on your mind the configuration of the rough cap-stones (fig. 102) for at a later stage they will be the only guide to the line of the lower aqueduct. Nine square vertical shafts permit you to follow the line of the tunnel over the hill. On emerging from the tunnel [3] the upper aqueduct continues up the Wadi Bijar, disappearing where the road crosses the bottom of the valley. This is the beginning of a 3 km tunnel leading to the spring. It is pierced by about 50 square shafts (some visible in the fields), which are used by the farmers and give the wadi its name, 'Wadi of the Wells'. The purpose of the tunnel is

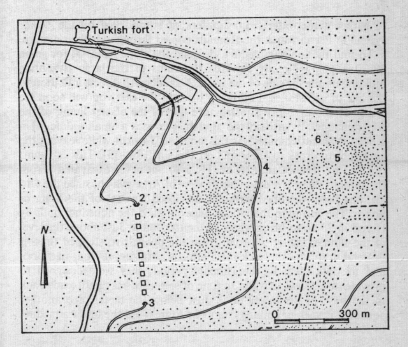

Fig. 101. Ancient aqueduct system around Solomon's Pools (after Schick).

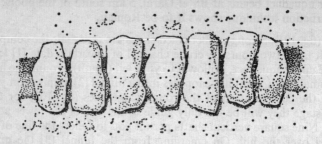

Fig. 102. Cap-stones cover aqueduct to prevent evaporation.

to gather extra water from aquifers; it is modelled on the *Qanat* system in Persia which the Romans copied throughout their empire.

To find the lower aqueduct, descend the slope from [3] for some 50–70 m going directly towards the ruins of the large Byzantine building on the far side of the wadi. A small cairn directs attention to the line of cap-stones. Following these to the east you will soon see traces of the masonry substructure and of the plaster lining of the water channel. Eventually the aqueduct crosses a small saddle [4] in a deep rock-cut channel. At this point it is worth while leaving the aqueduct to cross to the ruins on the small hill [5]. This is Etam; fortified by Rehoboam (2 Chr. 11: 5–6) but never excavated. From the summit there is a magnificent view of Artas which, since the C16 AD, has been identified with the 'enclosed garden' of the Song of Songs. The spring in the village once supplied the aqueduct built by Herod in 23 BC to bring water to the HERODION. Just above the level of the saddle, facing the road from the pools, two stepped tunnels descend deep into the rock [6]. Parallels at GEZER, HAZOR, MEGIDDO, and JIB date them to the Israelite period; they were designed to provide safe access to water in time of siege. An easy path leads back to the base of the lower pool. Just below the metal pipe another aqueduct is visible; coming from Ein Atan, it fed the lower aqueduct to Jerusalem.

SUBEIBE: *see* NIMRUD

SUSITA (O6)

Behind En Gev on the eastern side of the SEA OF GALILEE a high promontory juts out between two wadis (fig. 98). The flat top (2 km in length, averaging 500 m in width) is joined to the GOLAN by a narrow neck of land. If a little imagination suffices to see a camel in the hump of GAMLA, a much wilder flight of fancy is required to find the shape of a horse here. Yet, from the time of its foundation in the Hellenistic period (332–152 BC), the town was known as Hippos in Greek and as Susita in Aramaic, both meaning 'horse'.

The Seleucids of Syria were the first to recognize the natural advantages of the site but the Roman general Pompey, who in 63 BC removed it from the Jewish control imposed by Alexander Jannaeus (103–76 BC), gave the city its definitive form. He made it part of the Decapolis, the league of ten cities which he hoped would disseminate Graeco-Roman culture throughout the region, and had it rebuilt on a grid pattern. Even though new buildings were added in subsequent centuries, this street arrangement was always respected. Augustus granted the city to Herod the Great in 30 BC, but after the latter's death in 4 BC it was returned to the Province of Syria to the great satisfaction of the inhabitants.

The great prosperity of Susita in the Roman and Byzantine periods was due to its location on the Roman road linking Scythopolis (BET SHEAN) with Damascus; it controlled the one steep ascent and provided a convenient staging-point. Fine public buildings and four churches betray the wealth which the inhabitants were careful to protect by a massive wall ringing the summit. The city was abandoned after the defeat of the Byzantine army by the Arabs at the battle of the Yarmuk river (8 km to the south-east) in 636.

Visit. Unfortunately, the site is untended and badly overgrown; it is best to visit in summer or autumn when the sun has dried up the weeds. The climb up the zigzag track at the west end takes about 40 minutes; the new road in Wadi Jamusiyeh, following more or less the trace of the Roman road, will make it possible to drive to the east end of the ridge linking the city to the Golan plateau.

The track crossing the city from east to west follows the line of the Roman main street whose basalt paving is visible in places. An excavated area just south of the middle of this street is the site of the C5 cathedral. It was clearly destroyed by an earthquake, since all the columns lie pointing in the same direction. The apse has a mosaic floor with the sockets for a marble chancel screen. The baptistry built along the north side of the church in 591 has two features which make it unique: it is triapsidal and dedicated to special patron saints (the framed inscription in the south aisle mentions SS. Cosman and Damian).

Three other churches are located on the north side of the main street between the middle and the eastern end; the floor plans can be traced among the ruins.

West of the cathedral are a Roman nymphaeum, a Byzantine bath, and a large underground cistern with a vaulted roof. The water for these installations travelled in a great stone pipe beneath the main street from the basalt aqueduct crossing the ridge linking the promontory to the plateau of the Golan; it brought water from the spring at Afiq. The aqueduct entered the city by the East Gate; the north pier has disappeared but its southern partner is well preserved together with the city wall into which it is integrated. First erected by the Romans, this gate was rebuilt in the Byzantine period. The city wall is best preserved on the south side of the city, but significant traces can also be found on the west where there was a smaller gate.

TABGHA: *see* HEPTAPEGON

TEL AVIV – JAFFA (YAFO) (E14)

The confused urban sprawl of Tel Aviv belies the fact that the city was founded in this century. In 1909 a group of sixty Jewish families moved out of Jaffa to settle in the sand dunes to the north. At first a suburb of Jaffa, it became independent in 1921 and thereafter grew uncontrollably as new immigrants poured in. In May 1948, on the eve of the declaration of the State of Israel, Jewish forces took control of Jaffa.

The first settlements in the area between Jaffa and the Yarkon river date from the end of the Stone Age (*c.* 5000 BC), and evidence for continued occupation during the subsequent Copper and Bronze Ages has also been found. The name Jaffa appears for the first time in the list of cities captured by Thutmose III in his campaign of 1468 BC; the story of soldiers smuggled into the city in baskets supposed to contain tribute became a favourite Egyptian folk-tale. Letters conserved in the archives at Amarna show Jaffa to have been under Egyptian control in the C14 BC, and they retained it until the Philistines established themselves in the area *c.* 1200 BC.

According to 2 Chr. 2: 16 cedar wood for Solomon's temple came from Lebanon in great rafts which were brought ashore at Jaffa, but after Solomon's death the Philistines reassumed control of the port. It reverted to Israelite control during the reign of king Uzziah of Judah (769–733 BC), but later in that century it fell victim to Assyrian expansionism. Seeing the threat to his mountain kingdom, King Hezekiah of Judah (727–698 BC) took the death of Sargon II in 705 BC as the signal to organize a revolt in Palestine. One of his allies was Sidqia king of ASHQELON who occupied Jaffa and its hinterland. What happened thereafter is succinctly described on the famous Prism of Sennacherib: 'In the continuation of my campaign I besieged Beth-Dagon, Jaffa, Bene-Berak, Asor, cities belonging to Sidqia who did not bow to my feet quickly enough; I conquered them and carried their spoils away' (701 BC).

The collapse of the Assyrian empire came very quickly, and in subsequent centuries Jaffa passed from hand to hand, being occupied in turn by Egypt, Babylon, Persia, and Sidon. Under Alexander the Great, who campaigned in Palestine in 332–331 BC, it became a Greek colony. The book of Jonah was written about this time; the hero tried to escape God's command to go to Nineveh by taking ship from Jaffa (1: 3). The port remained under the control of the Ptolemies of Egypt until they were pushed out of Palestine by Antiochus III of Syria (223–187 BC).

When the Maccabees revolted against Syria two hundred Jaffa Jews were treacherously drowned and in reprisal (163 BC) Judas Maccabaeus burnt the port (2 Macc. 12: 3–7). The city was conquered by his brother Jonathan, and annexed to Judaea by his other brother Simon (1 Macc. 12: 34). In 63 BC Pompey restored its independence, but in 47 BC Julius Caesar returned the city to Jewish control. A besotted Mark Antony gave it to Cleopatra; on her death in 30 BC Augustus added it to Herod's realm.

Jaffa lost much of its importance when Herod built a new port at CAESAREA. After raising a woman from the dead, Peter stayed in the house of Simon the Tanner in Jaffa where he received the vision which showed him that pagans should be admitted into the church (Acts 9: 36–10: 23). After having suffered badly during the First Revolt (*War* 3: 414–31), the city was rebuilt by Vespasian and given an independent charter. Economically it could not compete with

Caesarea and remained a small place. When Jerome translated the *Onomasticon* of Eusebius in 390 he felt obliged to substitute 'town' for 'city'; he is also the last to mention the legend of Andromęda bound to the rock which was first associated with Jaffa by Strabo (*c.* AD 19).

As the harbour at Caesarea silted up, Jaffa regained its position as a port, and remained the principal point of entry into Palestine until this century. It played a critical role during the Crusades, particularly at the beginning; siege equipment landed there in the nick of time made the capture of Jerusalem possible in 1099.

Visit. There are two archaeological sites in Tel Aviv-Jaffa, both associated with museums.

Jaffa

Part of the archaeological history of Jaffa can be seen in an excavation (with excellent explanatory signs) across from St. Peter's Church on the high ground above the port. Finds from the dig are displayed in the Museum of Antiquities at 10 Mifratz Shlomo St. which is open 9 a.m.–4 p.m. Fridays 9 a.m.–1 p.m.; Saturdays and Holy Days 10 a.m.–2 p.m.

Tel Qasile

This mound, located on the north side of the Yarkon river just east of Derech Haifa, was apparently first settled by the Philistines in the C12 BC. It has not been identified with any site known from written sources, even though it was occupied until the C15 AD. The most significant discovery was a series of Philistine temples of the C12–C11 BC. In its most developed phase the complex included two court-yards, a central temple with a smaller secondary temple, and an altar. The numerous cult objects found in this sacred area are exhibited in a special section of the nearby Ha'aretz Museum Complex which in addition houses magnificent displays of ancient coins and glassware – open: 9 a.m.–4 p.m.; Fridays 9 a.m.–1 p.m.; Saturdays and Holy Days 10 a.m.–2 p.m.

TEL BALATA (K12)

Site of the biblical city of Shechem, the natural capital of the mountain region (E in fig. 92), it offers a unique opportunity to visualize the complex of buildings around a city gate of the Bronze Age.

Settled in the Chalcolithic period, the first city was founded in the C19 BC; its name appears in Egyptian texts. Abraham camped in its vicinity on his arrival in Canaan and received the promise of the land (Gen. 12: 6–7); there Jacob bought land to settle down and he was later buried there (Gen. 33: 18–20; Josh. 24: 32). The small city the patriarchs knew saw a great expansion in the C17–C16 BC, when its only rivals in Palestine were MEGIDDO and GEZER; it was a powerful city-state whose borders embraced the entire hill country. Aggressive leadership freed it in the C15 BC from the foreign domination imposed by Egypt in the previous century. It was strong enough to threaten MEGIDDO.

After the arrival of the Israelites in the Promised Land (c. 1200 BC) Joshua held a great assembly of all the tribes (not all Israelites were at Sinai) to swear allegiance to the new faith (Josh. 24). The abortive attempt of Abimelech to make himself king (Judg. 9) gives a vivid picture of life in the city during the C12 BC, and explains the violent destruction at the end of the Bronze Age.

When Rehoboam refused to grant tax concessions, the Shechemites would not recognize his right to succeed his father Solomon as king (1 Kgs. 12). Shechem thus became the first capital of the dissident northern kingdom. This privilege it lost to Tirza (TEL EL-FARAH), then to SAMARIA in 876 BC. The Assyrian invasion (724–722 BC) wrought terrible damage, and the city did not recover until the end of the C4 BC. After Alexander the Great expelled the citizens of Samaria for having burnt his governor alive (c. 330 BC), they returned to the old city and fortified it once again. Its tormented history came to an end in 107 BC when John Hyrcanus reduced it to rubble. No one ever settled there again because, in AD 72, Titus founded a new city (NABLUS) a little to the west in the centre of the pass.

Visit (fig. 103). The unmarked entrance is a path between two buildings on the road just north of the tel (E in fig. 92).

All the walls visible around the gate [7] are dated to between 1650 and 1550 BC, permitting the imagination to re-create the bustling life of the most important quarter of the city. The great cyclopian wall

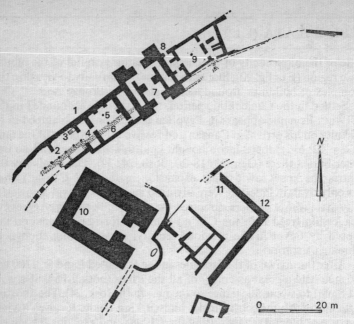

Fig. 103. Tel Balata. Area around the North-West Gate (after Wright and Dever).

[1], filled on the inner side, raised the city 10 m above the land outside. A ramp led up the main gate [7] in which sat the tax collectors and senior citizens; here the news was fresh, visitors could be inspected, and business was transacted (Gen. 23: 10; Prov. 31: 23). The guards who occupied the adjoining barracks [9] had a peephole [8], permitting them to anticipate problems such as might be created by the arrival of a notorious trouble-maker or a group too heavily armed.

The complex on the other side of the gate had a different function; it was the private temple of the ruler. The arrangement is not immediately obvious because, late in this period, a new wall [6] was inserted in order to create a new defence line. With the inner wall of the existing building it made a casemate, i.e. a double-wall designed to be filled with earth. If we ignore this intrusion the plan becomes clear. A reception hall [2] had a line of columns in the centre, supporting an upper floor (royal apartments?) reached by a staircase

[3]. The temple comprised three rooms (a model later adopted by Solomon for his temple in Jerusalem): an antechamber [4], a square room [5] whose roof pillars rested on squared bases (one now in the middle, the other in the base of the casemate wall) with an altar facing the entrance, and a small rectangular chamber.

This temple must have been for private use because just nearby was a large fortress-temple [10] to serve the general public. The width of the stone foundations shows that the brick walls must have risen to a considerable height. The standing-stone before the entrance was restored by the archaeologists to its original position. To do so they had to rebuild the courtyard. It is no less artificial than the original one, because in order to build the fortress-temple the Bronze Age occupants of the city had to cover a huge area [11] which had been the temple domain since the C19 BC. The wall [12] which had served to separate the sacred area from the rest of the city was re-used to retain the fill. The buildings in the bottom of the trench belonged to this earlier temple complex.

At the far side of the tel there is another city gate dated some 75 years after [7]; the single bay is constructed of four pairs of great flat stones. Some are worn on the inside, and sliding doors have been suggested.

TEL DAN (O1)

In the Old Testament, 'from Dan to Beer Sheva' appears as a stereotyped expression fixing the northern and southern limits of the land of Israel (Judg. 20: 1; 1 Sam. 3: 20; 2 Sam. 3: 10; 17: 11; 24: 2; etc.). Today the ancient city is the centre of an extensive nature reserve whose luxuriant vegetation is watered by one of the three headstreams of the River Jordan.

In the division of the land following the conquest by Joshua, the tribe of Dan received territory in the coastal plain inside Jaffa (Josh. 19: 40–6). When they found that they could not hold it against the chariots of the Philistines they moved to the north, and occupied a Canaanite city-state called variously Leshem (Josh. 19: 47) or Laish (Judg. 18: 27) whose name was then changed to Dan. Laish is mentioned in Egyptian Execration Texts of the C19 BC and in the mid-C15 BC list of cities conquered by Thutmose III; it also appears in documents from Mari across the desert on the Euphrates.

The Danite invasion took place about the middle of the C11 BC, but the city came into prominence only as a result of the political schism which followed the death of Solomon in 928 BC. In order to give his new kingdom a distinctive identity and to prevent his subjects from being propagandized when on pilgrimage to Jerusalem, Jeroboam (928–907 BC) 'made two calves of gold. And he said to the people, "You have gone up to Jerusalem long enough. Behold your gods, O Israel, who brought you up out of the land of Egypt." And he set one in Bethel and the other he put in Dan.' (1 Kgs. 12: 28–9.) To mark the new importance of Dan, Jeroboam erected a second line of fortifications outside the great C18 BC wall which ringed the summit of the mound; its monumental gate was on the south slope. The destruction of this gate is dated to the Syrian invasion of the north (1 Kgs. 15: 20) inspired by King Asa of Judah (908–867 BC). The city was rebuilt during the reigns of Omri (882–871 BC) and Ahab (871–852 BC); the last phases of the gate and of the huge podium on the northern part of the tel are dated to this restoration. Dan is not mentioned explicitly in the account of the Assyrian invasion of the north under Tiglath-Pileser III in 732 BC (2 Kgs. 15: 29), but it is highly probable that its inhabitants were deported with all others of the region.

The subsequent history of the site is shrouded in obscurity but the location of the city of Dan was never forgotten. In describing Lake Semechonitis (= Lake Huleh, now drained) Josephus says that 'its marshes extend as far as Daphne, a delightful spot with springs which feed the so-called little Jordan, beneath the temple of the golden cow, and speed it on its way to the greater river' (*War* 4: 3).

Visit. Open: 8 a.m. – 4 p.m.; Fridays to 3 p.m. The excavations can be reached only by passing through the Nature Reserve. At the entrance, which has a parking-lot (toilet facilities and a refreshment stand), one can obtain a map of the trails in the Reserve with a summary description of the trees and shrubs. The thick-trunked terebinth (Station 9 on the Reserve map) corresponds to [1] in fig. 104 from which a trail leads to the top of the mound at a point mid-way between the two main excavation areas.

The Southern Gate. The Israelite gate of the C9 BC is very well preserved. Anyone approaching the entrance [4] was forced to present his exposed right side (the shield being carried on the left arm) to the defenders on the city wall. A paved rectangular area nearly 20 × 10 m just inside the threshold might be 'the square at the gate of the city'

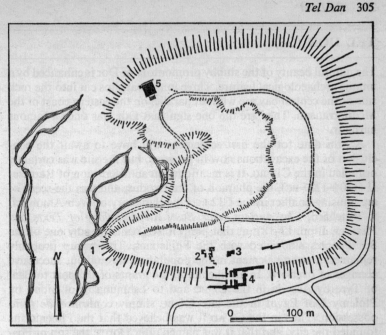

Fig. 104. Tel Dan. Excavated areas (after Biran).

(e.g. Judg. 19: 15; 2 Chr. 32: 6). The paved street which begins in the middle of the west side passes two guardrooms on each side before turning up the slope into what appears to be another gate [2] on the same level as the C18 BC wall [3].

The High Place [5]. The dominant feature is an almost square platform built in the classical Israelite masonry of the C9 BC. An 8 m-wide flight of steps on the south side led to the summit from a pavement with large slabs; the purpose of the pit is unclear. The sacred area was enclosed by a wall whose sole opening was on the south. This complex remained in use into the Hellenistic and Roman periods; the latest coins are dated to the C4 AD.

TEL DOR (G8)

The natural beauty of the stubby promontory of Dor is enhanced by a unique archaeological feature. Three long boat slips cut into the rock side of the central bay are without parallel on the eastern coast of the Mediterranean. They are the one sign that Dor was once a famous harbour.

A firm date for the first settlement will have to await the conclusion of the excavations now in progress, but the site was certainly occupied in the C15 BC. It is mentioned in an inscription of Rameses II (1304–1237 BC), the pharaoh of the Exodus, and was the scene of an amusing conflict in the C12 BC Egyptian story of Wen-Amon (cf. J. Pritchard, *The Ancient Near East. An Anthology of Texts and Pictures*, I, pp. 17–18); at that point it was controlled by one of the Sea Peoples associated with the Philistines. This group probably remained a strong element in the population throughout successive changes of overlord. In all likelihood the grants of the port to Baal of Tyre by Assyria in the C7 BC and to Eshmunazar of Sidon by Ptolemy I of Egypt in the late C4 BC simply confirmed *de facto* possession. Thus in the C1 AD it was believed that the Phoenicians founded the city, and that it was named after Doros, the son of Poseidon, the sea-god.

After a century of Ptolemaic control the Seleucids of Syria acquired possession in 201 BC. Taken by Alexander Jannaeus (103–76 BC), Dor was liberated by Pompey in 63 BC and accorded the right to issue its own coins. Since Josephus describes Dor as an unsatisfactory port where goods had to be transhipped by lighters from ships at sea (*Antiquities* 15: 333), it must have suffered from the development of CAESAREA (only 15 km away) under Herod the Great (37–4 BC). It is not mentioned by the geographer Strabo (*c.* AD 25), and Pliny the Elder (*c.* AD 70) describes it as a 'mere memory'. Yet in the reign of Agrippa I (AD 37–44) it had a Jewish synagogue and a sizeable pagan population (*Antiquities* 19: 300), and had its own mint from 64 to 222. The same ambiguity appears in later references. Jerome consistently describes Dor as deserted and in ruins, but later in the C5 the city appears as sufficiently important to justify a resident bishop. Either the city had a very curious history or certain authors did not check the facts. There is no mention of Dor in the early Arab period and its situation in the Crusader period is unclear.

Visit (fig. 105). Exit from the Tel Aviv–Haifa highway at Mehlaf Zikhron (if coming from the south) or at Mehlaf Atlit (if coming from the north). From the inner road take the turn-off signposted Nahsholim-Dor. After crossing the railway tracks take the first paved road to the right into Kibbutz Nahsholim. From the bathing beach it is possible to walk north to the tel. Alternatively one can drive round the kibbutz towards the fishponds and continue on a dirt road to the foot of the tel.

Precise archaeological information on Dor is lacking but this situation will be remedied by the major excavation begun in 1979. The three-aisled Byzantine basilica [1] is dated to the C5–C6 AD; flanked by colonnades paved with mosaics, it is surrounded by an atrium. The tomb at the east end of the south aisle exhibits a unique feature. Oil poured through a hole in the stone cover was sanctified by contact with the body within and ran through to a plastered basin outside.

Of the ancient port installations one can still see part of the quay walls [2] and the stub of a breakwater [3]. Until the end of the last century a tower stood on the mound [4] which may have been the

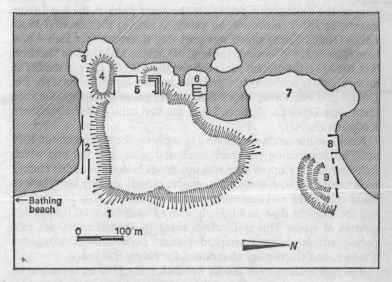

Fig. 105. Tel Dor. Excavated area

acropolis of the Phoenician city. Just to the north is the podium [5] of a great public building, probably a temple.

Each of the three slips [6] could take a 20 m boat with a beam of 4 m. They date from the Hellenistic period (332–37 BC) and are oriented so as to give the boats maximum protection from the sun. On either side are basins in which wood destined for the ribs was soaked to make it pliable.

The complex of large and small basins linked by channels [7] utilized both sea and fresh water. It covers an area of some 700 square metres and must have been used either for the dyeing of cloth or for the making of the purple dye from which the Phoenicians got their name.

The masonry [8] at the edge of the northern bay was probably part of a port installation; both Tyre and Sidon had double harbours which ensured a sheltered anchorage in most winds. Nearby are faint remains of a Roman theatre [9].

TEL EL-FARAH (L12)

One of the most scenic drives on the West Bank is the road from NABLUS to Jiftlik in the Jordan valley. It runs in the beautiful Wadi Farah (Nahal Tirza) which was probably the route by which Abraham (Gen. 12: 5–6) entered the land of Canaan and came to Shechem (TEL BALATA); the present route follows the line of a Roman road. The intense cultivation is made possible by two powerful springs, Ein Duleib and Ein Faria, which flow the length of the valley. Between them rises Tel el-Farah, once Tirza, the first capital of the Northern Kingdom (Israel).

Neolithic hunters were the first to settle by the springs about 7000 BC. This occupation was very small and poor, and the one which followed in the Copper Age was not much better. A sudden change took place c.3100 BC when a new people moved in; they knew how to build with stone and had experience of urban life. They fortified the site for the first time and built houses of mud-brick on foundation courses of stone. This civilization came to an end c.2500 BC, in a period which shows a marked decline in urbanism throughout Canaan, and the site lay abandoned for nearly 600 years.

The new settlers were few in number, but c.1700 BC there was an increase in population, but still not sufficient to occupy the whole area of the earlier town. They built a new wall which excluded the eastern section of the mound and, in the process, modified the position of the western gate. The most interesting building of this period is an underground sanctuary in which young pigs were sacrificed; in the ancient Orient such sacrifices were essentially related to magic and exorcisms.

Tirza is mentioned as one of the Canaanite cities captured by Joshua (Josh. 12: 24). In the early Israelite period (C10–C9 BC) houses of uniform quality lined well-marked streets; the city had the dignity befitting the capital it became when Israel seceded from Judah after the death of Solomon (1 Kgs. 14: 17). This city was brutally destroyed in the early part of the C9 BC. The timing fits perfectly with a series of events dated to 882 BC when Zimri assassinated King Elah and reigned for seven days in Tirza. When news reached the army the troops proclaimed Omri king, 'So Omri went up from Gibbethon, and all Israel with him, and they besieged Tirza. And when Zimri saw that the city was taken, he went into the citadel of the king's house, and burned the king's house over him with fire and died' (1 Kgs. 16: 17–18).

Omri reigned for six years in Tirza (1 Kgs. 16: 23) but the first four were taken up with the struggle against his rival Tibni. The delay this caused in the reconstruction of the city is betrayed by a hiatus in the archaeological levels. New buildings do appear, but the most important one was abandoned when only half finished; a dressed stone, almost ready to be put into position, was found as the stone-cutter left it. It is impossible not to relate this to Omri's decision to move the capital to SAMARIA (1 Kgs. 16: 24), taking, it seems, most of the population with him, because the site lay uninhabited for a short period.

Intensive occupation in the C8 BC is clearly attested. Israel enjoyed great prosperity under Jehoash (800–784 BC) and Jeroboam II (784–748 BC), and this flourishing period is represented here by rich private houses whose opulence contrasts vividly with the miserable hovels of the poor. Such social inequality, with the development of an urban proletariat, evoked the condemnation of the prophets (Amos 5: 10–13). The fire predicted by Hosea (8: 14) arrived in the form of the Assyrians who devastated the city in 723 BC (2 Kgs. 17: 5). Tirza became an open city and continued to decline until the site was finally abandoned *c.* 600 BC, possibly as the result of an epidemic of malaria which was endemic in the area until this century.

Visit. From the Nablus–Damieh Bridge (Gesher Adam) road take the turn to Tubas. Located 4·5 or 3·5 km from the main road (depending on which turn-off is used), the site is not marked in any way but is easy to recognize (fig. 106). Where the tarmac road bears sharply right after crossing a small stream in the bottom of a steep-sided valley, go left on to a dirt road which circles behind the mound. It is possible to drive right to the edge of the excavated area. Parts of the site have been excavated to a greater depth than others; fine lines

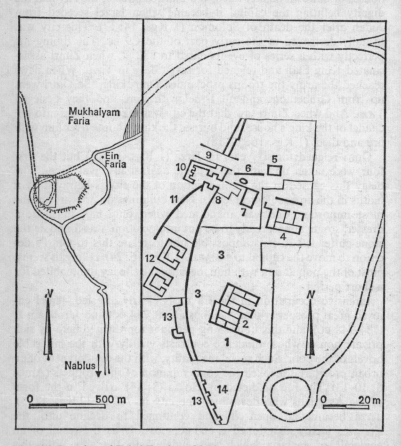

Fig. 106. Location of Tel el-Farah on Nablus–Tubas road with enlargement of excavated area (right) (after de Vaux). Fine lines indicate different levels.

show the edges of the different levels which can be used as orientation points.

The C8 BC level is the most natural one at which to start since it is nearest the end of the access road. The miserable houses of the poor [1] are separated by a long straight wall from two upper-class houses [2] whose plan is perfectly preserved. The single door gives access to a courtyard with rooms on three sides; some of the floors are cobbled. Around these houses are other buildings [3] of the Iron Age.

In the C9 BC a large building [4] was started but never rose above the foundation levels; no trace of a floor was found. Three rooms are disposed around a central courtyard entered from the north; on the west is a long hall with a wide entrance. Just beside the north-east corner is a dressed stone designed for the superstructure; now lying flat, it was discovered tilted at the stonecutter's angle as if the mason had been summoned abruptly to another job.

From the unfinished building go along the edge of the deep trench to the north-east corner where it is easy to get down. The wide stone walls of the underground sanctuary [5] stand out clearly; for some two hundred years (1750–1550 BC) pigs were here sacrificed to the gods of the underworld. The walls [6] nearby are the foundations of a house of the Early Bronze Age (3100–2500 BC); the upper courses were of mud-brick. In the centre a shallow circular pit about 2 m in diameter is all that remains of a hut of the Copper Age (4500–3100 BC); the walls were of mud mixed with rubble. Just beside is another Early Bronze Age house [7]; the two rows of stones in the centre were the foundations of wooden pillars supporting the roof. A similar house to the west was buried when the mud-brick city wall collapsed on top of it. The tumbled bricks can still be seen in the side of the baulk [8], and a cut in the side of the 2 m-thick wall clearly reveals the method of construction.

One can leave the Early and Middle Bronze Age level by the section [9] cut through the city wall; note that the original mud-brick wall was reinforced on the outside by stone facing. The structure of the city gate [10] is well preserved; it was of the indirect entrance type and was rebuilt many times, for it served the city for over 1,000 years (1700–600 BC). Running south from the gate is the curved line of the Middle Bronze Age glacis [11]. When complete, this covered the original Early Bronze Age gate [12]; its hollow square towers of mud-brick protected the city during the first part of the third millennium BC.

Continuing to the south the city wall [13], which was in use from

1700 to 600 BC, is clearly visible. The structures at the bottom of the triangular trench [14] are the foundations of Early Bronze Age houses.

TEL ER-RAS (K13)

The northern peak of Mount Gerizim towers above NABLUS (C in fig. 92). Coins minted in the reign of Antoninus Pius (AD 139–61), with the inscription 'Flavia Neapolis of Palestinian Syria', show a temple on the summit linked to the city by a long flight of steps (fig. 107).

With this clue archaeologists brought to light a great platform (65 × 44 m) on which stood a small temple (13·4 × 8·2 m). This is the temple dedicated to Zeus by Hadrian (AD 117–38). On the precise line indicated by the coins they found 65 steps cut into the rock of the mountain, as well as the foundations of the buildings on both sides

Fig. 107. C2 AD coin showing temple on Tel er-Ras.

shown in the coins. The temple was probably destroyed by an earth-quake in the C4.

In order to create their 7 m-high platform the Roman engineers utilized an earlier structure. Its dimensions are not very clear because the Romans buried it under thousands of tons of fill mixed with concrete. There was certainly one building, which can be visualized as a half-cube ($20 \times 20 \times 10$ m), and a perimeter wall. This structure was dated to the C3 BC. In the light of present knowledge it seems to be the temple built by the SAMARITANS in the C5–C4 BC and destroyed by John Hyrcanus in 128 BC.

TEL ES-SAMRAT (M16)

From the road which leads to its base it is only a small dusty mound (fig. 69), but from the top one looks down into the semicircle of Herod's theatre with the long rectangle (315×84 m) of the hippo-drome stretching out in front.

This site is intimately associated with three events which took place in the tense days surrounding the death of Herod the Great in 4 BC. There, lying on a couch because too ill to stand, he reproached the leaders of the Jews for an abortive uprising in Jerusalem, which he interpreted as base ingratitude. This hint of the temper of his people worked on his diseased mind and he had eminent Jews from through-out Judaea interned in the hippodrome with orders that they be killed at the moment of his death. This manic plan, to ensure that tears would accompany his departure, was ignored by his sister Salome, who instead used the hippodrome to win the mercenaries' loyalty to Archelaus (*War* 1: 647–73).

The tel is in fact an artificial platform of mud-brick projecting out from the back of the theatre. It supported a building (70×70 m) erected round a courtyard, probably a reception area. Jericho was a private royal estate, and those who attended the shows here would have been members of the court. They would have been comfortably accommodated in the 3,000–4,000-seat theatre with their backs protected against the cold north wind of winter; no benches have been found in the walled hippodrome.

The rigidly horizontal line on the nearby cliffs is the aqueduct which brought water from the springs near Naaran to the palace at UTLUL ABU EL-ALAIQ. Just below the aqueduct piles of excavation debris reveal the openings of a number of the rock-cut tombs. These were part of the great cemetery, stretching for some 10 km along the cliffs, which served Jericho between 100 BC and AD 68. The tombs are of a very common type: burial recesses are cut into three walls above a bench. In some of the recesses were remains of wooden coffins. Made of planks mortised to the four corner-posts, these generally had gabled covers and painted decoration.

TEL ES-SULTAN (M16)

The jagged outline suggests a badly kept rubbish dump, but the climb to the top is worthwhile (fig. 69). In a deep trench dug by the English archaeologist Kathleen Kenyon stands a great stone tower (diameter 8·5 m; height 7·75 m) with a perfectly preserved stairway running up the centre. Constructed about 7000 BC, this supreme achievement of a Stone Age people is without parallel elsewhere in the world.

The mound grew to its present height of 15 m as town after town was built on the same site. Hunters probably visited the spring (Ein es-Sultan) from time immemorial. In the Mesolithic period their camp included a small sanctuary. They lived in flimsy shelters which later evolved into mud-brick huts with domed roofs. Their tools were of flint, bone, and wood, and in place of pottery they used limestone utensils. Their construction of the tower and its associated defence wall in the first part of the Neolithic period attests a very high degree of communal organization which must have been reflected also in the agricultural and irrigation systems needed to support a town of some 2,000 inhabitants. Jericho was one of the places which saw human society move from its food-gathering to its food-producing phase.

Around 6800 BC the original settlers at Jericho were displaced by another Neolithic people who brought with them a much more sophisticated form of architecture; courtyards were surrounded by large airy rooms. It seems that they practised a form of ancestor-worship because ten skulls were found whose features were restored in plaster (these are to be seen in the Rockefeller Museum, Jerusalem). The delicate individualized modelling of ears, nose, and eyebrow, and the flesh-coloured tinting make them extraordinarily lifelike. A head sculpted in unbaked clay with shell eyes and hair marked by lines of paint is probably also from this period.

Having survived for some 2,000 years, these people disappeared as suddenly as their predecessors. Around 4500 BC they were succeeded by others whose architecture was inferior (they lived in pits or semi-subterranean huts) but who had discovered pottery. However, neither they nor any of the subsequent waves of immigrants ever produced anything as extraordinary (for their time) as the tower or the plastered skulls. Succeeding periods in the archaeological history of Tel es-Sultan are parallel to what has been discovered at many other sites. What Kenyon found in her careful stratigraphic cuts, and in the many undisturbed rock-cut tombs, augmented existing knowledge and made it more precise but without contributing anything unique. Two elements from these later periods are still visible. At the north end of the tel, facing the refugee camp, the Middle Bronze Age glacis, which steepened the angle of the slope to 35 degrees, is clearly evident in the side of the trench. Those with trained eyes can follow, around the summit of the tel, the mud-brick wall which defended the Early Bronze Age town. At one time these were thought to be the walls blown down by the trumpets of Joshua (Josh. 6) but they are now known to have been in ruins for 1,000 years before the Exodus took place around 1250 BC. Nothing subsequent to the end of the Late Bronze Age was found on the surface of the tel, but evidence for reoccupation in the C7 BC appeared on the sides. After the Babylonian exile the site was abandoned.

TIBERIAS (N6)

Although founded by Herod Antipas (4 BC–AD 39), the son of Herod the Great, and mentioned in the gospels (John 6: 1; 21: 1), Tiberias contains nothing of archaeological interest. Its claim to fame is spiritual (fig 98).

The west side of the Sea of Galilee was lined with villages in the C1 AD, and Herod Antipas's choice of a virgin site (*c.* AD 20) betrays his desire to emulate his famous father. He wanted to create a showplace that would be entirely his own. He named it after his patron, the emperor Tiberius, and endowed it with a stadium, a palace with a gold roof, and a great synagogue. Its location on the site of an ancient cemetery perturbed only devout Jews. By the middle of the C1 Jews were in the majority as well as being the ruling class. The city did not resist Vespasian, and played an insignificant role in the Second Revolt (132–5), whose failure reduced the Jewish population of Judaea to virtually nothing. Galilee thus became the Jewish sector of Palestine, and it was there that great scholars completed the labour of learning that preserved the identity of Judaism after the destruction of the Temple (AD 70).

Rabbi Jochanan ben Nappaha founded the great rabbinic school of Tiberias *c*. AD 220. He had been one of the last disciples of Rabbi Judah ha-Nasi (*c*.135–217), the compiler of the Mishnah (the organization of the oral code of law), and set himself to test the logical consistency of the Mishnah. He thus laid the foundations of the Gemara which was completed by his disciples in Tiberias *c*. 400. The Mishnah and the Gemara together constitute the Palestinian Talmud. Owing to Christian pressure the school of Tiberias began to break up in the middle of the C5. It came to life again in the C8–C10 when the five generations of the family of Ben Asher established the pointed text of the Hebrew Bible which won universal acceptance. To Tiberias we owe the classic forms of the written and oral Law.

Tiberias was taken by Tancred who made himself Prince of Galilee in 1099. Its capture by Saladin in July 1187 provoked the battle at the HORNS OF HATTIN which destroyed the Latin Kingdom of Jerusalem. In 1562 Suliman the Magnificent granted Tiberias to Joseph Nasi, a Marrano Jew from Portugal. Aided by his mother-in-law, Donna Gracia, he re-walled the town and tried to develop a silk industry with a view to establishing an independent Jewish enclave. The project failed, and the city became prominent again only in the C18 when a bedouin sheikh, Daher el-Omar, built the citadel from which he pushed the Turks out of Galilee. He was assassinated in 1775, and his fortress (today the 'Donna Gracia' restaurant) was ruined by the earthquake of 1837. The city received the Jews of the First Aliyah at the end of the C19 and since then has not ceased to prosper, expanding from the lake-front up the slopes to the west.

A serene park-like enclosure at the end of Hagalil Road, near the public garden, houses the tombs of the great Jewish sages: Rabbi Yohanan ben Zakkai (C1 AD), Rabbi Eliezer ben Hyrcanus (C2 AD), and Rabbi Moses ben Maimon (C12 AD), better known as the Rambam (from the initial letters of his name) or Maimonides. On the hillside above, a new white dome covers the cave-tomb of Rabbi Akiva (C2 AD) who acclaimed Bar Kokhba as the messiah; he was executed by the Romans.

TORON OF THE KNIGHTS: *see* LATRUN

TULUL ABU EL-ALAIQ (M16)

From even a short distance nothing is visible save two brown mounds separated by the Wadi Qilt, and a wide stretch of stony ground (fig. 69). Nonetheless for a century this was the winter playground of Jewish kings. Because of the dry climate they built in mud-brick which has now eroded to nothing, but great areas of the floors of their palaces have been revealed by recent excavations and more is still to come to light.

The site was occupied in the last part of the Chalcolithic Age (c. 4500–3100 BC), a period that is missing at TEL ES-SULTAN, but the first important buildings were erected by one of the Hasmonaean kings, possibly Alexander Jannaeus (103–76 BC). This complex comprised a large swimming-pool north of the wadi surrounded by buildings. An aqueduct brought water 6 km along the edge of the cliffs from the springs near Naaran. The first palace of Herod the Great (37–4 BC), no longer visible, was served by an aqueduct on the south wall of the Wadi Qilt. Some time later, apparently in the last decade of his reign, he incorporated the two earlier palaces into a great royal estate which spanned the wadi. The desert flowered in a sunken garden. Visitors were entertained in magnificent halls and baths, and a theatre and hippodrome were provided for their distraction. The great pools which cooled the atmosphere demanded another aqueduct on the north face of the wadi. It was to this verdant spot that Herod came in his last terrible illness, and here he died five days after killing his son and heir Antipater. His orders to throw the nation into mourning at his death by slaughtering the eminent Jews from throughout Judaea, who were penned in the hippodrome, were not carried out. His body was borne to HERODION for burial (*War* 1: 659–73).

According to Josephus, Herod's ex-slave Simeon, who claimed the crown, burnt the palace (*War* 2: 57), but it was magnificently reconstructed by Archelaus when his authority over Judaea was confirmed (*Antiquities* 17: 340). So far archaeology has not confirmed either of these events. The palace was in ruins by the end of the C1 AD when a Roman villa was built on the north bank of the wadi.

Visit. The complex falls naturally into three areas.

(1) *The buildings on both sides of Wadi Qilt* (fig. 108). The artificial mound dominating the sunken garden [1] raised a square building

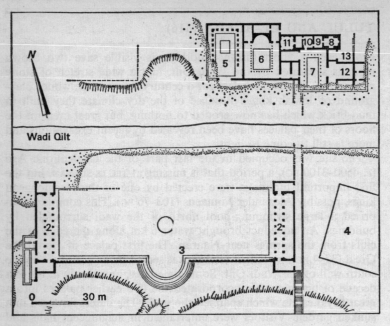

Fig. 108. Tulul Abu el-Alaiq. Buildings on both sides of Wadi Qilt (after Netzer).

containing a round hall (villa?, reception hall?, bath?) above the mosquito-laden vegetation. The columned porches [2], 2 m above each end of the sunken garden, are linked by a monumental façade [3] in Roman *opus reticulatum*. Flower pots were found on the steps of the central semicircle. The bridge crossing the wadi must have been between this garden and the great pool [4]; an entrance in the complex north of the wadi is in the line of the steps descending from the raised building. The varied negative impressions of the floor tiles hint at the sumptuous decoration of the roofed main reception hall [5]. Throughout the complex there is evidence of frescoes and stucco moulding. The columns of the two open courtyards [6 and 7] were of small segments of stone encased in plaster, producing the effect of marble but without the expense! Inevitably there was a bath area with its hot-room [8], warm-room [9], dressing-room and entrance [10], and cool-room [11] whose original floor was of plaster laid on wooden beams; there may have been a fountain in the centre. The big

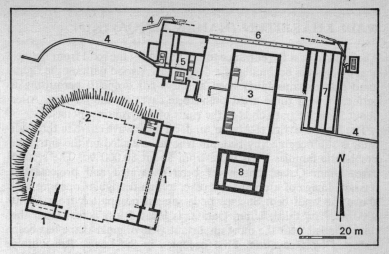

Fig. 109. Tulul Abu el-Alaiq. Structures near the Northern Mound (after Netzer).

room [12] may have been a dining chamber ajoining a service area [13].

(2) *The structures near the northern mound* (fig. 109). The structures [1] around the edge of the steep-sided mound come from the Hasmonaean palace; probably a central court surrounded by two-storey rooms in mud-brick. Herod inserted stone foundations, packed the rooms with fill from the wadi, and erected a large building on top [2]. Raised above the surrounding vegetation, it caught every breath of air. The double swimming-pool [3] is possibly that in which Aristobulus III, the last Hasmonaean, was drowned on Herod's orders in 35 BC. It was fed by one of the two aqueducts [4] coming from the cliffs. The Hasmonaean complex around the pool contained a number of stepped ritual baths [5], a peristyle [6], three long store-rooms [7] and a villa [8]. Herod buried all these under a layer of earth in order to create a garden around the pool.

(3) *The First Palace.* In the area between the above two complexes the archaeologists are bringing to light what they believe to be the first palace built by Herod on this site. They already have evidence of a great open court with a long chamber on the north side. Further south is a complete Roman bath and nearby a large swimming-pool.

WADI KHAREITUN (NAHAL TEQOA) (K19)

About 2 km past the entrance to the HERODION the road from Bethlehem crosses the beginning of a deep wadi. A good path on the right-hand side remains fairly level as the wadi deepens, permitting a perfect view of three great prehistoric caves on the far side. After about 3 km the path ends at the ruins of a Byzantine monastery.

The first cave, Erq el-Ahmar, under a huge wave curve in the wadi wall, is still occupied by bedouin who have walled up the entrance. Prehistoric families lived there from about 80,000 BC. The second cave, Umm Qalaa, has never been excavated and projects the classical image of a prehistoric cave, a high triangular opening well above the wadi bed. Surface finds suggest occupation from about 8000 BC. The third, Umm Qatafa, is located just across from the ruins and is by far the most important. The original shape has been distorted by excavation. First occupied in the Lower Palaeolithic period (500,000–120,000 BC), it provides the earliest evidence of the use of fire in Palestine. Large stones were arranged in a circle around a hearth, creating the conditions which fostered the development of language. On a flat ledge below the cave is a series of rock-cut basins. When these caves were occupied Europe was still in the Ice Ages, and this area enjoyed a climate similar to that of Europe today. The undulating areas on both sides were green and full of animals; the wadi was a river.

The monastery was founded by St. Chariton in the C4 AD and remained in use until at least the C12. The remaining ruins seem to be of this period but the reservoir with the stepped wall may be older.